FALLEN

Mick Conefrey is an award-winning writer and documentary maker. He made the landmark BBC series *Mountain Men* and *Icemen* and *The Race for Everest* to mark the 60th anniversary of the first ascent. His previous books include *Everest 1922*, *Everest 1953*, the winner of a LeggiMontagna award, *The Last Great Mountain*, the winner of the Premio Itas in 2023, and *The Ghosts of K2*, which won a US National Outdoor Book award in 2017.

MICK CONEFREY

FALLEN

George Mallory: The Man,
The Myth and the
1924 Everest Tragedy

ALLEN&UNWIN

First published in hardback and trade paperback in Great Britain in 2024
by Allen & Unwin, an imprint of Atlantic Books Ltd.

Copyright © Mick Conefrey, 2024

Maps by Adam T. Burton

10 9 8 7 6 5 4 3 2

A CIP catalogue record for this book is available from the British Library.

Hardback ISBN: 978 1 83895 979 1
Trade paperback ISBN: 978 1 80546 271 2
E-book ISBN: 978 1 83895 980 7

Printed and bound by CPI (UK) Ltd, Croydon CR0 4YY

Allen & Unwin
An imprint of Atlantic Books Ltd
Ormond House
26–27 Boswell Street
London
WC1N 3JZ

www.atlantic-books.co.uk

For Frank

Contents

Contents

Prologue

They fanned out across the slope, taking their time to survey the terrain. The wind was no longer so ferocious, but it was still cold and gusty. Back home, the experts referred to this as a natural 'terrace', but it was far from flat – a thirty-degree slope with steep cliffs at the bottom, the terrain a mixture of scree-covered rock and patches of snow. Just one slip could send you tumbling down the mountain, to be smashed to pieces on the glaciers below.

They were at 27,000 feet on the North Face of Everest, the lower edge of the 'death zone'. Five American climbers and mountain guides: average age thirty-two, two previous summiters, all eager and willing. At Base Camp, 10,000 feet below – near the tip of the Rongbuk glacier – other members of their team were attempting to follow the action through a powerful telescope.

It was 1 May 1999, day one of their search for Everest's Holy Grail: a camera that had gone missing seventy-five years earlier when George Mallory made his final, fateful attempt on

Everest. No one expected to find anything straight away – it was all about assessing the lie of the land, getting used to the oxygen sets and radios, figuring out how to work together as a team for a mission that was expected to take a week.

And then, fifteen minutes in, Jake Norton, the youngest climber on the team, spotted something: a blue oxygen cylinder, much bigger and heavier than their own, possibly a remnant of a Chinese camp set up in 1975. If it was, they were in the right area, so they carried on going, spreading out until eventually they were so far apart they needed their radios to communicate.

Each of the climbers had been given a small, spiral-bound notepad with instructions on how and where to look, but the search zone was vast – the size of about twelve American football fields – so they followed their hunches and intuition. If a body had fallen from a ridge high above, where would it have landed? Were there any obvious funnels or collection points?

Then at 11.00 a.m., about half an hour in, Conrad Anker spotted the first corpse, a twisted set of badly dislocated limbs wrapped in a washed-out purple suit. One arm stuck out rigidly, almost as if it were waving. Getting closer, he realized that the ravens had been there first, pecking off much of the skin from the dead climber's face. It was a gruesome sight, but it wasn't what he was looking for, the corpse clearly too recent.

'What are you doing way out there?' one of his teammates crackled over the radio. 'We need to be more systematic.' Anker ignored him and carried on going westwards. This was sacred ground, the North Face of Everest – mountaineering's most elevated and celebrated peak. All around were features named by previous expeditions; it was a privilege just to be here, heading for the Great Couloir that Edward Norton had attempted in 1924 and Reinhold Messner had conquered in 1980.

Then Anker saw a second body, this time in a blue-grey suit; again it was a confusion of broken limbs, the torso facing downhill. But like the first, the clothing was too modern for the expedition they were interested in. So Anker moved on, keeping a wary eye on the line of cliffs below until he stopped to take off his crampons. They weren't much help on steep downward-facing slabs covered in unstable scree.

A few minutes later, he spotted a piece of fabric fluttering in the wind and began climbing upwards to investigate. Blue and yellow, it too was probably modern but he needed to get closer to check.

And then he noticed it: a patch of white. Not snow, not rock; something that didn't quite fit. He moved closer and was stopped in his tracks. It was the powerful shoulders of a climber, his arms stretched upwards as if to arrest a fall, his partly clothed body seemingly fused into Everest itself.

Moments later, Conrad Anker took out his radio and called his teammates, but it was another twenty minutes before they all assembled, staring down at the mummified but clearly defined body. No one could quite take it in. On the first day of their search, Anker had discovered something totally remarkable, the solution to a mystery which had gripped the climbing world for the last seventy-five years. He'd found the remains of one of the great heroes of twentieth-century exploration: George Herbert Leigh Mallory.

In the now almost a century since he disappeared into the clouds with his young partner Andrew Irvine, George Mallory has become a legendary figure. Edmund Hillary and Tenzing Norgay may have been the first men to reach the summit of Everest, but their expedition has never quite roused the same devotion in Europe and America. Mallory has inspired biographies, epic poems, documentaries, works of fiction as well as works of fact, and countless magazine articles and other commentaries. His answer to the question 'Why climb Everest?' – 'Because it's there' – is probably the most famous quotation in the history of exploration, on a par with Henry Morton Stanley's 'Dr Livingstone I presume' and Neil Armstrong's 'A small step for Man'.

Everything about Mallory, from his looks to his skill with words to his athletic abilities, made him the ideal, quintessentially English hero. Even his name seemed to imply his destiny: George the dragon-slayer; Mallory an imperfect echo of Thomas Malory, the great chronicler of Arthurian legends. It's no wonder that his friend Geoffrey Winthrop Young dubbed him 'Galahad', after the legendary knight.

In general, most biographers and commentators have been very positive about him: he's portrayed as a Romantic hero, the incarnation of adventure, an idealist and a visionary. The only real exception to this hagiographic tendency comes in Walt Unsworth's monumental history, *Everest*, in which he described Mallory as someone 'who had greatness thrust upon him. The pity of it was that he had so little actual talent.' I suspect that Unsworth was being deliberately provocative, but a century after Mallory's disappearance how should we assess him? Was he the 'greatest antagonist that Everest has had – or is likely to have', as Edward Norton dubbed him in the official account of the 1924 expedition, or was he 'a very good stout-hearted baby', as Tom Longstaff, his teammate on a previous Everest expedition, memorably described him in a private letter?

Is there any fresh evidence that might help answer this question? The unexpected truth is that over the last decades a surprising amount of new material has become available – Mallory's letters to his penfriend Marjorie Holmes, John Noel's private archive, George Finch's papers, an enormous number of documents from the Mount Everest Foundation archive that have now been scanned and digitized – that enables Mallory's story to be told more fully. The picture that emerges is complex and nuanced: a fascinating individual, loved by his friends and family; idealistic, chaotic, narcissistic, generous, impulsive, indecisive, driven by the demons of risk and ambition, and continually reassessed and reappropriated by successive generations of climbers and adventurers of all kinds.

This book is not an attempt to tell the complete story of Mallory's life. Rather, the aim is to do two things: first, to look in detail at the events of 1923 and 1924 and understand the forces that drove Mallory and the third British Everest expedition, and second, to separate the man from the mythology that grew up after his disappearance and which continues to evolve, especially after his body was discovered in 1999.

It begins though, not on the slopes of the world's highest mountain, but on a small spit of rock by the seaside...

Pen-y-Pass, Snowdonia, December 1913. Siegfried Herford, a highly regarded rock climber, and George Mallory, photographed by Geoffrey Winthrop Young.

1

About a Boy

St Bees on the Cumbrian coast, the summer of 1895. Mary Jebb was getting more and more worked up, watching her grand-son, George, sitting on a rock far from the shoreline, the waves inexorably rolling in, soon to drag him out into the Irish Sea.

As with a lot of good ideas at the time, the nine-year-old George had been so confident that the water wouldn't rise higher than his rocky perch that he'd gone out dressed in his new school blazer, hoping to watch the sea swirl around him and then recede, before he returned to his family. He hadn't accounted for the high tides which still to this day can be deadly for unwitting tourists and locals alike.

Eventually, with no sign of George moving by himself, Mary raised the alarm and a local man waded out into the water to rescue him. It wasn't easy though, and took several attempts before the preternaturally calm and confident George was carried back to the shore. As his sister Avie told an interviewer many years later, he 'had no sense of fear' and the 'knack of making things exciting and often rather dangerous'.

George Herbert Leigh Mallory was born in 1886 in Mobberley, a small but prosperous village in Cheshire in the north of England. His seaside drama was a typical adventure for a young daredevil who loved shinning up trees and church roofs, climbing whatever was in the vicinity, whether a pier or a humble drainpipe.

His father, the Reverend Herbert Leigh Mallory, was the tenth child of another vicar father, also called George, and there were hopes that as the eldest son, young George might go in to the church and maybe even take over his father's parish one day. George's mother, Annie, was the daughter of another Anglican vicar but by contrast an only child. Unlike her more straight-laced husband, she had a free-spirited and unconventional side and was known for her sense of fun and her laughter, and the licence she gave her children to cavort and roam.

George had two sisters: Mary, the eldest, born a year earlier than him in 1885; and Annie Victoria, known as Avie, born a year after – a tomboy and occasional partner in George's childhood adventures. Trafford, his only brother, was six years younger, but he too was soon roped into the fun.

When it came to schooling, George had a conventional middle-class start, attending first a 'prep' school in Eastbourne and then Winchester College, the ancient public school, where he arrived aged fourteen in 1900 as a mathematical scholar. It was a prestigious award, which to his father's undoubted relief paid for most of the fees.

George enjoyed himself tremendously at Winchester. Though he clearly enjoyed the academic side, his time there was notable for his sporting achievements. He took part in the college's eccentric version of soccer, the complexity of whose rules was matched only by the ferocity with which it was played. He excelled particularly at gymnastics, and was very proud to be part of the school's successful shooting team. More importantly for his future career, it was at Winchester that Mallory first discovered mountaineering, when he encountered Graham Irving, a senior master and keen aficionado of the sport.

Climbing was by the end of the nineteenth century firmly established among the middle and upper classes. Its 'Golden Age' had been the 1850s and 1860s, when most of the high peaks of the Alps were climbed, many of the first ascents achieved by British climbers and their guides. Before long, Britain boasted the world's first climbing association, the Alpine Club, its first mountaineering periodical, the *Alpine Journal*, and by the end of the nineteenth century, a small but active community who regularly spent their holidays climbing in France, Switzerland and Italy.

As the first 'risk sport', mountaineering was not however universally approved of. In 1865, following the famous accident in Switzerland in which a French guide and three British climbers died after making the first ascent of the Matterhorn, with the casualties including a peer of the realm, Queen Victoria was moved to ask her prime minister Gladstone if there was any way to ban it. He advised her that there wasn't and mountaineering continued to grow in popularity, but the question of why it was worth taking such risks for the sake of nothing more than sport never went away.

For devotees like Irving, the answer was obvious: as he wrote in his classic book *The Romance of Mountaineering*, from an early age he knew that 'happiness... would be found in climbing mountains'. Like Mallory, Irving was a northerner, a childhood maths prodigy, and a technophobe whose 'ways with the old-fashioned collapsible candle lantern', as his obituary in the *Alpine Journal* stated, 'suggest that he would not have been good at repairing oxygen apparatus on Everest'. Mallory first came to his attention when Irving was recruiting boys for what he would later call the 'Winchester Ice Club'. George already had a reputation for climbing school buildings – including at one point, the front of the college where Irving, a house tutor, had his office.

Though sometimes criticized for exposing novices to excessive risks, Irving was unrepentant and the boys were undoubtedly keen. In August 1904, he took the eighteen-year-old Mallory and his friend Harry Gibson to the Alps for their first climbing season. It didn't all go perfectly – their first challenge, an attempt on Mont Vélan on the border of Italy and Switzerland, ended with bad weather bringing a premature halt to proceedings and Mallory and Gibson both vomiting with mountain sickness, but the rest of their Alpine holiday was much more successful. After less than a month, Mallory was able to return to Britain a veteran of three of the most famous mountains in the Alps – Mont Blanc, the Grand Combin and Monte Rosa – as well as several high Alpine passes. As Irving wrote in his account of their hard-fought ascent of Mont Blanc: 'It is impossible to make any who have never experienced it, realise what that thrill means. It proceeds partly from a legitimate joy and pride in life.'

Mallory was smitten, and though over the next year the only opportunities he would have to hone his climbing skills would come scaling nearby school buildings and the vicarage roof, the following summer he returned to the Alps with Irving and two more school friends, Guy Bullock and Harry Tyndale, to climb several mountains in the Arolla valley and the Dent Blanche – 'the one peak we had set our hearts on', as he told his mother.

Back home in Cheshire, family life was not quite as stable as it might have seemed. Though they both came from relatively wealthy backgrounds, his parents had tastes above their means and regularly were chased for unpaid bills. In 1904 the Mallorys left their large house in leafy Mobberley for the rather more urban setting of St John's in Birkenhead. Herbert tried to make the best of it, telling George that they were going to 'an exceedingly important parish', but the move came amid a swirl of rumours of affairs and murky ecclesiastical politics.

Mallory never really warmed to Birkenhead but nor was he often there. In 1905 he sat the Cambridge entrance exam, and again to his father's delight won a scholarship – to study not mathematics but history at Magdalene College. Winchester, whose old boys have included Hugh Gaitskell and Geoffrey Howe, had changed him from a budding scientist into someone who was more interested in politics and social debate. As his friend David Pye later wrote, in his first year at Cambridge Mallory became known as 'a very contentious, a most persistent and even derisive arguer' who would sometimes let his passionate opinions get the better of his sense of humour.

After three years studying history, he was awarded a second-class degree with merit, a slight disappointment after his previous academic success. Nevertheless, he decided to stay on for another year to write an essay on the Scottish writer James Boswell for an academic competition. He didn't win the prize, but he turned the essay into a short book, and a few years later managed to get it published.

Cambridge introduced Mallory to a very different artistic and cultural world than anything he'd ever previously encountered. He continued to excel at sport, rowing for Magdalene and eventually captaining their team, but by his second year he had assumed a distinctly Bohemian air, allowing his hair to grow longer and wearing bright colourful clothing. He joined the university's Fabian

Society, the left-leaning political club, as well as the Women's Suffrage Association, and made friends with future writers and poets, some of whom would become part of the fabled 'Bloomsbury Group' of writers, artists and intellectuals.

The first decade of the twentieth century was a time of artistic experimentation all over Europe. In art, Van Gogh, Gauguin and Manet were leading the post-Impressionist charge; closer to home, Henry James, E. M. Forster and Joseph Conrad were pushing the novel in new directions. In music there was Mahler, Stravinsky and Richard Strauss; in dance the Ballets Russes; in poetry the first Modernists. Mallory and his friends lapped it all up and argued well into the night about all the new movements in art.

In truth, Mallory was never a full member of the Bloomsbury set – their intellectual snobbery ruled him out as not being quite 'brilliant' enough, according to John Maynard Keynes – but their values and interests stayed with him throughout his life. Whenever he sailed off to India for an expedition, he would carry with him the latest books and would spend long hours in his tent reading intensely. On a lighter note, he was photographed several times naked or semi-naked after skinny-dipping in a nearby stream in Sikkim or Tibet, following the practice of the 'Neo-Pagans', a subset of the Bloomsbury Group who loved to bare it all.

Edwardian Cambridge was a place where same-sex relationships were commonplace, and it wasn't long before the strikingly handsome Mallory became the focus of a lot of attention. He met closeted older men, like his history tutor Arthur Benson, who had crushes on him which they were never likely to consummate, as well as younger students and alumni such as Lytton and Richard Strachey and the poet Rupert Brooke, who were much more open about their sexuality. When the future economist Maynard Keynes, the brother of Mallory's lifelong friend Geoffrey Keynes, returned to Cambridge in 1908 after a couple of years working in India, he wrote to his friend, the painter Duncan Grant, that 'practically everyone in Cambridge, except me, is an open and avowed sodomite'.

In those days, Cambridge was virtually an all-male domain. It wasn't until 1869, with the founding of Girton College, that the university had accepted female students, and even then Girton wasn't allowed to award degrees until 1948. Apart from sisters and occasionally friends, Mallory and his social circle did not encounter women very often, but nor did they want to be confined by traditional values or social mores, being as radical and experimental in their sexuality as they were in their politics.

Lytton Strachey, the future author of *Eminent Victorians* – perhaps the most 'out' of his circle and a central figure in the Bloomsbury Group – was enraptured by Mallory when they met in 1909, describing his body as 'vast, pale, unbelievable... a thing to melt into and die' and noting how his face possessed 'the mystery of Botticelli, the refinement and delicacy of a Chinese print, the youth and piquancy of an unimaginable English boy'. Lytton lusted after him, but to his frustration Mallory was more interested in his younger brother, James Strachey. Mallory declared his love and pursued him with characteristic relentlessness, until they ended up 'copulating' in a friend's bed. According to a letter from James to Rupert Brooke, it was no fun for either party – James confessed to having being bored by the whole thing, while Mallory, he wrote, seemed 'shocked [and] shewed no desire to repeat the business'.

With homosexuality a taboo subject, not least because homosexual acts between men were illegal in Britain until 1967,

Mallory's first biographers stayed clear of any mention of this aspect of his time at Cambridge, but it was clearly a crucial period for him. Many of the friends that he made, both gay and straight, stayed with him for the rest of his life.

Undoubtedly one of the most important of these was Geoffrey Winthrop Young, a significant figure in the development of British mountaineering and someone who would play a key role in Mallory's life. They met in 1909 at a dinner organized by Charles Sayle, a writer and poet who worked at Cambridge University Library. Sayle was known for the salons where he would bring together beautiful young men, or 'swans' as he called them, to discuss literature and art. He was also a founder member of the English Climbers' Club, set up to promote mountaineering in Britain – as opposed to the Alpine Club, who as their name suggests tended to focus on the Alps and the so-called Greater Ranges.

Young was a flamboyant, camp figure, distinctively dressed in bright colours and sharply tailored clothes, his upper lip invariably crowned with a well-trimmed walrus moustache. His background was wealthy and cultured, allowing him to regularly climb in the Alps. In the 1900s and 1910s he took part in several notable first ascents of difficult routes and like Mallory, he'd had a youthful penchant for climbing in urban as well as natural settings. His first book, *The Roof-Climber's Guide to Trinity*, both poked fun at Swiss guidebooks and provided hints and tips for anyone who wanted to tackle the high towers of Trinity College.

Aged thirty-two, and almost ten years his senior, Young was instantly taken by Mallory. There were soon rumours that the two men had become lovers, but their relationship was much more that of mentor and confidant. Young took Mallory to the Alps and then regularly invited him to the climbing parties that he organized in Snowdonia in North Wales, where he brought together friends and Britain's leading mountaineers to enjoy the challenging rock climbing of the local peaks and crags.

Modern mountaineers have a whole range of protection devices to mitigate the risks – cams, nuts, pitons and slings, to name but a few – but the pioneering rock climbers of Mallory's era had nothing more than flimsy ropes to make their ascents a little safer. To modern eyes they might look quaint, photographed in their hobnail boots and tweed knickerbockers, but they tackled difficult routes and took risks that many of today's climbers would find unacceptable.

Mallory learned fast, garnering a reputation as one of the most gifted climbers of his generation. Some of his climbs in North Wales have rarely been repeated. His impulsiveness occasionally came to the fore, with stories of forgetting to rope up in the Alps and a legendary incident in Wales when he left his pipe on a ledge high up on a cliff face and made a daring solo climb to rescue it over very difficult ground. More than anything else though, Mallory's friends were struck by the elegance and ease with which he climbed. Young was particularly impressed: 'His movement in climbing was entirely his own. It contradicted all theory... a continuous undulating movement so rapid and so powerful that one felt the rock must either yield, or disintegrate.'

Today it's possible for a few gifted individuals to become 'professional' climbers, aided by sponsorship from equipment manufacturers and money from lecturing and books, but until recently this simply wasn't an option. Climbing was a leisure activity that had to be supported by professional jobs or considerable family money. Mallory had neither.

When he arrived in Cambridge, he still harboured the vague plan that one day he might become a vicar or a country parson, but his questioning nature inevitably led him down a different path. He encountered too many priests whose sense of goodness seemed 'sometimes to displace their reason'. Instead he decided that education, and perhaps writing, would be his vocation.

When in the autumn of 1909 he finally left the gilded cloisters of Cambridge, Mallory headed for Europe, hoping to live off a small legacy while improving his linguistic skills to make himself more employable. His dream of returning to Winchester as a master proved to be just that, but eventually he did get a job as an assistant master at Charterhouse, a slightly less grand public school in Surrey. There he gained a reputation as a devoted but rather scatty teacher, who in addition to history lessons would lecture his boys on art – and like Graham Irving, occasionally take them on climbing expeditions. Robert Graves was one pupil who became a good friend. As he wrote in his memoir, *Goodbye to All That*, Mallory was an inspirational figure particularly to the boys who felt like outsiders. He introduced Graves both to the greats of English literature and to the pleasures of mountaineering, and most importantly treated him as an equal.

Mallory was throughout his life passionately interested in education, but he didn't like the prevailing culture of British public schools, with its emphasis on exams, games and corporal punishment. He disliked what he called the 'mechanical atmosphere' of Charterhouse, and when the traditionalist and disciplinarian Frank Fletcher was appointed headmaster, he grew increasingly disenchanted.

Mountaineering was his 'Great Escape', the sport he excelled at and which brought together the pleasures of physical activity, companionship and the sheer joy of being outdoors. Apart from a brief lull during his first couple of years at university, Mallory spent virtually every holiday climbing in the Alps or the Lake District or North Wales.

He joined the Alpine Club and the Climbers' Club and eventually began contributing to their journals. Unlike the previous generation of Victorian 'peak-baggers' whose articles tended to be very descriptive, Mallory took what he called a 'high line' on mountaineering. In his famous essay 'The Mountaineer as Artist', he explored the multiple levels of experience it offered – from the physical to aesthetic to spiritual – in the kind of language used to describe art rather than sport. 'A day well spent in the Alps,' he declared, 'is like some great symphony... The spirit goes on a journey just as does the body.' With all its intensity and variety, mountaineering could only be appreciated, he maintained, as a unified whole. Like all great art, it was a way of experiencing the sublime, allowing a climber to come 'to a finer realisation of himself than ever before'.

But mountains and literature weren't the only distractions from Charterhouse.

In the autumn of 1913, Mallory met Ruth – the daughter of Hugh Thackeray Turner, a prosperous architect with a passion for preserving ancient buildings. Turner's wife, Mary, had died unexpectedly six years earlier, leaving him to bring up his three daughters at Westbrook, a huge baronial mansion in Godalming in Surrey, close to Charterhouse.

All three women were very attractive, and they all seem initially to have been interested in the handsome schoolmaster their father invited into their lives, first to play billiards and then to accompany them on a family holiday to Italy in April 1914. George was as surprised as anyone with the way things were turning out. Apart from a brief encounter with Mary Ann 'Cottie' Sanders, whom he met first in the Alps and later at Geoffrey

Winthrop Young's climbing parties in Wales, he did not have a lot of experience with women. 'I am to stay in Venice with a family consisting of one man and his three daughters,' he wrote to Young in March 1914. 'Did you ever hear the like of that?'

Over the course of the week, George gravitated towards Ruth, Turner's middle daughter. In many ways they were ideally suited. She was very beautiful, with China-blue eyes and long Pre-Raphaelite hair – 'Botticellian' in his eyes, echoing Lytton Strachey's famous description of George himself. Ruth too was interested in art and design, and though not such a great reader or letter-writer, she was cultured and literate and game to go climbing and hiking with him. She didn't share George's political interests, but as he said many times, she was utterly honest and true.

On May Day 1914, barely a month after their week in Venice, George wrote to his mother announcing their engagement. 'What Bliss! And what a revolution! … she's as good as gold, and brave and true and sweet.' The whirlwinds continued to blow until 29 July, when they were married, with Geoffrey Winthrop Young acting as his best man and George's father officiating over a service at a local church in Godalming.

George wanted to go to the Alps for their honeymoon, but with Europe on the brink of war, they were forced to settle for a camping trip to the Sussex coast. In a moment of absurdity-cum-wartime-paranoia, they were briefly detained on suspicion of being German spies.

Back home in Godalming, with the help of Ruth's father they bought a house nearby, The Holt, but inevitably the First World War ruptured any thoughts of a family idyll. As a teacher, Mallory was in a protected occupation and not required to enlist. His headmaster at Charterhouse, Frank Fletcher, repeatedly refused him permission, leaving Mallory feeling guilty and frustrated. On the day he heard the news that Rupert Brooke had died with the British Mediterranean Expeditionary Force, he wrote to A. C. Benson, his former Cambridge tutor, that 'there's something indecent, when so many friends have been enduring so many horrors, in just going on at one's job, quite happy and prosperous'.

Eventually, in December 1915, Fletcher let him go, and he was commissioned as an artillery officer, arriving in France five months later to be assigned to the 40th Siege Battery. The first six months were the worst, with Mallory's unit involved in the Battle of the Somme, which saw 300,000 killed and over a million wounded. Mallory himself escaped unscathed, but several men under his command died. Eventually, like everyone, he became hardened to the sight of dead bodies, but as he told Ruth, it always distressed him to see the wounded.

In between bouts of action, which occasionally reminded him of Alpine expeditions in their camaraderie and 'code of conduct', Mallory found himself enduring the tedium of military life and the misery of the trenches, with all the mud, filth, vermin and parasites that involved. The only compensation was that he had the time to read, but inevitably it led to him examining his values. 'I wonder if you'll find me different,' he wrote to Ruth in August 1916. 'My mind is in a state of constant rebellion. I believe that always will be so.'

He started on a new project, *The Book of Geoffrey*, a novel about a father trying to teach his son what is 'good', but before he could really get going, he was pulled away from the trenches to see a very different side of the war, as a liaison officer between the British and French forces. He briefly returned to combat before being sent back to England in 1917 for an operation on his left ankle, after being told that an old climbing injury was much more serious than he had thought.

After some time to convalesce, Mallory was sent for artillery training near Winchester, a town he knew well from his schooldays. Life became much more domestic. He was able to see Ruth regularly, and that summer even went on a climbing holiday to Scotland with his friend David Pye. The pattern continued for most of the following year, with Mallory being sent on training courses, but never returning to the front line. 'I seem to be frittering away days and weeks in England,' he wrote to Ruth, 'as one only can do in the Army.'

At the beginning of 1918 he was best man at Robert Graves's wedding, and in July he managed to get away to Skye with Ruth and two friends. By the time he returned to active service in September, it was obvious that the war was coming to an end. On 10 November, Mallory and his Cambridge friend Geoffrey Keynes, who had spent the last four years as a military doctor, were reunited at Cambrai, a once beautiful city reduced to rubble by continual bombardment. Anticipating the armistice that would be declared the following day, the troops set off thousands of flares in an impromptu fireworks show. 'Engines whistled and hooted,' as Keynes later wrote. 'Discipline had temporarily vanished.'

The next day, Mallory was whisked off by his younger brother, Trafford – who had been a pilot in the Royal Flying Corps for the last three years – to a rather more sedate celebration at the officers' club. 'It was a good evening altogether, of the kind one would expect from the public-school type of British officer,' he wrote, 'with much hilarity and no drunkenness.'

Mallory finished the war feeling introspective. He had lost four years and some dear friends. Rupert Brooke and Hugh

Wilson, both fellow swans from Cambridge, were never coming back. Geoffrey Winthrop Young's left leg had been blown off, requiring an above-the-knee amputation, and several other members of the Alpine Club had been killed or maimed. In a letter to Ruth, written on 12 November, the day after the Armistice, Mallory looked forward to the future with their daughters Clare and Beridge: 'What a wonderful life we will have together! What a lovely thing we *must* make of such a gift! I want to lose all harshness of jagged nerves, to be above all gentle.' When he followed this with a letter to his father a few days later, he was in a rather more sombre mood: 'If I haven't escaped so many chances of death as plenty of others, still it is surprising to find myself a survivor, and it's not a lot I have always wanted.'

Back in 'civvy street', Mallory returned to Charterhouse in early 1919, but he was increasingly restless and disenchanted with the status quo. He corresponded and held meetings with Geoffrey Winthrop Young and his Cambridge friend David Pye, coming up with ideas for a more progressive type of public school in which there would be less emphasis on games and a much greater attempt to get boys to think for themselves and enjoy intellectual effort. Parents would be encouraged to play a more active role in their children's education and there would be opportunities to learn craft skills and encounter people outside their social class.

Mallory remained interested in politics, both in Britain and abroad. In the summer of 1920 he contacted Gilbert Murray – an Oxford academic heavily involved in the League of Nations, the forerunner of the UN – offering his services to the 'cause'. 'Perhaps the most important thing about me', he wrote, 'which I ought to tell you is that I think and feel passionately about

international politics.' Later that year, he travelled to Ireland
to get a first-hand view of the War of Independence and the
'Terror' the country was gripped by. Mallory saw fault on both
sides, but admired the idealism of the men and women fighting
for self-determination, and was shocked by the ransacked
rooms and lorryloads of soldiers driving around Dublin, and
the stories of 'secret and sinister chambers' in Dublin Castle.
Back in England he wrote an article entitled 'An Englishman's
Conversion', detailing his observations, but before it could be
published, another much bigger project intervened: Everest.

Though Everest lay on the border of Nepal and Tibet, two
countries outside the British Empire, from the moment it was
measured from a survey station in northern India, Britain had a
proprietorial interest in the world's highest mountain. Contrary
to the usual practice of retaining local names, it was christened
'Everest' after George Everest, a Welshman and previous
Surveyor General of India, who ironically pronounced his name
'*Ee-verest*' and was not happy with the act of cartographic
piracy. It wasn't long before British climbers were planning
expeditions to climb it, however the main challenge was not
the altitude but the obtaining of permission from either Nepal
or Tibet, countries who jealously guarded their borders and
refused to let outsiders in.

In 1920, after many years of diplomatic approaches and
rebuffs, the Tibetan government finally agreed to two British
expeditions. The first, in 1921, was billed as a reconnaissance
and survey; the second, a year later, a full-blown attempt. The
problem for the organizers, the Everest Committee, was finding
a suitable team. The First World War had robbed Britain of a

generation of Alpine climbers, who had been either maimed like Geoffrey Winthrop Young or killed, and there were only a handful of mountaineers with any Himalayan experience.

Impressed by his reputation as a ferociously talented rock climber, John Percy Farrar, a former president of the Alpine Club and a member of the Everest Committee, approached Mallory to enquire if he had 'any aspirations' to take part in the first expedition. Initially he wasn't at all sure. By the spring of 1921 he'd had enough of his job at Charterhouse, but with three children to support did not see the value of disappearing off for six months on an expenses-only expedition to the other side of the world. In the end it took Young's intervention to persuade him to go, arguing not only that it would be a great climbing adventure but also that, if Mallory succeeded, the fame that would follow would enable him to fulfil his literary and educational ambitions.

Though in theory he was a junior member, Mallory became the de facto leader of the climbing team when the Committee's choice, the fifty-five-year-old Harold Raeburn, fell ill during the crossing of Tibet and had to be sent back to convalesce. Mallory and his partner Guy Bullock, a school friend who had also been part of the Winchester Ice Club, were charged with exploring the glaciers around Everest and finding a viable route up the mountain.

Like most of the pioneers of Himalayan climbing, Mallory and the other members of the British team underestimated Everest, occasionally even imagining that on their very first acquaintance they might reach the summit. They were not unique. Initially, European climbers, from the Duke of the Abruzzi to Aleister Crowley and Jules Jacot-Guillarmod, treated the giants of the Himalayas and the Karakoram as if they were taller versions of what they had climbed in the Alps, and did not really take into account issues like altitude sickness and the much more extreme weather and topography.

Mallory and Bullock initially focused on the glaciers and northern approaches to Everest, before moving over the east side of the mountain. Apart from a quick peek over the West Ridge into Nepal, they did not cross the border. Then, after almost five months in the field, Mallory led a party of climbers and Sherpas to the North Col, the windswept pass at 23,000 feet that he had identified as the jumping-off point for the summit, 6,000 feet higher up.

As the wind roared across the desolate strip of icy, snow-covered ground, Mallory eyed the summit. Before he left, he'd been told in London, on the basis of minimal photographic evidence, that an 'easy slope' led to the top, but it was anything but. Later Bullock would estimate that the odds of reaching the summit were fifty to one against. Nevertheless, Mallory had done amazingly well, and though he never got on with the expedition leader, Charles Howard-Bury, it was his drive and determination that kept the party going when things got difficult. In the expedition book, he penned one of the great descriptions of Everest, calling it a 'prodigious white fang excrescent from the jaw of the world', and christened one of nearby mountains Clare Peak (later Pumori, or 'Mountain Daughter' in Sherpa), in honour of one of his daughters.

Mallory's first trip to Everest also showed up some of his less helpful characteristics. In his hurry to do the work as quickly as possible, he made a significant mapping error, missing the entrance to the East Rongbuk glacier, which later proved to be the best route to the North Col; and to his disgust, he flunked his photographic duties by exposing the wrong side of his camera's photographic plates, losing a week of work. These were 'rookie' errors, subsequently rectified by the team's official surveyor Oliver Wheeler and Mallory himself, who retook a lot of the images, but impatience and 'techno-phobia' and a slight sense of chaos would become recurrent themes in future expeditions.

Back in Britain, with the reconnaissance seen as a major success, the Everest Committee immediately set about organizing the main attempt in 1922. Mallory was top of their list to return, though they gave the climbing leader role to another older climber, Edward Strutt. Again, initially Mallory was diffident, telling his sister Avie that he had little faith that the Committee would find enough climbers to make it a viable attempt, and that if they didn't, 'I wouldn't go again next year, as the saying is, for all the gold in Arabia'. In the end, however, the organizers were able to put together a strong team, and it didn't take too much persuasion to get Mallory to sign up for a second time.

Led by General Charles Bruce and supported by a team of Sherpa and Bhotia porters, they swiftly crossed the Tibetan plain and set about laying 'siege' to Everest, setting up a series of supply camps up the East Rongbuk glacier before climbing back up to the North Col and then, for the first time, heading up the North Ridge towards the summit.

On their first attempt, on 19 May 1922, Mallory and two companions, Edward Norton and Howard Somervell, reached almost 27,000 feet, smashing the world altitude record by more than 2,000 feet. It was a significant achievement and a monument to their grit and determination, but they were still 2,000 feet short of the summit. As Mallory later wrote, their decision to turn back was all down to 'time and speed'. They could have gone further, but if they had done so, it would have meant abandoning all thoughts of sticking to a safe turnaround time. 'We were prepared to leave it to braver men to climb Mount Everest by night,' as he wrote in the expedition book.

A few days later, their record was broken by another few hundred feet, by Mallory's great rival on the British team, George Finch, an Imperial College London scientist climbing with the aid of artificial oxygen. Mallory persuaded Finch to join him for an oxygen-powered third attempt, but it was a disaster, with the whole team of three 'sahibs' (the Sherpas' term for foreign climbers) and fourteen porters swept away by an avalanche. By a stroke of luck, all the British climbers and seven of the porters survived, but the other seven were killed. Mallory was distraught, blaming himself for the accident. 'The consequences of my mistake are so terrible,' he wrote to Ruth, 'it seems almost impossible to believe that it has happened for ever and that I can do nothing to make good.' By the autumn, when the team held a homecoming meeting in London, the episode had faded from public memory and a new expedition was in the offing.

The Everest Committee had successfully petitioned the Dalai Lama for permission to stage a third and what they hoped would be final expedition, but there wasn't enough time to organize everything in just a few months, so instead of returning in 1923 they decided to defer for a year and use the time to raise money and recruit what they hoped would be an even stronger party.

Mallory was central to their plans, both as climber and ambassador. He delivered public lectures all over Britain, and when a New York agent, Lee Keedick, contacted the Committee, offering to arrange an American tour, there was no question of who they would choose to represent and tell the story of the British team – George Mallory, 'a gentleman of the highest character', as Arthur Hinks, the Everest Committee's honorary secretary, told the US visa office. 'His health is sufficiently guaranteed,' he added, 'by the fact that he climbed last May to 27,000ft.' Few could argue.

Mallory, for his part, was excited to go on his first trip to the United States, hoping to enjoy the sights and, as he told Hinks, earn some '£.s.d'.

America, however, would not be the cakewalk they had both hoped.

2 March 1923. George Mallory on Dartmouth Street
Bridge in Boston towards the end of his US tour. The
photographer was Helen Messinger Murdoch.

2

Go West

Lee Keedick thought he had a nose for a winner. Square-jawed and determined-looking, he was a former college baseball player from Iowa who set up a public speaking and press agency in New York in 1907 and kept it going until he was well into his seventies, billing himself as the 'Manager of the World's Most Celebrated Lecturers'. In the early 1900s, when the cinema was just getting going and television was a mere pixel in John Logie Baird's eye, there was a thriving lecture circuit all over the US, and audiences would come in their thousands to hear the famous men and women of their day tell their stories.

Initially Keedick's clients included American union leaders, magicians and big game hunters, but gradually he built up two specialisms: first, explorers such as his friend Roald Amundsen, the first man to reach the South Pole; and second, British personalities, ranging from the aristocratic Countess of Warwick, who lectured America on 'British Traits' in 1912, to famous writers such as Sir Arthur Conan Doyle, H. G. Wells and G. K.

Chesterton, who visited America in the early 1920s.

In the autumn of 1922, Keedick tried to bring those two specialisms together when he contacted the Everest Committee in London, inviting them to send a member of the recent expedition over for what he promised would be a lucrative lecture tour. It would be a big hit, he assured them, as long as the British chose someone who could tell the story 'in popular style to arouse public interest'.

The Everest Committee had no doubt that George Mallory was the right man for the job and he readily agreed. Honorary secretary Arthur Hinks didn't like the fact that Keedick wanted to take 10 per cent more in commission than his British counterpart, Gerald Christy, but he was keen to raise money and the next expedition's international profile.

So, in January 1923, Mallory set out for New York on the RMS *Olympic*, the pride of the White Star shipping line. It was Keedick's idea that he should travel in style, taking the *Olympic* rather than one of the cheaper ships Hinks would have preferred. If America was going to embrace Mallory as a star, Keedick maintained, he would have to play his part and behave like one. Mallory did not object. After spending much of the previous two years sleeping in a tent on the windswept plains and slopes of Tibet, the five-day voyage was a no-holds-barred immersion into the world of luxury.

The *Olympic* was a sister ship of the *Titanic* and at one time the largest passenger ship in the world. It had a swimming pool, gymnasium, Turkish baths, and several restaurants and bars. Initially, however, Mallory preferred to keep himself to himself, spending much of his time in his cabin, reading and writing. It would be his first visit to the United States and he was eager to see New York, visit Niagara Falls, and if everything went well, go as far west as California. The only downside was the people.

Like Charles Dickens, who had visited the US in 1842, initially Mallory was rather a snob about his transatlantic cousins. The first Americans he got to know were his nightly dinner companions on the *Olympic*, a family of tourists returning home after spending time in Europe. As he wrote to his wife Ruth, they were kind-hearted but naive. The husband in particular had 'disgusting' table manners and an accent that verged on caricature. At first Mallory could barely understand them, or they he, but gradually he tuned into their way of speaking and began practising his American accent, hoping that it would be of use when dealing with porters and 'such'.

Mallory's main preoccupation was to get as much writing as possible done for the official account of the 1922 expedition. His target was 2,000 words a day, but though he was happy to immerse himself in the details of his recent expedition on paper, he was not so keen on being recognized by other passengers. He kept off the subject of Everest with the American family, and managed to stay incognito until he bumped into a British general and his wife, who as luck would have it, had been on the SS *Narkunda,* the P&O ship that Mallory had taken back from India five months earlier. Fortunately, General Hughes was the soul of discretion and kept Mallory's secret safe. A few days later, on 17 January, the *Olympic* reached New York.

It was a bright, blue-sky morning but, fittingly, freezing cold with a vicious wind that reminded Mallory of Tibet. The *Olympic* anchored for a few hours just off the Hudson River while passports were checked, and then steamed past the Statue of Liberty into the New York docks. Like many before him, Mallory was immediately struck by Manhattan's skyscrapers, but he was probably the first to view them with a mountaineer's eye, describing the spearhead of tall buildings at the tip of the island as 'one of the most wonderful effects of piled up mass I have ever seen'.

Once the ship had docked, Mallory was whisked way to the Waldorf-Astoria, then New York's most prestigious hotel, and installed in a large room on the tenth floor with its own telephone and a luxurious bathroom. Keedick didn't give him much time to settle in: almost immediately he was introduced to a press agent, who briefed him on what to say and then hustled him into a room full of journalists.

American newspapers had followed the story of the British reconnaissance of 1921 and the second expedition a year later, but though Mallory was the best-known member of the British team, he was not nearly so well known as Amundsen or Shackleton. Arthur Hinks and the Everest Committee had always been uncomfortable with publicity, viewing newspapers as a necessary evil. Hinks trusted *The Times*, considering it a 'newspaper of record', but was very sniffy about other publications and was always uncomfortable with personalizing the expedition or creating any heroes.

The next day, the *New York Times* carried the first of several articles it would run on Mallory over the next three months. Under the headline 'Says Energy Faded on Everest Climb', it told how he had reached 27,235 feet (an exaggeration that would be repeated many times in the US press) but had turned back fourteen hours from the top when he and his party felt their physical and mental strength giving out. 'Would Everest ever be climbed?' the reporters had asked. 'It's a gamble,' said Mallory, tight-lipped.

Three years into Prohibition, American journalists were particularly keen to hear whether the climbing party had taken any 'alcoholic stimulants' and Mallory duly obliged, admitting that though the medical advice was against it, he and his partners had swigged back a little brandy at high altitude 'with good results'. The *New York Times* underestimated Mallory's age by six years and elevated his schoolmaster role at Charterhouse to that of a full-blown professor, but it was a positive start and the article mentioned his forthcoming lecture tour twice. There was less good news, though, from Keedick.

Despite his bullishness the previous autumn, it turned out that very few lectures had been booked. There had been many enquiries but hardly anything had been firmed up. Everything, Keedick said, depended on Mallory's first New York lecture, at the Broadhurst Theatre in early February. If he did well and got good reviews, the bookings would come in. If not... Keedick didn't elaborate. Prior to the Broadhurst, Mallory was engaged for some warm-up lectures in Philadelphia and Washington, but until then, Keedick advised, he was free to enjoy the Waldorf and two private New York clubs where he had been given temporary membership.

It was disappointing and slightly surprising, but Mallory was glad to be in America, and though he worried that he didn't know many people, in fact it turned out that he had several relatives and acquaintances on the East Coast. He still hadn't finished the chapters for the Everest book, and was keen to rework the British lectures that he had recently given to American tastes. He even hoped that he might have time to find an American publisher for his book on James Boswell.

A week after his arrival, Mallory left New York for the first of two lectures for the National Geographic Society in Washington. The venue was the Masonic temple, a large Neoclassical building that was a distinctly grander stage than the provincial British theatres Mallory was used to. Keedick resented the fact that the administrator at the National Geographic Society wanted Mallory to deliver both an afternoon and an evening lecture but was only willing to pay a single fee, but it was a good platform, especially as Mallory was going to be introduced by Robert Griggs, the famous American explorer and botanist who had made a daring visit to the volcanoes of Alaska.

Once enough hands had been shaken and publicity photographs snapped, Mallory began his lecture with a simple but provocative question: 'What is the use of climbing Everest?' His answer was succinct: 'It is of no use.' Reaching the summit of the world's highest peak, he declared, had no ostensible scientific value but was a product of the 'spirit of adventure and of pitting human intelligence against natural objects'.

Over the next hour, Mallory told the story of the 1922 expedition and the previous year's reconnaissance, illustrating the various stages of the journey and the two main attempts with black-and-white slides. He focused on the climbing difficulties but, mindful of contemporary America's obsession with alcohol, made sure to mention again the slug of brandy that he and the others knocked back at the end of their attempt. Having delivered many lectures in Britain, Mallory was a seasoned pro who enjoyed performing and working an audience, but he was nervous about his first foray into the American market. As he wrote to Ruth a few days later, the results were mixed.

'This afternoon they were the most unresponsive crowd I ever talked to,' he moaned, 'never a clap when I meant them to applaud, and almost never a laugh. They weren't comfortable with me, I don't know why.' The second, identical lecture – delivered that evening – got an utterly different response. 'From the first word to the last,' he continued, 'I did what I liked with them; they took all my points; it was technically better than any lecture I've ever given, either year, and had any amount of spontaneity, too.'

America was not going to be swept off its feet by Mallory in the way that Keedick or the members of the Everest Committee had anticipated, but there was some more positive press after Washington, and a few days later he delivered another lecture to a packed house of 2,000 in Philadelphia. Keedick's agency, however, saw no sudden rush of bookings. Everything, as he continued to insist, depended on what happened in New York on 4 February.

Back at the Waldorf, Mallory carried on working on his chapters for the 1922 expedition book in between social engagements and meetings with journalists and press agents. Some doctors took him for lunch and then persuaded him to come back to their laboratory, where they subjected him to breathing tests before pronouncing that his lungs had twice the 'vital capacity' of a normal individual. Another admirer, a wealthy stockbroker who'd had a good day at the Cotton Exchange, took him out for an expensive lunch at a penthouse restaurant, forty storeys up in an express elevator.

Mallory loved the energy of the city streets at night. At the University Club, he caught up on the latest books and devoured the weekly edition of the Manchester *Guardian* for political news. He arranged to visit the Pierpont Morgan Library, where he was thrilled to find a collection of original letters from James Boswell and unexpectedly met an old friend from Cambridge, the actor Reginald Pole, who was then in New York playing Hamlet's ghost on Broadway. Pole promised to be there when Mallory lectured at the Broadhurst.

As 4 February drew closer, Mallory was invited out by the American Alpine Club to a gala dinner. Forty members turned up, and after speeches were made and extracts read out from his account of the 1921 reconnaissance, Mallory was bombarded with questions about the problems and challenges of Everest. 'It went well enough,' he wrote to Ruth, but 'there was not much fun or fizz in it', and they served nothing all evening but water. An unexpected highlight came a few hours later, when Henry Schwab, an experienced Alpine climber and future president of the AAC, took him to the 'swellest of New York' clubs.

Mournfully, they processed down to the empty cellars now lined with lockers rather than wine racks. Then, to Mallory's great surprise, out of one of those lockers there emerged a bottle of gin, which was soon handed over to a barman to mix up a tray of Tom Collins cocktails. 'Quelle vie!' he exclaimed to Ruth. Perhaps Prohibition wasn't quite so bad after all.

The Broadhurst was never far from his thoughts. 'Everything depends on this for press reports,' he wrote nervously. Keedick continued to try to promote Mallory, sending a stream of journalists his way, but with the papers full of stories about Howard Carter's excavation of Tutankhamun's tomb in Egypt, it was not always easy to place articles on a British expedition which had done well on Everest but had not quite reached the top.

The *New York Times* continued to do its bit, with a piece on 3 February, the day before the big lecture. 'Mountain Climber Trains in Walk-Ups' proclaimed the headline, joking that Mallory preferred to keep fit in New York by taking the staircase rather than the elevator and was looking forward to climbing 'Mt Woolworth' before he left the city. On a more serious note, though not necessarily what the Everest Committee might have wanted, it confided to readers that funds were 'more or less assured' for a follow-up expedition in the spring of 1924.

The next day, Mallory finally took to the New York stage. Opened in 1917, the Broadhurst was a relatively recent addition to theatreland. It was slightly smaller than the huge hall in Philadelphia where he had given his last lecture but could still hold 1,200 people. Normally it specialized in revues and musicals, but on Sunday, 4 February 1923, George Mallory was the star attraction. A year earlier, he had been shuttling between his home in Godalming and London, getting ready to travel out to India and begin the first official attempt on Everest. Now he was facing a very different challenge. His pride – as well the hopes of the Everest Committee – was at stake.

The evening did not start well. The projectionist turned up late and initially didn't have enough electrical cable to power the slide projector. It wasn't quite as busy as Mallory had hoped, but as he looked out into the stalls, he could see the forty members of the American Alpine Club he'd dined with a few days earlier. Once again, they had turned out en masse to see him, along with several friends and acquaintances. Buoyed by their presence, Mallory gave a confident performance, focusing mainly on the three attempts made during the 1922 expedition, and showing images of what the *New York Times* later called the 'appalling peaks, crags and glaciers near the top of the world's highest mountain'. The audience went away 'fizzing, and I had reports of nice things said as they were going out', as he later reported to Ruth.

Sadly, Henry Schwab was not available for another round of cocktails, but afterwards Mallory and his entourage went out for celebratory ice creams at a local hotel. Reginald Pole, who'd arrived with an 'actress friend', told him that his delivery had been flawless and could not have been improved. Mallory was very grateful for the compliments, but when he went to bed that night, he knew that whatever his friends thought, all that really mattered was the reviews in tomorrow's papers.

In Britain, tempting the press and pulling in the crowds had never been too difficult. Even though mountaineering was still a relatively elitist sport, it had enough prominent supporters to keep its profile high, and there was already a small but viable 'armchair' audience who though they were never likely to visit the Alps, never mind the Himalayas, were keen to buy the books, read the articles and attend the lectures.

The situation was different in the US. In the 1900s, the press had followed the story of the first attempts on Denali in Alaska, America's highest peak, but climbing was much less popular than in Europe. There were a handful of clubs on the East and West coasts, but very few American mountaineers had climbed outside the United States and even fewer, if any, had been to the Himalayas. If the Everest Committee was going to sell its mountain to America, everything depended on George Mallory's performance at the Broadhurst.

And so, on the morning of 5 February, when he went down to breakfast, his first impulse was not to fill his cup or load up his plate, but to have a look at the morning papers and read what they said about his show the night before.

He was disappointed.

The *New York Times* had a large headline on page 4 and a third of a column devoted to the lecture, but as Mallory moaned to Ruth, 'the whole thing was turned into Anti-Prohibition propaganda', with the *Times* once again focusing on the restorative properties of a high-altitude brandy – which it repeated had 'cheered us up wonderfully'. It finished with Mallory's declaration that everything augured well for a further attempt, but the tone was more casual than epic, the article finishing: 'Most of the paths now being beaten, a few useful tricks and bits of local information having been picked up, the new attempt is very likely to prove successful, according to Mr Mallory.'

The rival, but less widely read, *New-York Tribune* had a longer, more flattering article, in which it described how Mallory and the other climbers had battled against 'almost unbelievable obstacles' and the 'terrors of avalanches', suffering intensely as they hacked their way towards the summit. Praising him for his 'unaffected manner of speech, which made him immediately a friend of the audience', the *Tribune* article was everything Mallory and Keedick could have wanted – if only it had been in the *Times*. Keedick's assistant ordered 100 reprints to send to prospective venues and clubs, hoping that it would help bring in the bookings nevertheless.

The following day, Mallory lectured at a private club just outside New York, but after that, apart from a solitary event in Montreal, the next two weeks were blank. It was all looking a little glum, until he met Basil Williams, a British historian then teaching at McGill University, who was a good friend of one of George's neighbours in Godalming. Mallory stayed with Williams in Montreal and spent a weekend with his sixteen-year-old son, John, learning how to ski at a cabin in the woods. After so many nights on his own at the Waldorf, he was very happy to be able to spend some time in a family home.

The East Coast was still gripped by ferociously cold weather. When Mallory reached Montreal, it was –23 degrees Celsius – so cold that one of his fingers that had been frozen on Everest started to show signs of frostbite again. The lecture went well though; despite more problems with a faulty slide projector, the audience was very good-humoured and complimentary, giving Mallory's confidence a welcome boost.

When he returned New York on 13 February, there was no good news. Though the agency had managed to set up new dates in Boston and Toledo, there hadn't been the hoped-for rush of bookings. As Keedick told Gerald Christy, his counterpart in London, the problem wasn't so much the speaker as the theme. 'Mallory is a fine fellow and gives a good lecture,' he wrote, 'but the American public don't seem to be interested in the subject.' After adding up all the box-office takings, it turned out that the Broadhurst show had only been half full. When Keedick contacted one of his regular clients, the Geographic Society of Chicago, all they offered was a measly $100 for a lecture to their thousand members. 'They say that there isn't any interest in Chicago in the Mt. Everest Expedition,' he lamented.

Keedick advised Mallory to abandon the tour and return home straight away, but he wanted to stay on. Though in his letters home he told his wife Ruth how much he missed her, there was still so much to see in America; and even if public appearances were limited, he enjoyed performing and being the centre of attention. 'After a lecture about half the audience is intent on shaking one's hand and making a little speech. They do know how to say nice things and make one feel happy with them,' he wrote to a friend back in England. As a concession to economy, Mallory vacated his suite at the Waldorf-Astoria and moved to the more modest Hotel Flanders on West 47th Street, a regular haunt for actors and performers with rooms at a quarter of the price.

Part of the problem was Keedick's business model. The 'Manager of the World's Most Celebrated Lecturers' didn't want to drop his prices and offer cheap talks to schools and clubs. Mallory was not so picky. He too had a vested financial interest in the success of the tour and would have preferred to deliver as many lectures as possible, even if some were paid at a lower rate. After expenses had been deducted and Keedick had taken his cut, he would get 30 per cent of the profits, with the rest of the money going to the Everest Committee. Though he was usually billed as a professor at Charterhouse, in fact he had left his job a year and a half earlier and his only income was from lectures and the occasional paid article for a magazine. Ruth received a generous allowance of £750 per year (about £37,000 in today's money) from her wealthy father, but with three children, a cook and a nanny, there wasn't a lot of money around, especially for a couple with relatively expensive tastes. The Mallorys had recently bought a car, a luxury item in the 1920s, and were having a garage built for it. As he admitted to Ruth in a letter on 15 February, 'We shall be poorer than I hoped for a bit.' For all his disappointment though, and his regular declarations of how homesick he was, Mallory was by then enjoying himself in America and wanted to stay on for as long as he could.

In late February and early March, the bookings finally started picking up and he found himself 'gyrating' from Boston to Chicago to Toledo to Iowa. He made a second trip to Philadelphia and spoke to a capacity crowd of 1,200 at the Penn Museum. He addressed the Harvard Union and the Travelers Club in Boston; had his portrait taken by Helen Messinger Murdoch, the celebrated photographer; and delivered lectures at two of America's most prestigious schools, Dartmouth College and St Paul's in Concord.

As the tour went on, Mallory loosened up and lost some of his British reserve and reticence about talking up Everest. 'It is a crazy thing to do,' he told an audience in Rochester, 'but I guess we all are a little bit crazy in some respects and surely this has

the thrill of adventure that breaks the humdrum life.' A couple
of weeks later he returned to the same theme in Iowa, trying
to explain to the audience why it was worth repeatedly risking
life and limb for something that had no ostensible scientific
purpose. 'You may think we were crazy, but isn't everyone crazy
sometimes? And craziness often accomplishes results.'

The most important event on his American tour, however,
was not a lecture or a speech but an interview by an unnamed
journalist which appeared in the *New York Times* on Sunday,
18 March 1923. Under the bold headline 'Climbing Everest Is
Work for Supermen', it began with a simple question, 'Why
did you want to climb Mount Everest?' and an equally laconic
answer: 'Because it's there.' In the century since it was first
printed, Mallory's reply has become one of the most well-known
quotations in the history of exploration, if not *the* most, repeated
by everyone from fellow mountaineers to John F. Kennedy, in his
famous speech at Rice University on America's space programme.

Some commentators have doubted whether Mallory actually
said it, or asked what the phrase really meant. Was 'Because it's
there' just a clever phrase dreamed up by a reporter – or the
response of a bored public speaker, desperate to shrug off a
question that had been put to him many times before, and get
to the bar? It is possible (though in the midst of Prohibition,
most bars were hardly an attractive prospect), but looking at
all his American press coverage in 1923, it's more likely that
Mallory actually did say it – and meant it. This was the fourth
article about him in the *New York Times*, and by far the longest.
Whereas the first three had tended towards the flippant, focusing
on the brandy and the candy, this one took him much more
seriously, allowing him to talk about both his philosophy and
the nitty-gritty of getting up and down Everest.

The bare simplicity of 'Because it's there' echoed the starkness of 'What's the use of climbing Everest? It's of no use' – the rhetorical question he often began his lectures with. And, as he went on to explain, it crystallized one important aspect of his approach to Everest and his need to climb it: 'Its existence is a challenge. The answer is instinctive, a part, I suppose, of man's desire to conquer the universe.'

From his childhood scrambles up church towers and school walls to his first proper mountaineering adventures in the Alps and North Wales, Mallory had always been instinctively drawn to challenges, especially of the vertical kind. As he had shown in 1922, he was fiercely competitive and wanted not just to climb Everest, but to be the *first person* to do so. The idea that mankind wanted to master the universe and so was magnetically drawn to Everest was a theme that had been repeated many times by Sir Francis Younghusband, the Chairman of the Everest Committee, but Mallory took this one step further, arguing that as a mountaineer he literally felt *compelled* to do so. 'I suppose we go to Mount Everest', he wrote in one set of lecture notes, 'because – in a word – we can't help it.'

Though it frequently appeared under a rather cruder headline, 'He-Man's Job to Climb Everest', this last *New York Times* article was the most widely syndicated of all the Mallory pieces that appeared that spring in America's newspapers. The new publicity arrived too late to enable him to extend his stay, but the last few weeks of his tour were among the busiest and most enjoyable. He paid a visit to Princeton, spent three 'wild days' in New York, and then returned to Boston where he spoke to a thousand-strong audience at Jordan Hall, a final lecture that was the direct result of the 'fizz' generated by his earlier appearance in the city.

With just three days before he boarded the *Saxonia* for the voyage back to Britain, Mallory was getting 'de-mob' happy, telling his Boston audience that the only way to be truly confident of reaching the summit was to be 'shot there' as a human cannonball. On a more serious note, he talked about the importance of improving their oxygen sets and how it would be necessary to establish a last camp 2,000 feet closer to the summit than their final camp in 1922. With better equipment and a higher starting point, he argued, next time they really would have a fighting chance of getting there.

As Mallory contemplated his return, he told Ruth that he'd enjoyed his trip and had reversed his earlier opinion of Americans. The United States was 'intensely interesting' and he now discerned a modesty and humility behind its citizens' sometimes brash façade. As for America, it too had eventually warmed to Mallory, despite his plummy British accent and his initial reticence and reluctance to sensationalize.

Back in Britain, Mallory knew his lectures would probably always get a more enthusiastic reception, but he wasn't quite as confident or certain of his future as he might have seemed. The Everest Committee owed him around £180 from his earlier British appearances, and he was expecting a further £250 from his American tour – a total of around £21,000 in today's money for six months of public speaking. Other than that, and a small amount from magazine articles, he had no other money coming in. True, he had just written several chapters for the forthcoming 1922 Everest book, as well as several others for the official account of the 1921 reconnaissance, but knowing how parsimonious the Everest Committee was, he'd have to put up a real fight to get any royalties.

As for taking another crack at Everest, though he had spent months talking about nothing else, he felt ambivalent about going back. Put Mallory on a mountain and all he thought about was getting to the top, but climbing wasn't the only passion in his life. If he was ever going to become that professional writer, found that progressive school, or change the world for the better, he would have to stay home with his wife and children and friends and put an end to his ceaseless travelling. He loved mountaineering and felt magnetically attracted to Everest, but as someone who had been there twice, he knew that the odds of reaching the top were slim and the odds of dying, or simply wasting a lot of time, much higher.

But that wasn't all. Though over the course of his US trip American newspapers had frequently referred to Mallory reaching 27,235 feet on his final attempt, struggling upwards with an oxygen set on his back, in fact neither of those things was true.

Mallory had never used oxygen in 1922 and the honours for the highest altitude on Everest had gone to his great rival, the second 'George' on the 1922 team: George Ingle Finch. If Mallory was the Everest Committee's 'Golden Boy', Finch was its black sheep – an assertive, sometimes abrasive Australian-born scientist who frequently, and justifiably, felt aggrieved by the behaviour of his teammates. Mallory had led the first attempt on the summit, reaching 27,000 feet, but Finch had done even better, climbing 200–300 feet higher and several hundred yards closer to the summit with Geoffrey Bruce, a novice climber he'd shepherded up and down the mountain. Every time an American newspaper printed that Mallory had reached 27,235 feet on Everest, he must have known that this was in fact Finch's record altitude, not his own.

In some of the earlier British lectures Mallory had been directly pitted against Finch, one representing 'science', the other 'spirit'. It was likely both he and Finch would be invited to return in 1924, but could he endure the struggle and the limelight with him? Would he be willing, as he'd been asked in 1921, to share a tent, real or metaphorical, with Finch?

I wouldn't care who I shared with, he had replied, 'as long as [we] got to the top', but the next couple of months would turn out to be far more complicated and unpredictable than either George had envisaged.

3

The Two Georges

At 4.00 p.m. on 22 March 1923, while Mallory was in Boston preparing for another round of press interviews, the Everest Committee met at the Alpine Club on Savile Row in Mayfair. In the chair was Norman Collie, an esteemed professor of chemistry at University College London; the other attendees were Lord Ronaldshay, the former governor of Bengal and current president of the Royal Geographical Society, Sir Francis Younghusband, the famous soldier-explorer, and Lieutenant-Colonel Charles Howard-Bury, the man who had led the Everest reconnaissance in 1921. Unusually the joint secretaries, Sydney Spencer and Arthur Hinks, were both also present, perhaps because it was the first meeting in three months and there was important business at hand.

Today, mountaineering is a private affair. Largely speaking, anyone can climb any mountain; all they need is enough money to support themselves and enough skill and energy to get to the top. For most mountains in the Himalayas you have to obtain a permit and pay a 'peak fee', but you don't have to pay anything at all to climb in the Alps. In the case of Everest, the vast majority of people join a commercial expedition where all the staffing and transport has been organized in advance, stumping up around £50,000 to become part of an ad hoc team in which everyone expects to get to the summit.

Arthur Hinks, the honorary secretary of the Everest Committee.

Francis Younghusband, the Chairman of the Everest Committee.

From the 1920s to the 1950s it was very different. Himalayan mountaineering was a true team sport, where several mountaineers would work together to put one or two of their party on the summit. They didn't generally have to pay for the privilege of taking part, but nor did they have that much control over the personnel or the staging of the expedition. In the case of Everest, the early British expeditions were ruled over at first by the Everest Committee, and then, after the Second World War, by the Joint Himalayan Committee.

The purpose of both bodies was to organize and finance what were complex and expensive undertakings. In the first instance the Committee worked behind the scenes to obtain official permissions and raise money. They selected the climbers, procured the equipment needed, and liaised with the press before and during the expedition. When they reached Everest, senior members of the team like George Mallory might be expected to play a major role in the decision-making, but prior to that, the Committee was in charge.

Its ranks were drawn from 'the great and the good' of two bodies: the Royal Geographical Society and the Alpine Club. The RGS was bigger, had a more prestigious address and more distinguished patrons, but both organizations were very well connected to the British establishment. As Mallory once quipped: 'Speaking as a member of the Alpine Club, I must describe it as an association of men who climb mountains, and the Royal Geographical Society as an association of men who want to have them climbed.'

In 1921, the reconnaissance had been billed as a dual-purpose expedition, its two aims being to map the geography and geology of the Everest region and work out how to climb the mountain. Subsequent expeditions were supposed to be purely for mountaineering and therefore should have been largely controlled by the Alpine Club, but the RGS had no plans to relinquish control over proceedings.

The public face of the Committee, Sir Francis Younghusband, was a quintessentially Victorian man of action, with thinning hair, a huge moustache and dark intense eyes. Born in British India in 1863 into a military family, he had spent several

decades exploring and travelling in central Asia. In the 1880s
and 1890s he trekked 1,200 miles through the deserts of China;
made the first crossing of the fabled Mustagh pass, the gateway
to K2 and the Karakoram mountains; and explored Ladakh
and the remote city of Kashgar. Later, in 1903, he led the rather
less noble British invasion of Tibet.

Younghusband was one of the first men to declare an
ambition to climb Everest, concocting a plan to conquer the
world's highest mountain on a polo field in Chitral on the
North-West Frontier in 1893, with his friend and fellow officer
Charles Bruce. Neither the Tibetan nor the Nepali government
were willing to let any foreign climbers into their country
at the time, but when several decades later Britain finally
got permission from the Dalai Lama, it was no surprise that
Younghusband was at the forefront of the small group of men
who made it happen. Once he'd got official approval in 1920,
Younghusband delivered speeches, glad-handed officials and
wooed the press to raise enough money for the expedition that
would give mankind 'increased pride and confidence in himself
and in his struggle for ascendancy over matter'.

Younghusband was the chief banger of the drum, but on a
day-to-day basis the most important member of the Committee
was much less visible: the joint secretary, Arthur Hinks. Trained
as an astronomer at Cambridge, he had become Secretary of the
Royal Geographical Society in 1915. Tall and bespectacled and
rather portly, he was someone who liked to be in control and
didn't suffer fools gladly. In theory he was just an administrator,
but Hinks was the main organizer and letter writer – the man
who got things done.

On 22 March, the most important items on the agenda
were the selection and leadership of the new team for 1924,

and something much more embarrassing: the embezzlement, or 'defalcation' as it was quaintly described in the minutes of the meeting, of a considerable amount of the Committee's precious funds by Charles Eric Thompson, a former clerk at the RGS.

Thompson had been taken on in 1922, initially as a shorthand typist. The fact that he came from the Association for the Employment of Ex-Officers but had never been an officer did not cause undue concern. He seemed like a hard worker and was soon promoted to accounts assistant and then cashier. What he didn't tell anyone was that he'd recently left his wife and two children and had shacked up with his mistress in Chelmsford in Essex.

His pilfering started small, with £10 stolen from petty cash, but gradually he took more and more until, as the magistrate later declared, he had stolen £1,400 (around £70,000 in today's money). Though he later denied in court that he had squandered it on betting and carousing, he was sentenced to twelve months of 'such hard labour as he was able to perform'.

Among the climbers, Hinks and the Committee were known for their stinginess yet it had been easy for Thompson to steal from expedition funds because their financial management was incredibly sloppy. In theory, all Everest expedition cheques had to be signed and countersigned by the RGS's treasurer, the banker Edward Somers-Cocks, and Captain J. E. C. Eaton, Hinks's opposite number at the Alpine Club. In practice this rarely happened, and there was very little oversight of the account.

The only crumb of comfort for the Committee was that, after a thorough check, it appeared that Thompson had stolen just over £700, about half of what he had been accused of, but with money tight and Mallory's US tour not having gone as well as they had hoped, it was still a huge hole in their finances, especially amid planning for the 1924 expedition.

In recent years it has become commonplace to describe the 1920s expeditions as 'grand imperial gestures', but it would be a mistake to think that they were directly funded by the British government. The British Army did supply some of the personnel and some logistical support, but most of the money came from the membership of the Alpine Club and the RGS, supplemented by smaller donations from the general public and funds raised through lectures, films and the sale of newspaper rights. Eventually, the Committee's shame-faced treasurer, Somers-Cocks, offered to refund half the money Thompson had stolen, but expedition funds were still £350 down.

Planning for the second attempt had begun almost as soon as the failure of the previous expedition was announced in July 1922. Initially the Committee wanted to send out a new team in 1923, and the fifty-nine-year-old Younghusband had even offered to take all the stores to base camp, but as the months went by, the Committee began to doubt that they would be able to raise enough money or find strong enough candidates. They did manage to secure permission for another attempt from the Tibetan government, but decided to postpone it to 1924, by which time they hoped sufficient cash would have been raised. In Hinks's estimate, it would cost approximately £1,000 to equip and support each European climber, a surprisingly similar figure to what it costs today, if inflation is taken into account.

The Committee wasn't keen on repeating the general appeal to the public or their fellows that they had made in 1921. Instead, they hoped that book royalties and substantial profits from British lectures and the expedition film would soon be coming in. In the meantime, the most important issue at hand was to get on with selecting a new team.

Though he had not been officially appointed, everyone assumed that General Charles Bruce would once again be in charge. Bruce, like Younghusband, was a quintessentially British figure, both large and larger than life. Thickset, moustached and immensely strong, he was the fourteenth child of Baron Aberdare. Educated at Harrow and then Repton, he had joined the British Indian Army in 1888 and spent decades in the Punjab, patrolling the Northern and North-West frontiers before being seriously wounded at Gallipoli in 1915.

As a climber Bruce was a regular visitor to the Alps and one of the most experienced Himalayan travellers of the era. He had been to Nanga Parbat on Albert Mummery's last expedition in 1895, and had explored the Karakoram and later Nanda Devi, India's highest mountain. In his late fifties, he was too old to go high on Everest, but in 1922 he had led an exemplary march across Tibet to Base Camp and proved himself to be as popular with the Sherpa and Bhotia porters as he had been with the Gurkha soldiers he had commanded for so many years. He was their kind of man: a Nepali speaker who was as fond of a joke as he was of a drink; a raconteur and wit who loved to tell tall stories as much as rude ones.

The arch-bureaucrat Arthur Hinks was a little wary of Charlie Bruce. They'd had their run-ins in the past, but by 1923 Bruce was 'part of the furniture'. The only question mark over his leadership was whether he would get through a Harley Street medical or whether his war wounds and his liver – so big he joked that two boys were needed to carry it – would rule him out. Bruce, who for the last three years had been in

charge of a Welsh Territorial Army association, clearly wanted
to go back for another crack and had already started choosing
the climbers who would be going with him.

Top of the list were the three men who had made the first
summit attempt in 1922 – George Mallory, Howard Somervell
and Edward Norton. Bruce, like the other more experienced
members of the 1922 team, had been very critical of Mallory
at the end of the expedition, blaming his poor judgement for
the deaths of seven porters in the avalanche that put paid to
the third attempt. 'He is a great dear but forgets his boots on
all occasions,' he wrote in a confidential report. In the months
that followed, Bruce had forgiven Mallory, but there was never
any question of making him leader, or even deputy, of the
1924 climbing team. That role instead would go to Norton,
a highly regarded army officer whom Bruce described as the
'discovery' of 1922. The other climber who had impressed him
most was Somervell, a surgeon from the Lake District whom
Bruce called 'a wonderful goer'.

His initial list also included his nephew Geoffrey, another
officer in a Gurkha regiment, and two 'new boys': the geologist
Noel Odell, who had a very good record in the Alps, and
Bentley Beetham, a schoolmaster from Durham. The most
interesting and most complicated entry on the list, though,
was George Finch. At the end of the 1922 expedition, Bruce
had described him as 'probably the best snow and ice man on
the expedition', but though Finch had been invited to join the
fold and become a member of the Alpine Club, he never quite
fitted in.

Finch was an Australian by birth but had been educated
and taught to climb in Switzerland. Unlike Mallory and the
other former public-school boys and soldiers on the team, who

Everest Base Camp, 1922. George Finch wearing
his specially designed down jacket.

did what they were told, Finch was assertive and independent
minded. He had very quickly come into conflict with Arthur
Hinks, with whom he shared a strong, mutual antipathy. In
1921, Finch had initially been chosen for the reconnaissance
but was rejected at the last moment, supposedly on medical
grounds. In 1922 he'd been invited to take part, but because of
his scientific background he'd quickly been cast as the team's
oxygen champion and made fun of by the other members of
the team – as well as Hinks, who had once declared that 'only
rotters would use oxygen'.

Despite all the barbs, Finch had proved himself to be
both resourceful and industrious. As well as looking after the
oxygen sets, he had designed a prototype duvet jacket, found

a way to laminate maps, and taken and developed hundreds of photographs. The other members of the team had laughed at his padded coat until they realized that it was much warmer than their tweeds and wool. As for the oxygen, Mallory for one had refused to take part in Finch's training drills and scorned its use, until Finch broke his altitude record by 200–300 feet, at which point Mallory started to take an interest. He invited Finch to join him on the doomed third attempt, but with no time to recover from his exertions, Finch was too exhausted to take part and had to retire early.

Back in England, Finch delivered around eighty lectures for the Everest Committee in the autumn of 1922 and the following spring. While Mallory was travelling up and down the East Coast of the US, Finch brought the Everest story to Workington, Harwich and Huddersfield. Like Mallory, he was a confident and popular lecturer. There are several letters in the Everest Committee's archives from venues which had been so pleased with his performance that they waived their own expenses and chose to offer the Everest Committee the complete takings.

Despite all this, the 'problem' with Finch was that he was just too assertive and self-possessed and could be arrogant and abrasive. Charlie Bruce might have admired his engineering skills and his mountaineering prowess, but he never warmed to him. When he sent his initial list to Sydney Spencer, the Secretary of the Alpine Club, Bruce put a note next to his name: 'Finch: I am very sorry to say.'

For his part, Finch never tried to ingratiate himself with the Committee or the other climbers, though he clearly expected to be part of the 1924 team. When Mallory asked if he could borrow some copies of his photographic slides for his lectures,

Finch refused, telling him rather patronizingly, 'my style of lecturing is, as perhaps you know, essentially different from yours and is, amongst other things, chosen to set off my slides to their best advantage'.

There was one issue on which both he and Mallory agreed: money.

The membership of the Alpine Club and the Royal Geographical Society was largely middle- and upper-middle-class. Climbing was an expensive sport which required both time and money, and Arthur Hinks frequently behaved as if prospective Everest climbers were all independently wealthy. In 1921 he had reluctantly handed over a clothing grant to the climbers, but had baulked when Charles Bruce had asked for a stipend to cover his wages. The leadership that year had gone to Charles Howard-Bury, a well-heeled Anglo-Irish aristocrat who had offered to cover his own costs.

Finch and Mallory were undoubtedly middle-class but neither was wealthy. Mallory's father, the Reverend Herbert, was frequently overstretched and did not have a lot of spare cash for his children. Finch had been born to a well-to-do family and was highly educated, but most of his inheritance had been invested in the imperial Russian railway. After the 1917 Revolution, his Russian shares were worthless, and to make things even more difficult, he had recently married for the third time and had alimony payments to cover. Prior to joining the Everest team in 1922, Finch had regularly lectured about his climbing adventures to supplement his university salary. He was happy to lecture on Everest for the Committee, but not so happy with the split of profits they offered.

He'd argued about lecture fees with Hinks in the autumn of 1922, and though they reached an agreement, in the spring of 1923 new battle lines emerged when Finch was offered a series of lectures in Switzerland, his old stamping ground. Hinks did not approve. The film of the 1922 expedition was about to be released on the Continent, so Hinks said no, arguing that Finch's proposed lectures would compete with and devalue the film, and that the contract everyone had signed in 1922 forbade him from lecturing without the approval of the Committee. Finch refused to back down, buoyed by messages from his Swiss friends, who were confident that he would get a good audience.

While Finch wrangled with Hinks, Mallory had his own money worries. His wife Ruth continued to receive the annual allowance from her wealthy father, but Mallory had no definite career prospects other than the fantasy of working, as he told his sister, at a 'minor provincial university'. Then, out of the blue, shortly after he had returned from the US, Arthur Hinks appeared as an unlikely fairy godmother.

In March 1923, Hinks had bumped into an old friend, the Reverend David Cranage, who was then the director of external studies at Cambridge University. Cranage told Hinks that he was looking for a dynamic new colleague to deliver evening lectures and organize summer schools. Hinks suggested Mallory and within a month he had the job, beating out a crowded field and some better-qualified rivals.

Mallory was overjoyed. Not only did it offer a good starting salary of around £500 – more than he had ever earned as a schoolmaster – but it was an ideal job for him, teaching adults in a joint enterprise between the prestigious university and the Workers' Educational Association. A position at the extramural department at Cambridge would bring him back to a city he knew well and where several very good friends lived, and for a Fabian proto-socialist, bringing education to the working classes felt like a worthy enterprise. Within six weeks, he had started work and had moved to temporary lodgings in Cambridge, where in between lectures and days in the office he went house hunting, planning to move Ruth and their three children in the autumn.

There was only one problem, but it was a big one: Everest.

Mallory had just come back from America, where he had spent three months talking up the next expedition, and prior to that he had spent almost a year getting to and from the mountain itself. In the eyes of the public, he was 'Mr Everest'. Only a few weeks after accepting the job in Cambridge, he was asked to address the RGS's annual dinner and propose the toast to the president. 'The Society gathers us together,' he declared, 'before sending out another expedition.' His words, however, belied an ambivalence over Everest, which was more profound than ever.

In 1921, Geoffrey Winthrop Young had worked hard to persuade Mallory to sign up for the reconnaissance, arguing that it would bring him into the public eye and give him a 'label' which might be useful to help him realize his other ambitions. Now, in the summer of 1923, that strategy had begun to bear fruit with the job in Cambridge. 'Few things,' Young wrote on hearing of Mallory's appointment, 'could have given me greater delight!' His great friend David Pye, now a neighbour in Cambridge, noticed how he had matured: 'He seemed to have developed quite a new kind of serenity, and to have sloughed off his old impatience, his hatred of caution and stupidity, and to have developed a gentleness and sympathy.'

The stakes were higher than ever: Mallory had the university job that he had always wanted, and after two years of virtually non-stop travelling was looking forward to spending the year with his wife and three young children. He loved gardening, the English countryside and the chance to model a new family home. He was impressed by the students he encountered at his evening lectures, the 'young men and maidens in various walks of life between teachers and boot-making hands'. Could he really desert them, his family and his friends for another six months for the slender chance of reaching the summit of Everest?

One intriguing insight into Mallory's thinking at this point comes from a very unexpected source: a collection of ten letters that he wrote to Marjorie Holmes, a nineteen-year-old teacher from Yorkshire, which came to light in 2015 when they were sold at Bonhams for £12,500. The pair never met, but in late 1922 or early 1923 they began corresponding regularly, their letters an odd mixture of epistolary romance interspersed with paternal advice, digressions on the art of letter writing, and discussions about Marjorie's future career. It is not clear what initiated the correspondence, and none of Marjorie's reciprocal letters to George have survived, but viewed today the correspondence is a particularly interesting one because Marjorie was not part of his profession or social circle, so he could be totally candid with her about certain things.

In one letter, dated 26 May 1923, just before Mallory moved to lodgings in Cambridge, he told her how his new job would take him travelling around England and that, though it had had prompted some soul-searching and angst, 'I'm convinced it's the job I want'. It was difficult, he admitted, to uproot Ruth and make her leave Godalming where her father and sisters still lived, but it was a different type of 'adventure'. He added:

'I hope I shan't become less interesting to you if, as now seems probable, I don't go again to Everest – but you might go on liking me even so.'

Ironically, while harbouring considerable private doubts that he would ever return, Mallory had been invited to join a special subcommittee at the Alpine Club to help select the new Everest team. On 1 May the subcommittee made its first formal recommendations with names that echoed Charlie Bruce's initial list: George Mallory, Howard Somervell, Edward Norton or his brother Jack, and the two new prospects, Noel Odell and Bentley Beetham. One name was not included: that of Mallory's great rival, George Finch.

The idea that the man who had got highest on the mountain in 1922, had been the team's oxygen expert, and was thought of as one of the best climbers in Europe might not be included seems quite astonishing, but it tells you something about the politics and prejudices of the era. Even though he'd served with distinction in the Royal Army Ordnance Corps and was highly regarded at Imperial College in London, Finch was just too different, too 'other', perhaps too Australian, to be accepted whatever his merits.

The game wasn't quite over though. About a month later, in early June, both Georges were invited to appear in front of the Everest Committee, to argue out the case for and against oxygen. Even though Finch had proved its value in 1922, it remained a divisive issue. As well as the controversy over the 'sporting' ethics of using 'artificial aids', puffed up by the non-climber Hinks, there were other, more pragmatic objections: oxygen sets were primitive in design and heavy and awkward to wear when climbing. Their use significantly increased the logistical challenge of any attempt, because large numbers of oxygen bottles had to be carried to Base Camp and then high on the mountain.

Finch, of course, was still very much in favour. He advocated using oxygen from 21,000 feet upwards, and argued that a large number of bottles should be carried to a camp at the Shoulder, the point at around 27,500 feet where the North Ridge meets the North-East Ridge. From this dump, the summit parties would strike out for the top equipped with sufficient oxygen to get them there and back.

Mallory took a different position, maintaining that well-acclimatized climbers might be able to reach the summit without any additional oxygen at all, or with a minimal amount for the very last stage. The meeting broke up without any definite conclusions, but before long Finch's disagreement with Mallory over oxygen would become academic, when for the second time he was thrown off the team.

The final straw was the continuing arguments over Finch's proposed lectures in Switzerland. Initially he had been happy to appear under the auspices of the Committee, sharing any profits with them, but after Hinks's outright refusal to let him lecture at all, Finch had decided to go ahead anyway.

From Finch's point of view, this was perfectly reasonable. Over the last year he had worked very hard, undoubtedly raising as much funds as anyone else. He had written chapters and provided photographs for the 1922 Everest book without any payment in return, and had done many official lectures. Furthermore, he had played an instrumental role in building the oxygen apparatus in 1922 and had offered to continue working on it for the next expedition. He was adamant that his Swiss lectures were a private affair and did not need any official approval.

So, after months of wrangling, Finch sent Hinks a letter on 28 June 1923 informing him that he had sought legal counsel and would no longer be bound by the contract that he had signed in 1921. If Hinks or the Everest Committee objected, they should contact his solicitors, Messrs Warren, Merton, Miller & Foster.

The letter, predictably, caused uproar. Hinks was away on holiday, but it soon reached Sydney Spencer, his opposite number at the Alpine Club, and then Charlie Bruce, just as he was preparing to leave for a climbing trip in the Alps. Bruce was livid. On 30 June he got straight back to Spencer with a furious reply, denouncing Finch and his actions: 'He's torn it now. I have one compensation for everything and I think this action on his part explicitly rules him out of the next expedition... What an absolute swine the man is – I now regret the necessity there was for putting him up for the Alpine Club.'

Like most of the other documents from the period that deal with anything controversial and potentially embarrassing, this letter was subsequently removed from the main archives of the Everest Committee by Thomas Blakeney, the assistant secretary of the Alpine Club. It presently resides in Blakeney's private papers at the British Library.

Finch's friend, Percy Farrar, a highly regarded climber and former member of the Everest Committee, was also shown the letter. He had always supported Finch, but he too was shocked by his tone and persuaded him to withdraw his first letter and resubmit his request in more emollient tones, removing any reference to lawyers. When Hinks got back, he sent a long, detailed reply reiterating his contention that the original contract Finch had signed bound him to follow the Everest Committee's rules *until the mountain was climbed*, a clause which seemed entirely unreasonable to Finch.

The argument was not unprecedented. It was common for expedition members to be bound by contracts that severely limited their 'media' activities. Exploration was an expensive business, and organizers expected to use the royalties from books and lectures to pay into expedition funds. In this instance though, you can't help but feel for Finch. He'd done his bit for the team and had become exasperated by Hinks's refusal to bend. The argument wasn't just about money – it was about control. Hinks and the Committee didn't just want their share of the proceeds, they wanted to determine when and where team members lectured about Everest. As Farrar wrote in a letter to Spencer at the Alpine Club, Hinks's bureaucratic intransigence was bound to rub up against 'men of independent spirit'.

Over the summer, Finch did go to Switzerland. He climbed the north face of the Dent d'Hérens with some friends – then considered a daring enough ascent to be reported in *The Times* – and went on to deliver the lectures that he had promised. At one stage he stayed in the same hotel as Charlie Bruce. You can only imagine what the atmosphere was like.

Just before he got back to London, Finch wrote to Hinks again from Zurich, reiterating his willingness to lecture for the Committee, even though by then he knew he would not be returning to Everest. He finished his letter on a plaintive note: 'I understand indirectly that for reasons doubtless sufficient to the Committee I am not to be asked to join the next expedition, notwithstanding the relative success gained by my own party and my subsequent very willing services in connection with the improvements to the oxygen apparatus.'

It is impossible to know what the other climbers thought of this. There are no records of anyone either fighting Finch's corner or approving his expulsion, apart from another letter now also residing in Blakeney's files at the British Library. It's from Alice Bullock, the American wife of Guy Bullock, who had been Mallory's climbing partner on the 1921 Everest reconnaissance.

In 1960, Bullock's expedition diary was reproduced in the *Alpine Journal*, prompting a number of letters between his widow, Alice, and Blakeney, who was also an assistant editor of the *Alpine Journal*. Alice Bullock was rather negative about Mallory, because, she said, her husband thought that during the reconnaissance he had taken 'unwarranted risks with their still untrained' Sherpas and did not take criticism well. As for Mallory's relationship with Finch, she made a revelation: 'In the second expedition, Finch as a physiological chemist considered that Mallory did not know what he was talking about in his opinions on the use of oxygen at high altitudes. The result of this was according to Mallory's own statement to me, when the third [1924] expedition was being prepared, Mallory refused to join it, if Finch were to be a member.'

There's no doubt from the tone of Alice's letter that she was no fan of Mallory, but there is plenty of evidence that Mallory did not like Finch and saw him as a rival. When Finch was controversially excluded from the reconnaissance in 1921 on medical grounds, Mallory had not supported him; and in letters sent back to Ruth in 1922, he was frequently critical of Finch – complaining about everything from the shape of his head, which 'seems to go out at the sides where it ought to go up', to Finch's insistence that everyone should practise using the oxygen sets. But would Mallory really have refused to take part in 1924 if Finch had been invited, especially when he had doubts about his own participation?

Apart from Alice Bullock's letter, there's no evidence of this. Mallory was undoubtedly competitive and did not like Finch, but he rarely seems to have been malicious. In 1922 he had persuaded Finch to take part in the abortive third attempt of the season, and even if he didn't like him, he still regarded him highly as a climber. Finch was an arrogant, abrasive character, and to an extent his exclusion from the 1924 expedition did produce a more harmonious team, but in retrospect it's hard not to conclude that this was a massive own goal for the Committee, which arguably had a very significant impact on what happened at the end.

In the summer of 1923, apart from his friend Percy Farrar, no one seemed to care that much about Finch. The Everest team had got rid of one of its most talented members and its oxygen expert; and the other George still hadn't committed to the next expedition and was looking increasingly unenthusiastic. To make matters worse, the Committee lost yet more money when news came in that the Alliance Bank of Simla had gone bust, taking with it another £700 of their funds that had been retained in India.

The show had to go on though, and for once, there was good news from an unexpected quarter: Captain John Noel.

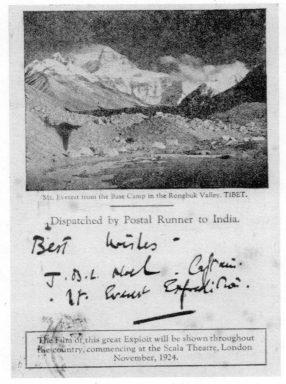

Mt. Everest from the Base Camp in the Rongbuk Valley, TIBET.

Dispatched by Postal Runner to India.

The Film of this great Exploit will be shown throughout the country, commencing at the Scala Theatre, London November, 1924.

Postcard produced by John Noel for the 1924 Everest Expedition. Members of the public were asked to provide their addresses and some stamps. In return Noel agreed to send them a specially produced postcard from Everest Base Camp, with an Everest stamp. The card also served as an advert for the Noel documentary (*The Epic of Everest*) and its first showing at the Scala Cinema in November 1924.

4

To Go or Not to Go

J ohn Baptist Lucius Noel, to give him his full name, is one of the great 'characters' of the Everest story. Tall, thin, blue-eyed and eternally inventive, he outlived all the other British members of the 1924 team, dying at the grand old age of ninety-nine in 1989.

Noel was the official cameraman for both the 1922 and 1924 expeditions, but his interest in the world's tallest mountain started much earlier, when in 1913 as an officer in the Indian Army he made two illicit forays into Tibet. His aim had been to get a good look at Everest with a view to one day climbing it, and though he was eventually forced back by a Tibetan official – backed up by a party of soldiers – he managed to get closer than any previous European. The First World War put paid to any thoughts of further excursions, but it was Noel's lecture to the RGS in March 1919 that kicked off the whole Everest bandwagon and ultimately led to the 1921 reconnaissance and the first attempt.

By 1922, Noel was no longer so interested in climbing Everest but it was still at the forefront of his mind. He had discovered a new passion – cinema. Appointed the expedition's photographic officer, he set off for Tibet with no less than sixteen cameras and came back with some exceptional stills and panoramas as well as enough material for a documentary film.

Climbing Mt Everest was released in late November 1922 to decent reviews. It did well in London but was not a commercial success. The Everest Committee had made the mistake of trying to distribute it themselves, mainly in non-cinema venues so it was hard to pull in the crowds. Hinks and Noel were its managers, but both were unfamiliar with film distribution and didn't do a brilliant job of it – particularly with the German rights, which they sold twice, to their great embarrassment and financial cost.

Notwithstanding all the problems with the first film, in June 1923 Noel made the Everest Committee an incredible offer. He and a consortium of business friends, including the Aga Khan and the industrialist Arthur Nettlefold, would buy the photographic and cinematic rights to the next expedition for the princely sum of £8,000. Unsurprisingly, they said yes. Virtually in a stroke, the Everest Committee's financial woes were over. The 1922 expedition had cost roughly £11,000 but there was some money left in the bank, and a lot of new income had by then come in from Mallory and Finch's British lectures.

Why Noel decided to do this is slightly mysterious. Obviously, like a lot of other people, he was optimistic that Everest would be climbed in 1924 and that this would make great material for a film; but considering everything that could go wrong, and knowing the disappointing box office from the first film, it's surprising he took the risk. Perhaps he was simply a dreamer, or a gambler, but either way the £8,000 he raised was an enormous boost to the Committee.

The Times, which had bought the exclusive rights to print and distribute the official dispatches from the previous two expeditions, behaved rather differently. They had paid £1,000 per expedition in previous years for the British rights, but when one of their managers, William Lints Smith, contacted the Committee in October 1922, his proposal for the next expedition was less generous. 'Public interest will be limited,' he warned, 'until they reach the summit.' Instead of offering £1,000, with no strings attached, *The Times* was only willing to offer £500 for the first set of dispatches and a bonus of £500 when, and *if*, the summit was reached.

Ultimately, *The Times* doubled their offer, after selling the American rights to the *New York Times*, but they still insisted that a second payment would only be made if the team was successful. If no one reached the summit, the Committee would not get their second instalment. It was hardly an endorsement, but buoyed by all the money coming in from John Noel and his investors, the Committee agreed and included a paragraph in the expedition contract which explicitly forbade team members from talking to any other newspapers.

As for those members, there were several developments over the summer. Howard Somervell took three prospective candidates to the Alps: a young climber called Frank Smythe who was said to be promising; Bentley Beetham, who was a friend of Somervell's from Barnard Castle; and A. J. Rusk, a young Scottish climber. The aim was to assess their climbing skills and test out a new improved oxygen set. Somervell was rather negative about Smythe, a future star, describing him as a 'bad mountaineer, always slipping and knocking stones down... his incessant conversation makes others tired', and not totally impressed by Rusk who was a 'good man' but not an exceptional climber. His old friend Beetham was, he was pleased to announce, 'a phenomenon'.

When it came to the new, supposedly improved, oxygen sets, Somervell was distinctly lukewarm after a day testing one. As a doctor he was interested in the effects of altitude and the theoretical benefits that supplementary oxygen could offer, but as a climber he hated how heavy and awkward the sets were. In a report to Percy Unna, the engineer and Alpine Club member who had helped Finch in 1922 and was now in charge of the development programme, Somervell wrote: 'The apparatus as at present constructed would add tremendous difficulty both to ascent and descent. Everest is nearly impossible with a weight like the one we took.' There was clearly plenty more work to be done, but with Finch gone, none of the team members seemed to be that interested.

The selection committee had better luck recruiting new climbers, further boosting the team with Richard Graham, a powerful mountaineer from Lancashire with a lot of Alpine experience. The most intriguing new candidate of all was a tall and strapping twenty-one-year-old student from Oxford, Andrew 'Sandy' Irvine. He was no mountaineer but he was considered a great all-round sportsman and a prodigious rower.

From their earliest meetings in 1921, the Everest Committee had talked about the importance of recruiting young talent and done the opposite, appointing men like the fifty-five-year-old Harold Raeburn and the forty-seven-year-old Edward Strutt as their climbing leaders. Now, for once, they decided to take a chance on a relative novice, hoping that he would turn out to be an inspired choice. Mallory was intrigued by the handsome athlete. 'Irvine represents our attempt to get one superman,' he told Geoffrey Winthrop Young, 'though lack of experience is against him.'

By early October the selection committee was convinced that it had a very strong team, but there was one key member who still refused to commit: George Mallory. He was by then firmly ensconced in his new life and job in Cambridge. Over the summer he had worked hard to prepare dozens of lectures and run two summer schools. In between assignments, his house hunting had borne fruit and he had found a large property on Herschel Road in central Cambridge that was far bigger and better appointed than the Mallorys' cottage near Godalming. Herschel House had seven bedrooms, an acre of land, and its very own squash and Eton fives courts. It cost £4,000 for a sixty-eight-year lease, but his father-in-law, George Thackeray Turner, was willing to put up the money as long as the house was in Ruth Mallory's name.

In the middle of October, the Alpine Club selection committee made their final recommendations and included Mallory, putting him in a very awkward position. Not only had he failed to mention the possibility of going to Everest at his job interview, he was really enjoying the work and it was clear that the Cambridge board liked him. To make matters worse, he was in the final stages of his house move. In a few weeks Ruth would have to sign the lease on Herschel House and leave Godalming, where her father and sisters still lived. As George put it in a letter to Hinks, 'I'm having a terrible time on the tightrope.'

Hinks too was in an awkward position. Having so heartily recommended Mallory to his friend Cranage in Cambridge, he now had to ask for a leave of absence for at least six months. In the end, the needs of the expedition trumped any embarrassment he might have felt. Hinks wrote to Cranage emphasizing that everyone on the Committee thought Mallory vital to the team. 'You ask a very difficult thing do you not?' his friend replied, refusing to agree until he had spoken to his colleagues on the Cambridge board.

Sensing a moment of potential leverage while his membership of the expedition hung in the balance, Mallory finally plucked up the courage to write to Francis Younghusband to ask for some money for the 70,000–80,000 words that he had written for the last two Everest books. 'My work for the Everest Committee has as a matter of fact involved a good deal of time which if it hadn't been spent that way would have been free for writing for my own purposes.' He asked for a percentage of the book's profits but didn't have the temerity or the self-assurance of Finch. There were no threats of legal action and he even offered to pay the money back if the Committee lost money in 1924. Younghusband didn't reply but passed the letter on to Hinks to ponder upon it.

While waiting for the men on high to make their decisions, Mallory frantically discussed the expedition with his friends and family. What was more important, he asked his father, Herbert – loyalty to the team and his desire to 'have a part in the finish', or the pull of his new job and the family he was about to uproot? This time Geoffrey Winthrop Young advised him against going, and agreed to take him to see Kathleen Scott – the widow of Robert Falcon Scott, who had died in 1912 on the way back from the South Pole. She was a sculptor who had charmed everyone from Auguste Rodin to Aleister Crowley, and had remarried Young's brother Wayland. There was nothing particularly radical about her art, but she shared Mallory's Bohemian sensibility and was known for her spiritual sense and occasional moments of clairvoyance.

Whether Mallory saw a direct parallel between his struggles on Everest and Robert Scott's doomed expedition to the South

Pole, it is difficult say. There is no transcript or correspondence regarding his meeting with Kathleen, but on the taxi ride home Mallory admitted to Winthrop Young's wife that he didn't really want to go to Everest. He could of course have been decisive and turned down the Committee's offer directly, or at the very least put off Ruth and his family's move from Godalming to Cambridge, but instead he seemed to be waiting for someone else to make the decision for him, hoping that either Cranage or Ruth would put their foot down.

In the end, neither was willing to say no. Ruth agreed both to move house and to let George go back to Everest. Cranage and the extramural department offered him six months' leave, and even agreed to pay half his salary while he was away – after all, how could they say no to an important national committee? On 24 October, the Everest Committee sent Mallory a formal invitation to join the expedition, subject to him passing the usual Harley Street medical.

It was a deeply unsettling time. In a letter to his young confidante, Marjorie Holmes, George tried to be positive. 'My chief feeling is we've got to win the top next time or never. We must get there and we shall.' He went on to describe his feeling of being at the mercy of both fate and his own risk-taking nature: 'What a funny mixture life is – of fate pushing or pulling one along (like running behind and holding on to a milk-cart when I was a small boy) and great gambler's throws not knowing in the least what will turn up.'

His final hope for a last-minute reprieve came when he visited Messrs Larkin and Anderson of Harley Street for his official pre-expedition medical, but there was no escape there. Larkin pronounced Mallory 'fit in every way' and Anderson agreed. David Pye, Mallory's first biographer and one of his closest Cambridge friends, later wrote that he would have been 'profoundly relieved if the whole expedition had been called off', but there was no chance of that.

In late November, Mallory wrote to his father again, telling him that the decision had been made and that he was looking forward to going out. 'Life is full of interest, and we're all very happy.' There was nothing to do but make the best of it, but he could not stop feeling uneasy. When he and Ruth went climbing at the end of the year with Julian Huxley and his wife, Juliette, tensions were high. 'Both he and Ruth had a premonition of disaster,' Juliette later wrote, 'but he felt he couldn't refuse, and she feared that to try to dissuade him would leave him with a deep sense of frustration.'

There was not very much time left. While trying to fulfil his obligations to the extramural department and the Climbers' Club, whose journal he was now editing, Mallory started thinking concretely about the forthcoming expedition. He began corresponding with Norton about a plan of attack on the mountain, commissioned some new boots, and wrote to Sydney Spencer at the Alpine Club with suggestions for the expedition larder. Mallory had encountered Grape-Nuts, the breakfast cereal, in the US, and thought it would be an ideal high-altitude food. There's no record whether or not it was taken, but by the 1950s boxes of Grape-Nuts were a Himalayan staple. Mallory's other suggestion, sodium phosphate, he described as a 'pick-me-up', similar to cola or caffeine. Fortunately, it does not seem to have been taken, as Mallory failed to mention that it was also a powerful laxative.

Norton, now officially the team's deputy leader, was also busy thinking more systematically about equipment and logistics. The previous two expeditions had been very ad hoc, and Norton was determined to adopt a more rigorous approach. In 1921, when Mallory was invited to take part in the Everest reconnaissance, he had been given a £50 clothing allowance and told by the climbing leader, Harold Raeburn, that he should bring 'ordinary Alpine outfit on a liberal scale'.

Norton was much more detailed, sending each climber a four-page memo in which he listed what was needed and where to get it from. Each man was expected to provide their own cold-weather trousers and jacket, but in addition they were offered Shackleton-style windproof suits to fend off the vicious winds of the North Ridge. Climbers were advised to bring at least three different pairs of boots, the high-altitude versions being a new experimental style designed, ironically, by George Finch, with a nailed leather sole and a thick inner lining made from felt. Thinking ahead to their creature comforts and the occupational hazards of operating in extremely cold weather, they were advised that 'a felt bedroom slipper cut like a "gouty" or snow boot is a convenience in camp, and if frostbitten'. As for bigger items of equipment, Norton would supply all the tents and bedding, including for the first time a large mess tent. Individuals were invited to bring, or ideally share, a portable bath.

At one point there was talk of taking a radio to Base Camp, but the most complex pieces of equipment that made it to Tibet were undoubtedly the oxygen sets. Inexplicably, despite their rejection of Finch and their previous qualms about using oxygen on 'sporting' grounds, the Committee decided to invest a lot of money in the design and manufacture of oxygen apparatus for 1924, spending £1,024, or about £50,000 in today's money – three times as much as they had in 1922. Before he left London, Charlie Bruce was given specific instructions that as 'the Committee had gone to considerable expense to send out the best oxygen outfit procurable, the members of the expedition were expected to make the best possible use of the outfit supplied'.

As with the previous expedition, the Committee collaborated with an Anglo-German company, Siebe Gorman, who specialized in deep-sea diving gear, and the Air Ministry, whose aviators had started using oxygen for high-altitude flying. The basic design for 1924 was very similar to that used by Finch and Bruce in 1922, with a set of oxygen bottles connected to a mask via a regulator, which reduced the pressure coming out of the canister. A flow meter allowed a climber to control the amount of oxygen they were breathing in at any point.

The biggest innovation for 1924 was a larger type of oxygen bottle made from light-weight 'Vibrac' steel, which could be pressurized to a greater degree and hold more gas. In theory, it would give the climbers a greater range, but though the new bottles were supposed to be lighter, fully loaded with four cylinders the sets still weighed 32–33 pounds and were bulky and awkward to carry. The other problem was that, whereas in 1922 Finch had taken the oxygen apparatus from the laboratory to the field, getting to know its workings intimately, in 1924 there was no one really in charge.

Percy Unna did most of the liaison with Siebe Gorman, but the team's latterly appointed 'oxygen officer', the geologist Noel Odell, was ironically not that keen on using oxygen and was away in Persia during the first two months of 1924, when most of the work was done. In his absence, one of the 1922 oxygen sets was sent to Sandy Irvine in Oxford, so he could tinker with it in his workshop and get to know the basic principles, but Irvine too felt very ambivalent about oxygen and did not have Finch's working knowledge or his passion.

As the autumn wore on, and the departure date grew closer, the Committee met more frequently and the organizers grew busier and busier. But there was still room for one more controversy. It centred not on Finch, but on one of the climbers brought in to replace him: Richard Brockbank Graham. This time Mallory did make a stand.

Graham was a well-known and highly regarded climber from the Lake District who taught at a school in Reading. He had been on the selection committee's shortlist from early on, and in October 1923 was formally invited to join the team. Graham went to Harley Street for the usual medical tests and was pronounced 'absolutely fit in every respect', so he arranged with his school to take a term and a half off, signed his expedition contract, and sent it back to Hinks on 19 November. Then, about three weeks later, he resigned.

Officially it was a private decision, but rumours soon spread that he had been forced out after an anonymous team member objected to his inclusion. As a Quaker, Graham was a conscientious objector and had refused to fight in the First World War. Instead, he had finished his studies at Oxford and become a schoolmaster. Graham had been approved by Charlie Bruce, who was by no means a pacifist, and confirmed by the Alpine Club's selection subcommittee, most of whom had also served in the forces – but, so the rumour went, someone didn't want a 'conchie' on the expedition, and Bruce had been forced to act.

When in early December Graham wrote to Mallory to tell him that he had been asked to resign by Bruce, Mallory was outraged and immediately leapt to his defence, writing to the general: 'Graham put it that the reason of your request to him is that the feeling in the party is very strongly against him. I must register my view, if that is the fact, that the sooner members of the party who feel such things learn to control their feelings and make the best of the party as they find it, the better it will be for all of us.' Though he admitted that his letter was written in haste and anger, Mallory stated his opposition to anyone who had 'agitated' against Graham on the record, and asked Bruce to reconsider.

When Howard Somervell, a bloodied veteran of the Somme, found out, he was so furious at the way Graham had been treated that he threatened to resign from the Alpine Club, and was only assuaged when Bruce promised to make a 'full confession' when they met in Darjeeling.

Somervell was convinced that the 'agitator' was someone outside the expedition who wanted to replace Graham. Mallory was not sure but, either way, Graham was not allowed to withdraw his resignation letter, and he was replaced by one of the official reserves, John de Vars Hazard, a former artillery officer.

Much later, in February 1924, Mallory was told by his friend Geoffrey Winthrop Young that the 'agitator' was Bentley Beetham, Howard Somervell's friend from Durham. Mallory was worried that this would put him off someone with whom he was about to share a two-week voyage to India.

There's something about this story that doesn't quite ring true though. In the first instance, Beetham hadn't served in the war, because as a schoolmaster he was in an exempted profession and, unlike Mallory, he hadn't insisted on joining up. To object to Graham would have been rank hypocrisy as everyone would have realized. More than this, it doesn't seem quite credible that one of the new boys, who lived far away in remote Durham and was very rarely down in London, could have swayed the other members of the team. Clearly Mallory hadn't objected to

Graham and nor had Somervell or General Bruce – so who was the real culprit? The resignation story has all the hallmarks of an Everest Committee stitch-up, even if Beetham might have played some part.

Graham had committed not one but two sins. In the first instance he had been not just a conscientious objector but a prominent one, whose battles with his local conscription tribunal were widely reported. Like George Finch, Graham was a very self-assured individual who was never shy of speaking his mind. His second sin was in the eyes of Hinks probably just as serious: he had gone to the press in November 1923, before the names of the new Everest team had been officially released. There had been several articles about Graham being chosen for Everest in Midlands and northern newspapers, all of which referred to his Quaker background. Apart from the fact that this would have violated the agreement between the Committee and *The Times* that they would be first to get expedition news, Hinks had always hated publicity and especially any individual climber claiming the limelight.

On 5 December there was a meeting of the Everest Committee in London, after which Sir Francis Younghusband was tasked – not officially but in his 'private capacity' – to have a quiet word with Graham. Shortly afterwards, Graham resigned.

Off the mountain, the climbers never really had any control over the British Everest expeditions. From the 1920s all the way up to the 1950s, it was the Committee who were in charge; and as George Finch, Richard Graham and later Eric Shipton, the deposed leader of the 1953 expedition, found out, if you fell foul of the Committee, you were out.

Despite this last-minute fracas, preparations picked up pace. In the middle of January 1924, the Army and Navy Stores in

Victoria held a small exhibition of photographs from the 1922 expedition flanked by examples of the foodstuffs and supplies that were about to go out to Tibet. At the end of the month, Charlie Bruce's first official dispatch appeared in *The Times*, just before he sailed off for India to select high-altitude porters and make all the necessary local preparations. As ever, he was in exuberant form: 'It is possible that certain branches of science may benefit from the experiences of the party, but the dominant note of the whole undertaking, first, last, and for most, is a great adventure – almost now become a pilgrimage. Did we not explain to the great Lama of Rongbuk, the Sang Rinpoche, that it was for us an attempt to reach the highest point on earth as being the "nearest to heaven"?'

The Times was a little less excitable in its own editorial, but was equally sure that a new expedition was valuable, not necessarily because it was bound to end in success but because Everest was such a challenge. 'Hard things are an end in themselves,' the editorial climaxed, 'even with the possibility of failure and no material gain in view.'

Mallory, meanwhile, was intensely busy trying to get as much work done as possible before he left Cambridge. In an anxious but typical moment, in the middle of February, just a few weeks before he was due to depart, he realized that his passport was out of date, and he had to send it up to London to get a clerk at the Everest Committee to have another one hurriedly issued.

Then, at the end of the month, he and Ruth travelled north to Birkenhead to board the SS *California* and meet Irvine, Beetham and Hazard, who would be sailing out on the same ship to India. The regional newspapers were very proud that two local boys, Mallory and Irvine, were part of the latest Everest expedition, and the nearby climbing club, the Liverpool

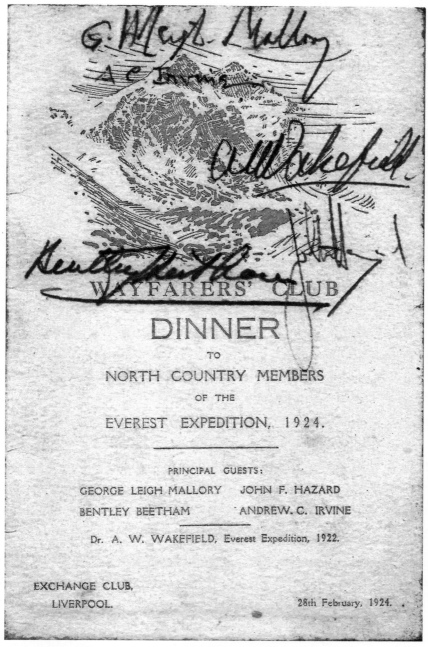

WAYFARERS' CLUB

DINNER

TO

NORTH COUNTRY MEMBERS

OF THE

EVEREST EXPEDITION, 1924.

PRINCIPAL GUESTS:

GEORGE LEIGH MALLORY   JOHN F. HAZARD

BENTLEY BEETHAM   ANDREW. C. IRVINE

Dr. A. W. WAKEFIELD, Everest Expedition, 1922.

EXCHANGE CLUB,
LIVERPOOL.   28th February, 1924.

Menu card from a dinner staged by the Wayfarers' Club in honour of the Everest team and A. W. Wakefield, a member of the 1922 Everest Expedition. Mallory and Irvine signed their names at the top.

Wayfarers, staged a gala dinner in their honour the night before they were due to leave. There were speeches and toasts and a special commemorative menu with a hand-drawn picture of Everest at the centre. Mallory and Irvine hit it off immediately. When asked for their autographs, they signed the menu card, putting their names at the top of the image close to the summit. Hazard and Beetham had to make do with the bottom.

The next day, on 29 February, Ruth went down to the docks to wave George goodbye, but it was so windy that the tugs assigned to tow his ship out were forced back, almost as if nature was echoing Mallory's uncertainty about leaving Britain.

Ruth didn't wait. She said her goodbyes and headed back down to Cambridge, but before they finally parted, Mallory asked her to get in touch with George Finch to invite him and his wife over for a weekend when he returned from the Himalayas. Having spent months failing to come to Finch's assistance when it mattered, he'd belatedly decided that his rival had been badly treated by the Committee and he wanted to make amends and go climbing with him in the Alps. It was pure Mallory.

At 8.30 p.m. the ship finally got underway, and for the third time in four years, Mallory was off on the long voyage to Everest, aiming to meet his old friends and the other members of the team at Darjeeling. It was the strongest party assembled so far, better equipped and better prepared than ever, climbing a known route to what would hopefully be a successful outcome. What could possibly go wrong?

5

The Long March

It wasn't a hard decision: chop wood for hours on end, or work as a high-altitude porter on the latest British attempt on Everest. Ang Tsering was twenty when he signed up for his first ever mountaineering expedition in March 1924; in the following four decades he would take part in many more, until in 1961 he finally stopped.

Though the vital role that Sherpas play in high-altitude climbing has long been recognized, until very recently their own voices have rarely been heard, largely because they came from an oral rather than written culture. Ethnic Tibetans who had migrated to the Solukhumbu region of Nepal, close to Everest, in the fifteenth century, Sherpas were natural-born mountaineers who quickly established themselves as ideal high-altitude porters in the early Himalayan expeditions.

It wasn't until the 1950s, with the publication of first Ang Tharkay's and then Tenzing Norgay's biographies, that their voices first appeared in print, mediated via ghost writers. Ang Tsering is the only Sherpa ever to have been interviewed about

the 1924 expedition, in an article for the *Himalayan Journal* in
1996. Then aged ninety-two, he couldn't recall that much but did
remember being relatively well paid and being issued with nailed
boots. As a very junior porter, Ang would not have come into
that much contact with the team, but he did remember George
Mallory, though for his height rather than his climbing skill.

Whereas Mallory and the other 'sahibs' climbed for pleasure,
for the Sherpas and other porters, expeditions were a source of
employment – more dangerous than the other work on offer, but
exciting too, and as far as most of them were concerned, not such
grindingly hard labour. Ang Tsering's story was typical. He was
born in the small village of Thame in the Solukhumbu region,
and like Tenzing Norgay, who grew up in the same village, he
spent his early years looking after his family's yaks. Then, in his
late teens, he made the 300-odd-mile trek to the bright lights
and paid jobs of Darjeeling, the famous Indian hill town.

Originally part of the small Himalayan kingdom of Sikkim,
Darjeeling was by the early twentieth century one of the busiest
towns in the Himalayas. It was a tourist resort and summer
residence for officials of the British Empire escaping the heat of
the Indian plains, and a bustling local trade centre, surrounded
by highly productive tea plantations.

By the 1920s it also had another, rather more niche identity:
the capital of high-altitude climbing. The infamous British
climber and occultist Aleister Crowley, 'the Great Beast 666',
was one of the first British mountaineers to visit, taking up
residence for almost a month in 1905 to recruit porters and
buy supplies as he prepared for the world's first attempt on
Kangchenjunga. Crowley hated Darjeeling and its damp climate,
describing it as 'lousy with young ladies whose only idea of
getting a husband is to practise the piano... The food itself is

as mildewed as the maidens', but, sitting close to the borders of Tibet and Nepal, it was the gateway to the Himalayas, where you could buy everything from cold-weather clothing to tubes and piping that could be used to repair an oxygen set, as George Finch had done in 1922.

Darjeeling was also a very cosmopolitan town, home to several different ethnic groups as well as the colonial British. There were Lepchas from Sikkim, Indians and Nepalis, Sherpas from the Solukhumbu and Tibetans who had emigrated directly, known as Bhotias. All of them worked at various stages on European mountaineering expeditions, but by the mid-1920s the Sherpas had established themselves as the pre-eminent group. They were hard-working, good humoured and tough, and because they had grown up in the foothills of Everest, they were used to high altitude. Unlike today's Sherpas, who do a lot of the lead climbing and route establishing as well as the carrying, in the 1920s they were only expected to play a supporting role as high-altitude porters, but nonetheless their contribution would be crucial if Everest was to be climbed.

In January 1924, Geoffrey Bruce, Charlie Bruce's nephew, had written to David MacDonald, the official British trade agent operating for Tibet, asking him to put the word out that a new expedition was coming that needed sixty strong local men. Two months later, the general himself arrived with Edward Norton, his deputy. They found plenty of candidates eager to be hired. There was Pu, who was hoping to work for the British for a third time; Lhakpa Chédé, Bruce's former personal Sherpa; and several other men who had been with them in 1922. The sahibs offered decent pay and clothing and a food allowance on the way into the mountains, as well as provisions for the whole time they were on Everest. Married men got an advance of a month's wages, and some were also offered a monthly stipend, to be paid to their families while they were away.

In an era when eugenics was in fashion, Edward Norton had strong ideas about the ideal physical type for both sahibs and Sherpas. The model climber, he thought, should be about five foot eleven and weigh about eleven and a half stone, fitting the profile of Mallory, Somervell and Geoffrey Bruce. John de Vars Hazard was a little thinner and Odell and Norton were taller, but the only real exception was the short and stocky Bentley Beetham, who Sandy Irvine once memorably described as looking like a cross between a pudding apple and Judas Iscariot. The best Sherpas, Norton believed, were those who were light and wiry, even if they didn't always look particularly strong. The ones to be avoided, he maintained, were the 'old soldiers', in army speak – the veterans of previous expeditions who had worked out how to play the system and do as little work as possible.

Charlie Bruce was less scientific in his approach but he was a very good linguist and popular with all the locals. A Gurkha officer for many years, he could curse fluently in Nepali and was very at home in British India. He knew from experience that Sherpas could occasionally be hard to deal with when they'd had a drink or three, but he loved their spirit and work ethic. 'We have tested, and found not wanting, a race of people who seem to be practically impervious to cold and fatigue and exposure,' he wrote in *The Times*, 'and in whom we also discovered, although as yet in an early stage of development, the seeds of those great qualities which are so clearly distinguishable in the great pioneers of the Golden Age of Alpine Exploration – cheerfulness under all conditions and a willingness to undertake any task for employers in whom they have confidence.' The Sherpas in turn liked and respected him, and even in the 1930s when his climbing days were long over, Bruce was fondly remembered in Darjeeling as the 'Burra sahib' (or 'big boss').

Of course, by 1924 everyone knew that it was dangerous work. The 1922 expedition had ended with the deaths of seven porters, and one sahib, Alexander Kellas, had died on the reconnaissance in 1921. But as Ang Tsering recalled many years later, the British were fair and behaved well in the event of any casualties, compensating the families of any Sherpas who were killed.

Somewhat to the surprise of Charlie Bruce, Angtarké, one of the two who had narrowly avoided death in the 1922 avalanche and been dug out unconscious from a crevasse by Mallory and Somervell, even signed up, but ultimately he was so traumatized by the experience that he didn't make it beyond Phari, the first major town on their way into Tibet.

Three expeditions into Britain's Everest obsession, the Himalayas were no longer *terra incognita*. As well as porters, Bruce recruited several other men who had worked for him two years earlier: Karma Paul the translator, Moti the cobbler and Rhombu the naturalist. By 1924 there was almost a set pattern for who to see and what say: dinner at the Planters' Club, a visit to the local Hillmen's Association, a special blessing for all the porters from the local priests. All their days seemed to be full.

Gradually, as Bruce and Norton got on with the logistics, the other team members began to turn up from the far-flung corners of India and the Middle East: Noel Odell from the oilfields of Persia; Richard Hingston, the team's Irish doctor, from the RAF hospital in Baghdad; and Howard Somervell from Kerala in south-west India. After the 1922 expedition

Mallory and Irvine on board the
SS California, on the way out to India.

he had travelled through India and been so moved by the lack
of medical care for the local Indian population that he had
decided to abandon his well-paid job in London to move to a
small mission hospital in the town of Travancore. Somervell
loved the work, but Bruce wasn't sure that doctoring in tropical
Kerala was doing his mountaineering any good, noting that he
didn't look nearly as fit as the last time he had seen him. For
Somervell, the expedition was an escape from the stifling heat
of South India, and a welcome chance to see his old tent-mate
George Mallory, with whom he'd spent a lot of time in 1922.
He knew, though, that he would have to wait a few days before
Mallory arrived with the last members of the team, who were
still on the way.

After Mallory and the others finally left Liverpool docks on
29 February, the stormy weather had continued, but by the time
the Rock of Gibraltar was in sight, it had grown so hot and
humid that in one very surreal moment, a vast cloud of recently

hatched butterflies suddenly congregated on the deck of the SS *California* and then fluttered off into the sun.

The two-week voyage would take them through the Mediterranean, past Spain's Sierra Nevada on the left and Morocco's Atlas Mountains on the right, down the Suez Canal and, after a stop at the port of Aden, into the Indian Ocean. Mallory's most magical moment came when they steamed towards Gibraltar at dawn. 'We were aiming straight for this little hole in the skyline where the light was brightest. I had the most irresistible feeling of a romantic world, we had only to pop through the hole like Alice through the garden door to reach a new scene and whole kingdom of adventures,' he told Ruth in his second letter home.

For Mallory, the voyage to India was a time for reading and writing, and getting fit. His collection of books included a biography of Shelley, his favourite poet, by the French writer André Maurois, and a semi-autobiographical novel by the Russian writer Sergey Aksakov – not quite airport thrillers. This time he didn't have any chapters to write for an expedition book, but he did have a 3,000-word article to finish for the Scottish publishers Blackie and Son's magazine.

Most of the other passengers were Scottish tourists, on an early Thomas Cook package tour to witness the wonders of ancient Egypt in six days. The deck was festooned with bunting and coloured lights, and there were nightly dances and entertainments. As the only well-known member of the team, Mallory found himself pestered by fellow passengers wanting to have their photograph taken with him. He tried to avoid them wherever possible and tended to hide out at the edges of the ship.

Mallory had asked to share a cabin with Irvine, but for whatever reason the message didn't get through to the Everest

Committee and he ended up with Hazard, the former artillery officer who had replaced Richard Graham. Tall and thin, with a regulation military moustache and a distinctly formal bearing, initially Mallory found Hazard a strange fish. He told Ruth that he seemed overexcited and was forever 'bursting with information about the tittle tattle of travel, how many knots the ship will travel per hour and whether one should wear a Topie in the Mediterranean and so on'. Eventually Hazard calmed down and turned out to be an easy-going companion.

Over recent decades, historians and journalists have speculated about Mallory's relationship with Sandy Irvine and asked if a romantic attraction to him might have influenced his decision to take him on his final, fateful climb. Mallory's sexuality has always been a tricky issue for his biographers. In his 1927 book, Mallory's close friend David Pye did not give any hint of George's sexual orientation, and nor did his son-in-law David Robertson in his 1969 biography. Audrey Salkeld and Tom Holzel opened the door on his gay relationships at Cambridge in *The Mystery of Mallory and Irvine*, but it wasn't until 2000, with Peter and Leni Gillman's *The Wildest Dream*, that the issue was really explored.

No one now disputes that Mallory did have at least one full-blown homosexual romance at Cambridge with James Strachey, who would go on to win fame as a translator and authority on the 'father' of psychoanalysis, Sigmund Freud. After Cambridge, there's no record of Mallory being involved in any specific relationships with men, but he did keep in touch with his gay and bisexual friends. At the British Library in London there's a whole set of rather risqué letters from Mallory to James's brother Lytton Strachey, dating from their earliest encounter at Cambridge in 1909 to Mallory's first Everest expedition in

1921. In May 1914, shortly after he had become engaged to Ruth, he wrote to Strachey, insisting that nothing had changed: 'It can hardly be a shock to you that I desert the ranks of the fashionable homosexualists (And yet I am still in part of that persuasion) unless you think I have turned monogamist. But you may be assured that this last catastrophe has not happened.'

Sexual acts between men might have been illegal at the time, but homosexuality and bisexuality were widespread in every sphere of life – including in the mountaineering world. Charles Howard-Bury, the leader of the Everest reconnaissance of 1921, spent his final years with his actor lover, 'Sexy Rexy' Beaumont, moving between a castle in Ireland and a villa in Tunisia. John Morris, one of the Everest team's transport officers in 1922, was a tortured soul who was so disturbed by his 'problem' that he publicly declared in his autobiography, *Hired to Kill*, that he ceased all sexual activity in his early forties. Mallory's great friend and mentor Geoffrey Winthrop Young was, like many men of the period, married but bisexual. He had several children and was deeply in love with his wife, Eleanor, but they maintained an open marriage and she was aware of his bisexuality.

Mallory did undoubtedly find Andrew Irvine physically attractive – writing to his pen pal Marjorie Holmes that he was 'a splendid specimen of a man... he is completely modest and has a nice voice which reminds me strangely of Rupert Brookes' – but his appeal seems to have been more aesthetic than sexual. When the Everest historian Walt Unsworth asked Mallory's close friend, the painter Duncan Grant, about his sexuality, he replied emphatically that Mallory 'was <u>not</u> a homosexual', but added that if he had to choose between potential climbing partners he might very well have chosen the more attractive one. Mallory was certainly drawn to Irvine, but there's no evidence of any romance between the men and no sense at all that Andrew Irvine reciprocated. Irvine was very much in the red-blooded male mould, enjoying japes and scrapes with his sporting pals at Oxford, and a scandalous affair with his best friend's stepmother, a former chorus girl.

When it came to both mountains and people, Mallory was more of an aesthete than a sensualist, an appreciator of beauty rather than hands-on sensual pleasure. He clearly found Irvine physically attractive, but Irvine's principal appeal was something very different, and in a way much more surprising: his role as the team's oxygen expert.

In 1922, Mallory had been the most outspoken of the anti-oxygen faction on the Everest team and had been openly dismissive of George Finch and his attempts to train the team members on how to use the oxygen apparatus. When in May 1922 it looked as if Finch might actually do better than Mallory's party, he had written to Ruth that even if Finch reached the summit, 'The whole venture of getting up with oxygen is so different from ours that the two hardly enter into competition.'

By 1924 Mallory had undergone a reluctant but profound conversion. Perhaps Finch had convinced him, or perhaps with Finch out of the way, he was able to take a more objective view; but either way, he had become the 1924 team's least likely but most fervent advocate of oxygen. In the same letter to Marjorie Holmes in which he compared Irvine to Rupert Brooke, he also outlined his feelings about supplementary oxygen. 'I <u>want</u> to go without oxygen,' he wrote, 'but am inclined to believe that it will be easier with oxygen, provided the instrument for using it works alright. So there we are. Anyway it will be a tremendous struggle.'

Though officially Noel Odell was the team's oxygen officer, in practice Irvine was much more interested and more involved in the maintenance of the sets. On previous expeditions Mallory had made a name for himself for losing things and misunderstanding equipment, but Irvine clearly both enjoyed and was good at tinkering with all kinds of machinery, so Mallory elevated him to his oxygen genie – who would prepare and maintain the sets that would take them both to the summit.

Irvine played the role perfectly. He was a natural engineer who was both good on paper and handy with a toolkit. When he was sent plans of the oxygen sets in the autumn of 1923, he had immediately set about redesigning them and had even asked for a 1922 set to be sent to his lodgings in Oxford to disassemble and experiment with. Siebe Gorman, the company that manufactured the equipment, did not however pay any attention to the twenty-one-year-old Irvine's ideas or take up any of his technical suggestions. Perhaps they did not take him seriously. When, during the voyage, a couple of oxygen sets were brought up from the hold, Irvine was not at all impressed, and as soon as he found time and space, he began a ground-up rebuild.

Unlike the thirty-seven-year-old Mallory, who was on his third voyage to India, this was Irvine's first time – and unsurprisingly he was hugely excited, writing home about everything from the squalor of Egypt to the amazing phosphorescence of the Red Sea. He shared a cabin with Bentley Beetham, though he usually dined with Mallory. In his physical prime, Irvine enjoyed deck sports and the fun of the voyage, while Mallory was much more concerned about maintaining his fitness, spending time in the onboard gymnasium and running around the deck. Not that the ship was that big – it took ten circuits to cover a mile.

When the SS *California* reached Port Said, it all became a little easier when their 'cargo' of 200 Scottish tourists disembarked for their six-day sightseeing tour, leaving behind a much emptier ship. Mallory relaxed a little more and even agreed to lecture on Everest to the remaining guests. Ruth and his family were still very much on his mind, though. He had left her with plenty to do while he was away. As well as selling their old house in Godalming, there was building work to oversee in Cambridge and creditors to be kept at bay. As Ruth admitted in her only surviving letter to George from the 1924 expedition, written on 5 March, the months before he left had been difficult. 'I know I have rather often been cross and not nice and I am very sorry but the bottom reason has nearly always been because I was unhappy at getting so little of you. I know it is pretty stupid to spoil the times I do have you for those when I don't.'

Mallory felt guilty about leaving her and fantasized about having Ruth with him on the ship, to discuss the habits and foibles of the other passengers. He signed off his letters 'your ever loving George' and told her how much he longed for her to be with him, lying on deck under the stars, but whether his sweet words made up for his absence and all the work he had created for her, it's impossible to know. His letters home from 1924 are noticeably more intimate and warmer than his America correspondence of the previous year. If all went well, Mallory hoped to return triumphant at the end of the summer and resume his job at the extramural department at Cambridge. First, though, he would have to climb Everest, and in 1924 getting to the foot of the mountain was an expedition in itself.

Today a hard-pressed climber can fly into Kathmandu and get up and down Everest in just twenty-one days on a so-called 'flash' expedition, but in 1924 everything was a lot more time-consuming and arduous. Just getting from Liverpool to Darjeeling entailed a two-week voyage, followed by a three-day train ride from Bombay to Darjeeling, in the searing heat of the Indian plains. As Irvine noted in a letter home, it was at times 37 degrees in the shade, before they transferred from the main line at Siliguri to the famous narrow-gauge 'toy' train that took them 6,500 feet up through tropical forest to the end of the line in wet and humid Darjeeling, where they arrived on Friday 21 March, three weeks after they had left Liverpool.

Mallory, like Aleister Crowley, had never been that enamoured by Darjeeling, but was pleased to meet his old friends Howard Somervell and Geoffrey Bruce, and the new members of the team. He immediately warmed to expedition doctor Richard Hingston, who had arrived two weeks earlier and had been busy vaccinating porters and preparing for his secondary role as the team naturalist. A short man with a sensitive face and a calm temperament, Hingston had won the Military Cross during the First World War, and though he did not consider himself a mountaineer, he was very interested in the physiological effects of climbing at high altitude. He had brought specialist equipment with him, and as Charlie Bruce joked was 'bursting with energy and enthusiasm to test every member of the Expedition with every terror known to the RAF authorities'.

In a last-minute setback, John Morris, the popular Gurkha transport officer from 1922, had been declared medically unfit. His replacement, Edward Shebbeare, was new to Everest, but by no means new to India. Like Mallory, he was a vicar's son, and he had attended Charterhouse, the public school where Mallory had taught for three years. An officer of the Imperial Forestry Service, Shebbeare spoke several indigenous languages and was expected to be a lot of help with the porters. In a progress report for the Committee, Bruce advised that their new transport officer was a famous elephant catcher and that if anyone wanted one, all they needed to do was forward him sufficient stamps to cover postage.

Mallory liked both of his new colleagues, but he had barely had time to start to get to know them before everyone rolled out of town early in the morning of 26 March – heading for Kalimpong, the last major town before the vast rainforests of Sikkim. Each of the sahibs had a personal allowance of 160 pounds, which was comfortable enough for most of them but not so easy for Irvine, whose baggage included tools and soldering equipment. Charlie Bruce was given a ride in a chauffeur-driven car and soon found himself on the steepest roads and the narrowest turns that he had ever encountered. The others left in two Willys Overland saloons, but after six miles the track was so poor that it was quicker to get out and walk.

Next morning, as in 1922, the team visited a nearby orphanage where Bruce read out a speech written by Robert Baden-Powell for the children of the local Scout troop. The latest Everest expedition, he told them, should be an inspiration. 'I'm sure you will wish them God-Speed on this great Scouting adventure. They are giving you Scouts a splendid example in carrying out your mottoes: "Stick to it" and "Never say die till you're dead".'

The orphanage had been set up in 1900 by Dr John Graham, a Scottish missionary, to look after the sons and daughters of British fathers and local mothers – or as Mallory put it in a letter to Ruth, 'bastards or children of ne'er-do-well parents'. The speech to the children had become a ritual, and even if Mallory was not so keen, Dr Graham was a friendly and hospitable host.

Over the next five days, the plan was to stay in Dak bungalows, set up for travelling officials and members of the Indian postal service (or *Dak*). Nominally Sikkim was a British protectorate with its own ruler, but effectively it was part of the empire. The bungalows generally had their own caretakers and sometimes even a cook, but they were only big enough to cope with six sahibs, so the team split into two parties, with Bruce leading the first and Norton the second.

For everyone who had been on the last attempt, these were nostalgic days. Charlie Bruce was pleased to revisit a small tea house run by an old lady and her sons where he had stopped, on the way in and out, in 1922. The children were much bigger but the tea and home-made bread tasted just as good. For Mallory, the trek through Sikkim, the land of 'the lotus-eaters', was his favourite part of the approach march. He loved the intense green of the rainforest, interspersed with the occasional explosion of colour from tropical plants. The air was hazy with fires set by local farmers, but a few days in he got his first view of a Himalayan giant, Kangchenjunga, the third-highest mountain in the world. Even more exciting was the moment when, out walking with Shebbeare, he saw a wild jungle cat.

Andrew Irvine was equally impressed, and couldn't contain his excitement in his letters home. 'It's an awfully fascinating country,' he wrote, 'and everything is on an awfully big scale.' He took a lot of photographs and sketched everything from the huge Buddhist prayer wheels and altars to the wooden swings he saw in some of the bigger villages. Mallory had no compunction about stripping off Neo-Pagan style and jumping in naked whenever he found a suitable stream or pool. Irvine was more circumspect, improvising some 'bathers' out of two handkerchiefs and a belt.

Everything went smoothly, apart from an incident when two porters got very drunk and beat each other black and blue. Next morning Somervell patched them up, amid protestations that they were best friends really. On 31 March, they finally crossed from Sikkim into Tibet. Charlie Bruce led the first party over the Jelep La, the 14,400-foot-high pass that had been used for hundreds of years by merchants and pilgrims to cross from Sikkim into Tibet. On the summit, prayer flags fluttered in the wind, but visibility was poor and it was too cold to stop for long.

The next day, when Mallory and Norton crossed with the second party, the sky was much clearer. They could see Chomolhari, the striking mountain that soared above Phari, and looking further on, the bare Tibet plain, where snow was falling. Two years earlier they had spent several difficult days crossing it in blizzard conditions – not an experience that anyone particularly wanted to relive. For now though, descending from the Jelep La into the warm Chumbi valley, they were able to stick to their solar topees and shirtsleeves as they trotted down towards the British trading post at Yatung, where the two parties were reunited.

General Bruce had arrived a day earlier but was ill and in bed. Prior to the expedition, the Everest Committee had sent him for a formal Harley Street medical like everyone else. One of the doctors had pronounced him fit, the other had serious reservations. Even though they had excluded previous candidates who had fallen foul of the medics, the Committee were so convinced of the general's value as the 'father' of the expedition that they allowed him to go if his personal physician approved, but with two provisos. He had to agree to go no higher than 15,000 feet, and also submit to an examination by the expedition doctor, Hingston, once he reached India.

It was obvious to Mallory from early on that Bruce wasn't fit. He told Ruth that 'entre nous' Bruce hadn't looked quite right at the start of the march. By the time he reached Yatung, after several days of ascent and descent, he was suffering from headaches and what looked like mild altitude sickness. In just a few days, it would be his fifty-eighth birthday. Bruce's brother had sent out a bottle of 150-year-old rum to celebrate the great day, but things weren't looking promising. For the moment, though, Hingston was not especially worried. He'd given Bruce the all-clear in Darjeeling and two of the younger men, Odell and Beetham, also seemed to have mild altitude sickness. As a precaution, he asked Bruce to stay an extra day.

On a more positive note, they met their old friend John MacDonald, the son of the British trade agent for Tibet who had been so helpful in 1922. He greeted them warmly and arranged for a great tamasha to be put on in their honour by a company of acrobats. The display lasted for over four hours and was, as Irvine wrote in his diary, 'rather monotonous', even though it was accompanied by copious quantities of Chang beer and a stronger spirit called arak.

For Mallory, Yatung's biggest thrill was the large consignment of mail waiting for the expedition. There were letters from his daughters, Clare and Beridge, as well as a second letter from Ruth and notes from friends. Mallory had enjoyed the march through Sikkim and the 'holiday feeling' he shared with his teammates, new and old, but his head was still in Cambridge, and news from home was always welcome.

He wrote to Reverend Cranage, his boss at the extramural department, to discuss lecture arrangements for the autumn. It was unlikely, Mallory told him, that he would return in time for the summer schools, but he was confident that he would be back by the end of August. Mallory warned Cranage that he would be expected to lecture about Everest in addition to his work for Cambridge, but promised that any bookings would be organized around his Cambridge timetable. In the meantime, he sent his best wishes to all his colleagues at the extramural department and looked forward to his return to England.

There were plenty more miles to go before that happy day, and news from Tibet was not good. Yatung was located in a pleasant, almost Alpine valley, but further ahead on the Tibetan plain, there were reports that two and a half feet of snow had recently fallen. General Bruce, however, wasn't worried by the weather – he knew that he was in for a different sort of battle when they reached Phari, the first big settlement en route to Everest.

At 14,100 feet, it was one of the highest towns in the world – a collection of low-roofed turf houses on a hill that was home to hundreds of people as well as large herds of pigs and yaks. With piles of dung and bones everywhere, Phari was famous for its stink, but General Bruce had other things on his mind when he arrived on 5 April 1924. All the team's general stores and supplies had been sent to the settlement in advance, but now he had to arrange transport for the next stage and he knew from past experience that it was not going to be easy.

According to the expedition's agreement with the Tibetan government, local officials were required to provided transport for the team at the going rate, but no one could agree what it was and two years earlier the negotiations at Phari had been particularly difficult. Once again, the dzongpen, or local governor, and his gyembus (posse of officials) wanted to charge as much as possible, but Bruce was determined to pay no more than he had in 1922. Mallory watched on as for almost two days the arguments raged back and forth, with both Charles and

Geoffrey Bruce and the translator, Karma Paul, doing their best to get the prices down. The dzongpen wouldn't budge, however, and knowing that Bruce was in a hurry to beat the oncoming monsoon, he held the upper hand.

Then, with the clock ticking down, Bruce visited the telegraph office to send a dispatch to *The Times* and check for expedition mail. Phari was the last station before the line turned north to Gyantse and then Lhasa – the capital of Tibet. Apart from a personal telegram for Irvine, with the bad news that his Oxford team had been walloped by Cambridge in the Boat Race, there was nothing else for the team. Then, by chance, Bruce spotted something very interesting: a recent telegram from the Tibetan government to the dzongpen, ordering him to give the British expedition every assistance possible. It was a decisive moment. Bruce returned to the fray, publicly holding a new telegram aloft which he promised to send to the Dalai Lama, to tell him that the dzongpen of Phari had disobeyed orders and had not been at all cooperative. Knowing that harsh retribution would follow if he continued to be obstinate, the dzongpen had no option but to capitulate.

The next day the British expedition trooped out of Phari with 250 yaks and 80 mules, heading for the Kyang La pass, but only after another morning of wrangling. General Bruce was not with them. He had won the battle of Phari but he didn't feel up to a steep ascent followed by long march across the brutal Tibetan plateau. Instead, he and Hingston were going to take an easier, slightly longer route that would be less taxing and would enable Hingston to continue his work collecting flora and fauna. They left camp at midday on 7 April with Karma Paul and a handful of porters, and were soon immersed in a vast desolate landscape that reminded Hingston of the deserts of Iraq.

That night they stopped at the small village of Tuna. Bruce seemed to be well, but the next morning, when Hingston returned to camp after a few hours collecting insects and plants, he found him shivering violently. The doctor had seen enough attacks of malaria to know what the problem was. He put Bruce back to bed, turned some soup dishes into improvised hot water bottles, and dosed him up with aspirin, quinine and Dover's powder – a potent mixture of opium and ipecacuanha, a South American herb.

By nightfall, Bruce's spirits had lifted but his temperature had not gone down. Before long he was in the middle of another attack of violent shivering. It was a difficult moment for Hingston, but he acted decisively. The following morning he sent Karma Paul back to Phari, telling him to find a stretcher and return as soon as possible. Bruce would have to be taken all the way back down to Kalimpong to receive proper medical care – assuming he made it.

Meanwhile, the rest of the team was wending its way across the Tibetan plain, oblivious to Bruce's travails. It would be many decades before Himalayan expeditions were routinely equipped with radios and satellite phones – and besides, they had problems of their own. The weather had turned exceedingly cold. On the night of 9 April, two days into the next stage, the overnight temperature dropped to −18 degrees Celsius. Irvine recorded in his diary how during the day the only way to keep warm was to don several layers of clothing: thick woollen underwear, a flannel shirt, a sweater, a windproof coat with a fleece lining, a leather waistcoat and, on top, a three-ply Burberry overcoat. Together his outfit was so heavy that he found it exhausting to get on his mule.

There was no firewood to be found nearby, so their food had to be cooked on fires stoked with dried yak dung or 'shing'.

Its thick black smoke flavoured their food and soon permeated everything. Beetham fell ill with severe dysentery and several other members of the party had decidedly 'seedy' stomachs, with Mallory suffering from severe abdominal pains. No one was prepared, though, for when a porter arrived at the camp with news that Bruce was seriously ill and might not be able to go on. Surely the man who had led them in 1922, survived Gallipoli and countless battles on the North-West Frontier, and spent several weeks in the Alps but a few months ago, would soon return, cracking jokes and organizing the Sherpas?

Back at Tuna, the stretcher arrived on 11 April along with eighteen men to act as bearers for the long march back to Yatung. It was a surreal journey through the desert-like landscape, with Bruce carried aloft wrapped in his sleeping bag and Hingston continually amazed by mirages of distant lakes and mountains. When they arrived three days later, Hingston immediately sent a telegram to the Everest Committee in London, telling them that Bruce was ill.

The Committee cabled back asking if he would return to the main party soon, but Hingston's reply was terse: 'Bruce anxious re-join expedition I insist relinquishment'. In a more expansive accompanying letter, he explained that the general had a dormant malarial infection which had been rekindled by the cold and harsh winds of Tibet. Bruce, he admitted, wanted to get back to his team as soon as possible, but the general had lost almost two stone and had an enlarged spleen. If the malaria were to return in a remoter location where it would not be so easy to evacuate him, then the consequences could be much more serious. His plan was to escort Bruce to the nearest hospital in Kalimpong, and then ride hard to return to the expedition as soon as possible.

Back on the main trail, the team had reached their next major stop, Kampa Dzong, one of the most striking fortresses in Tibet, a crossroads where the trail turned north to Lhasa or continued on to Everest. On the second day, John MacDonald arrived at the camp to announce that Bruce would almost certainly not be coming back, but Norton had some bad news of his own and immediately sent a note back to Hingston, telling him that Beetham's dysentery was so bad that he too would probably have to be evacuated, accompanied by Howard Somervell. Even worse, Mallory was sick.

Though during the first week of the approach he had felt supremely fit – better, he told Ruth, than in 1921 or 1922 – for the last few days Mallory's stomach had been so bad that he had been existing on a meagre diet of jam and biscuits. With Hingston away tending to Bruce, Somervell had taken over the role of expedition doctor. Initially he thought it was an attack of colitis, but when Mallory's pains got worse, he began to worry that it might be appendicitis.

Two weeks out of Darjeeling, it looked for a moment as if the expedition was about to fall apart, with its leader and two of its top climbers out of action and potentially both expedition doctors forced to return as sick nurses. Fortunately things weren't quite as bad as they seemed. Beetham and Mallory started to improve, and though everyone missed Bruce, they knew that Norton was a very competent deputy who was more than capable of getting everyone safely to Base Camp, and the general's nephew, Geoffrey Bruce, was almost as good with the Sherpas as his uncle.

In an excited letter home, a newly revived Mallory told Ruth that with Bruce's illness they had 'lost a force' but he was very pleased to announce that Norton had appointed him his second-in-command and the leader of the climbing team:

'I'm bound to say,' he wrote, 'I feel some little satisfaction in the latter position.' Immediately he and Norton began intense discussions on the best way to organize the summit attempts.

Norton had started his deliberations back in late January, sending Mallory and Bruce what he called a 'cock-shy', or rough plan of attack, with key dates that he hoped to hit. If everything went perfectly and they managed to establish basic camp in late April, he thought it feasible that they might reach the North Col in the first week and reach the summit after just three weeks, on 18 May. They had lost a couple of days or so after all the argument at Phari, but Norton still thought that they were on track to arrive at the Rongbuk glacier at the end of April and be ready to make an attempt on the summit in the middle of the following month.

On most points Mallory and Norton agreed. The only bone of contention was how many camps they would need above the North Col, the jumping-off point for the summit. Mallory favoured at least two more, but initially Norton was worried they might not have the manpower to put up more than one, especially if one of the summit teams was going to be climbing on oxygen and would need a lot of cylinders to be carried high up the mountain. When it came to the specifics of the route, Mallory favoured taking the North-East Ridge all the way to the top, but Norton was worried that there were a couple of sections that looked very difficult, and thought, like Finch in 1922, that it would be better to traverse out onto the North Face and then head diagonally up towards the summit. That decision would probably be made much later, when they were high on the mountain, but for now they agreed to continue their deliberations and in a few days announce to the rest of the team what each of their roles would be.

The next morning they started off with a new set of yaks and yak drivers, heading once again onto the bare Tibetan plateau. Irvine continued to be amazed by the scale of the landscape and the endless horizon that surrounded them on all sides. They passed huge lakes covered in ducks and geese and birds of all description, fought their way into the wind escorted by the spiralling 'dust devils', and threaded their way gingerly past marshes and quicksands.

In his letters home Mallory continued to tell Ruth how much he missed her and how the most exciting moments on the trip were when the 'English mail' arrived in camp with letters from friends and family. He was surprised that though the weather was unsettled, it was generally much warmer than in 1922; but as on previous expeditions, Mallory was never that interested in the sights or sounds of Tibet. All he really cared about was arriving at Everest with the best climbing plan possible, getting to the top, and then returning home as quickly as he could.

On the evening of 21 April, after one final meeting, Mallory and Norton gathered everyone in the mess tent to announce their plan of attack and each man's role once they reached the mountain. During the first week, everyone would work together to re-establish two supply camps along the Rongbuk glacier and an advance base at the foot of the North Col. Once it was fully equipped and stocked with food, fuel and oxygen, they would move into the 'assault' phase, climbing up to the North Col and then establishing their high camps on the North Ridge. As Mallory had suggested, there would be at least two further camps, the highest at around 27,500 feet – 1,500 feet below the summit.

Then, once everything was in position, Mallory and Irvine would make the first attempt climbing on oxygen from around

26,500 feet; the second, 'gas-less' party would be led by Somervell and start about 1,000 feet higher. His partner would be either Norton or Hazard, depending on who was fitter at the time. Geoffrey Bruce and Odell would help establish the high camps and then act as reserves.

Mallory was elated. He wrote to Ruth that the plan, which he felt largely responsible for, was so sound that it was 'almost unthinkable... that I shan't get to the top'. Yes, he acknowledged, Sandy Irvine had not done a lot of climbing, but he clearly understood the oxygen sets, and the only other option, Noel Odell, did not seem as fit or as well acclimatized. 'He [Irvine] will be an extraordinarily stout companion,' Mallory wrote, 'very capable with the gas, and with cooking apparatus; the only doubt is to what extent his lack of mountaineering experience will be a handicap; I hope the ground will be sufficiently easy.'

Irvine was equally thrilled, but disturbingly he admitted to his diary, 'I'm awfully glad that I'm with Mallory in the first lot, but I wish ever so much that it was a non-oxygen attempt.' Whether his objections were on sporting or pragmatic grounds, he didn't reveal, but Irvine, more than anyone else, knew that the oxygen sets were in poor condition.

In 1922, George Finch had also spent a lot of time modifying and working on the oxygen sets before his attempt, but the 1924 models were supposed to be a new improved apparatus and yet in some ways they were worse. In particular, the larger-capacity oxygen cylinders were chronically prone to leakage. In a confidential report written by Noel Odell, he revealed that when first checked in India, of the ninety cylinders sent out fully charged from Britain, twenty-one were either empty or significantly depleted. They were refilled and topped up in Kolkata, but when he and Irvine checked for a second time, in the middle of the trek, thirty-eight had leaked 'more or less badly'. It was a sorry tale, and something that could not be remedied in the wilderness of Tibet.

As for the apparatus, all eleven sets leaked to one degree or another, and six had serious defects 'due to faulty design and workmanship or bad material'. Over the course of the approach march, Irvine rebuilt virtually all the sets, attempting to repair the faults and lose some of their weight, but it was a far from ideal situation.

The result – what he called his 'Mark V' oxygen set – was tested by Mallory and Somervell when they reached the settlement of Shekar Dzong a few days later. Mallory approved of Irvine's modifications. He had shaved off 4–5 pounds and his redesign seemed easier to use. For the final attempt, Mallory intended to take as few cylinders as possible, having criticized Finch for overburdening his attempt in 1922 with too much oxygen. He was still worried that climbing with a heavy and awkward set might not be easy on very steep rock, but overall he remained confident that supplementary oxygen would help him reach his goal.

Shekar Dzong, 'Shining Glass Fort' in Tibetan, was the last big town before they reached Everest, another huge military outpost adjoining a monastery. It was home to hundreds of monks and nuns and was one of the most important religious sites in Tibet. In 1921, Charles Howard-Bury had stopped at Shekar on the Everest reconnaissance and photographed the elderly head lama, who was known as a living god. Howard-Bury had been amazed to be shown a huge fifty-foot-high gilded statue of the Buddha, as well as countless other treasures.

1924 was the third time a British team had visited. As a gift they presented the monks with two partially empty cylinders which could be used as gongs, each with a different note. To demonstrate the magical power of bottled oxygen, someone opened one of the taps and released it onto a bowl of charcoal and incense, which immediately burned bright. Irvine was very keen to get a photo of the famous gilded Buddha, admitting to his diary that he had knelt down and pretended to worship it in order to get a long enough exposure for a good shot.

Once the yaks had been swapped for the last time on the approach march, they left Shekar on 25 April, stopping the next day at the Pang La pass. It offered an awesome view of Everest, now just thirty-five miles away. In 1922, the British team had become embroiled in a slightly comical debate over which peak was Everest, but this time round everyone knew precisely what they were looking at. Visibility was so good that it almost seemed as if the whole of the Himalayas were ranged in front of them like a vast panorama, with Kanchenjunga on the far left, Shishapangma on the far right and Everest in the middle.

Mallory and Irvine took out their binoculars and spent an hour scouring the North Face for potential sites for high camps. There was nothing obvious, but the closer they got to Everest, the more confident Mallory seemed to be. 'I'm eager for the great events to begin,' he told Ruth four days before base camp. 'The telegram announcing our success if we succeed will precede this letter I suppose; but it will mention no names. How you will hope that I was one of the conquerors! And I don't think you'll be disappointed.'

After a stop at Cho Dzong, the last village they stopped in, they finally reached the Rongbuk valley, their highway to Everest. It was so bare and desolate that it reminded Norton of the battlefields of northern France. As in 1922, they spent their first night camped outside the Rongbuk monastery. Following

The Rongbuk glacier. View of Everest from Base Camp.

the lamas' request, they had brought a yak-load of cement to help mend the large obelisk, or chorten, outside the monastery, but this time Dzatrul Rinpoche, the head lama, was ill and unavailable to bless the expedition. Norton was disappointed, realizing how important an audience with the head lama would have been to the Sherpas, but there was nothing he could do.

Instead, they trekked a further four miles up the valley to the same site at 16,800 feet where two years earlier they had made their Base Camp. It was 11.30 a.m. on Tuesday 29 April, more than a calendar month since they had left Darjeeling. They had started off with high hopes of getting there a lot earlier, but after all the problems with Bruce's illness and the repeated delays organizing transport, they were only two days earlier than in 1922.

General Bruce was still sorely missed, but otherwise confidence was high. They had a strong team and a well-developed plan.

If everything went perfectly, the first climbers would reach the summit and leave the mountain well before the monsoon hit. What no one realized though was that this year the weather would be far worse than in 1921 or 1922. If the altitude and the climbing difficulties weren't enough, within days they would be enduring the coldest temperatures and the worst conditions that any of them had ever encountered.

Everest was not going to give in easily.

May 1924, the Rongbuk glacier. The third British Everest team: (back row, left to right) Irvine, Mallory, Norton, Odell and MacDonald; (front row) Shebbeare, Bruce, Somervell and Beetham.

Cold Comfort

E very year the tension starts rising in April and May. As the heat builds over the Indian plains and the winds drop, hundreds of thousands of rupees are staked on bets with legal and illegal bookmakers, with vast sums being placed on everything from the date when the Indian Meteorological Department will make its official announcement to precisely how much precipitation will fall in a particular hour on a particular day in a particular place.

Then, finally, it hits: the monsoon, one of the world's most important weather events, a three-month-long rainy season which dominates virtually every aspect of South-East Asian life – from agriculture to hydroelectric power production to levels of crime, which tend to increase when rainfall is unusually low and temperatures unusually high. In a good year the monsoon brings relief, wealth and prosperity. In a bad year it can cause devastating floods or, if it is late, terrible famines.

In the Himalayas it's generally too cold for rain, but the arrival of the monsoon is a crucial moment in the spring climbing season, bringing huge dumps of snow and unsettled weather, making mountaineering dangerous and sometimes virtually impossible. Today, modern expeditions invest significant amounts of money and resources in getting the best and most up-to-date weather information, planning their summit bids around optimal 'weather windows', but until comparatively recently it was all really a question of guesswork.

So, when on the morning of 30 April 1924, Mallory looked out of his tent onto the frigid wastes of the Rongbuk glacier, his hunch was that he had about three to four weeks to get up Everest before the monsoon hit, somewhere around the end of May. In the best-case scenario, the snows would hold off until the second week of June; in the worst, they would arrive in the middle of May.

Mallory knew from bitter experience how devastating the monsoon snows could be. Two years earlier, in June 1922, he had persuaded General Bruce to let him stage a third attempt after the first two failed to reach the summit. He hadn't even made it to the North Col after being stopped in his tracks by a huge avalanche, which swept everyone off the mountain. Mallory and the other sahibs miraculously survived, but seven out of their fourteen porters died. 'Why, oh why could not one of us Britishers have shared their fate,' lamented Howard Somervell, voicing the huge guilt they all felt.

Mallory had even taken the precaution of writing to his sister Mary, who then lived in Colombo in Sri Lanka, to ask for regular updates and advance warning of any impending changes to the weather. The monsoon starts in the Bay of Bengal and then heads up past Sri Lanka before making landfall on the southern Indian coast. If she could send him a postcard every five days and a cable when the heavy rains started, they would get some advance warning.

It was an optimistic thought. Modern-day Everest expeditions have access to satellite-based data and virtually instant communication to the outside world. The odds that a postcard would make the 2,500-mile trip from Colombo to their Rongbuk Base Camp by means of ship, train, mule and runner, in time to have any meaningful effect were not that much better than the 'finger in the air' method of weather forecasting.

The only thing they could control, or so they hoped, was the logistics of getting all their supplies up to the North Col. No porter could be expected to carry a load the full twelve miles from base camp at 16,800 feet to Camp 3, their advance base – 3,700 feet higher, near the foot of the North Col – so the plan was to set up two intermediate camps, on the same sites used in 1922, and carry everything up in stages.

The first was a three-mile hike from Base Camp to Camp 1 at 17,000 feet, very close to the junction of the main Rongbuk glacier and its first significant spur, the East Rongbuk. It was a relatively comfortable spot – a sheltered terrace covered in pebbles, surrounded by strange rocky pillars, sculpted by the wind, which from a distance looked like men.

Camp 2, dubbed the 'Frozen Lake' camp by Captain Noel in 1922, was another three hours and 2,000 feet higher up the East Rongbuk glacier. As its nickname suggests, it was a much colder spot, next to a huge ice-cliff by a frozen pool. The final march, though only another 1,500 feet of elevation gain, was another four miles of toil and the hardest and least predictable part: a long slog up the middle of the East Rongbuk glacier, past a succession of strange ice pinnacles that seemed to rear up from the ground.

The plan was to use locally recruited Tibetan porters to do the first two stages of the carrying, taking everything from Base

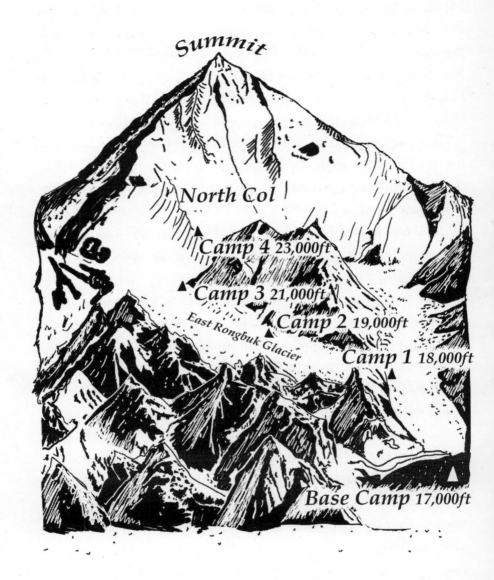

Camps on the Rongbuk glacier

Camp to Camps 1 and 2. Then the better-equipped Darjeeling Sherpas would do the final push up to Camp 3, where they would build a stockpile, before moving into the second phase of the climb.

In 1922, General Bruce had been continually frustrated by local Tibetan farmers who had offered to work as porters but had come and gone at will, making it impossible to plan. This time Norton had organized everything in advance, so when they arrived at Base Camp a small army of men and women was already waiting for them. Everything augured well on the first morning when a long column of 150 porters plodded out of Base Camp heading for Camp 1, each carrying a load of roughly forty pounds. Three Gurkha NCOs – Tejbir, Hurke and Shamsher – accompanied them to make sure that everything ran smoothly and to look after the camps. According to Norton's 'movement' chart, the next day seventy-five porters would return to pick up a second batch of supplies, while the other seventy-five would carry on to Camp 2.

The climbers and Sherpas meanwhile had a lot to organize. Base Camp was located in a small hollow surrounded by huge heaps of rocky moraine carried down the valley by the Rongbuk glacier. Nearby there was a small stream, which initially was frozen over but would grow bigger and noisier over the course of the expedition. Everywhere there were piles of wooden boxes in various stages of unpacking, which were gradually taken over by rooks and pigeons, eager to pick up any scraps. As ever, the two main focuses of camp life were the cook tent and the large green mess tent – 'Norton's special child', as Mallory called it – close to which everyone slept.

It was not quite home from home. Though protected to some extent by the surrounding rocks, Base Camp was often very windy and cold, particularly in the afternoons. Apart from a few tufts of coarse grass, there was no vegetation or source of firewood. Instead, the cooking fires were still fuelled with malodourous shing, consignments of which were regularly brought in by local merchants and farmers. At the high camps, they ran their stoves on Meta – solid blocks of paraffin – but at Base Camp and the first two stops on the glacier, the thick acrid stink of burning dung was the dominant smell, blackening the canvas of the cook tent and giving all their hot food a distinctly pungent flavour.

On 1 May the team was still in celebratory mood, enjoying a five-course meal washed down with champagne. After thirty days of riding and marching they had finally reached their goal, and the weather seemed to be holding. As Sandy Irvine, the youngest of the expedition's new boys, wrote to his nine-year-old friend Peter Lunn: 'The mountain looks wonderfully easy from here in the evening light... We are all sitting in the Mess tent writing letters for tomorrow's Dak [mail runner] or eating bulls eyes to help digest the yak meat we had for dinner tonight. It's great fun this expedition, you would love it if you were a bit older.' While he worked on the oxygen sets, Norton composed a dispatch for *The Times* and everyone else organized their kit and the equipment that would have to go up the mountain.

The next morning, the *Boys' Own* adventure stopped and the ordeal started.

The first problem, as in 1922, was the local porters. Everyone on the team had tremendous respect for their toughness and hardiness. Some were men, some were women, a few had even come with young babies on their backs. They wore heavy outer clothing in which they slept at night, not needing tents at Base Camp. But when they got onto the glacier, even the hardy Tibetans couldn't cope with the fiercely cold and snowy conditions. Despite the relatively high wages on offer, 52 out of the 150 recruits deserted after the first night. The remainder seemed in better spirits and carried their loads up to Camp 2 before returning to Base Camp, where Norton rewarded their hard work with a bonus meal. Six of them were hired as general assistants, leaving the others to return to their farms.

On 3 May, accompanied by Irvine, Odell and Hazard, Mallory set off at the head of the first party of twenty Sherpas, aiming to hump the stores left by the local Tibetans up to Camp 3. It was a bitterly cold and windy day, the sky overcast with heavy, threatening clouds. Mallory was the only veteran of 1922. Irvine was planning to go with him as far as Camp 3, and the other two new boys, Odell and Hazard, were going to carry on up 1,700 feet higher to the North Col to establish Camp 4, the jumping-off point for the summit attempts.

The route followed a narrow trail that ran between huge piles of rock, or lateral moraines, on the left-hand side of the Rongbuk glacier. Though in theory most of the supplies and equipment should have gone up already, Mallory noticed that several of the Sherpas seemed to be carrying very heavy loads, with their own belongings and bedding perched on top of the sahibs' precious oxygen bottles.

At Camp 1, no tents were needed. Instead, both the sahibs and the Sherpas slept in sangars, the rough low-walled shelters made from rocks gathered nearby that they had put up in 1922. The next morning, after a few hours reorganizing the Sherpas' loads and abandoning anything that wasn't totally necessary, Mallory once again led them out of camp, the rocky trail continuing up the lateral moraine before moving onto the glacier itself.

Mallory had 'a devil in him', as Irvine wrote in his diary, setting a furious pace which left his young partner breathless. Before they had set off from Base Camp, Somervell had taken blood samples from everyone to see how they were adapting to the altitude. Irvine had been pleased to see that he had the highest concentration of red corpuscles – vital to carry oxygen around the body – but he admitted in his diary that he found the going very tough, comparing keeping up with Mallory with competing in the Boat Race.

Just after midday, they reached Camp 2, next to the frozen lake. It was 'extraordinarily uninviting', as Mallory later wrote to Ruth. The sahibs and the Gurkha NCOs had tents, but the Sherpas had to scavenge for more rocks to build new sangars, topping them with tent flysheets to keep a little warmer. Mallory was shocked at how unenthusiastic they seemed, apparently so overwhelmed by the conditions that they did not care about their own creature comforts.

He had brought a Hindustani grammar to help him communicate, but Mallory never bonded with the Sherpas and in his letters home rarely mentioned any of them by name. Though like everyone else he admired their hardiness, he was very critical of how easily they seemed to lose heart when conditions got tough, often comparing them to children. In comparison to the previous expeditions, the Sherpas hired in 1924 were better clothed and equipped, but they hadn't been issued with the same quality of boots as Mallory and the sahibs and had to provide their own inner clothing. Carrying heavy loads across the freezing cold Rongbuk glacier, it's easy to see how they might have become 'listless', in Mallory's words.

The next morning, the real problems started. It had been an appalling night, with heavy snow, strong winds and the temperature dropping to −17 degrees Celsius. Everyone emerged from their tents late, and three of the Sherpas said they felt so bad that they couldn't carry on. After a long noisy argument between Mallory and one of the 'old soldiers' over what he should carry, which climaxed with Mallory threatening him with his fist in his face, they finally got away at 11.00 a.m.

The going was extraordinarily difficult. The wind had blown most of the snow cover off the ice, leaving it rock-hard and even more slippery. Occasionally between icy pinnacles there were piles of fresh, powdery snow, but nothing that offered a good grip. The expedition had brought crampons, but they hadn't been issued yet, so everyone moved achingly slowly. Mallory did the route-finding, occasionally falling back to the rear to check up on everyone and urge them on.

A few hundred yards later, they reached the Trough, a huge dip in the ice, about fifty feet deep, that Mallory remembered from 1922. On clear sunny days it could become intolerably hot and airless, prompting a strange 'glacier lassitude', but mercifully that morning the Trough was cloudy and overcast. It was crevasse-free, but with the porters still moving slowly, they roped up into three parties, a 'device' that Mallory hoped would help pick up the pace, even though there was no real need. When they emerged a few hours later, the wind was behind them, but when they passed Changtse, a lesser mountain in the Everest massif, the wind changed direction and hit them full on, slowing the Sherpas to a crawling pace.

Powering ahead of Irvine, Odell and Hazard, Mallory reached Camp 3 alone. It was, he confided to Ruth, a 'queer sensation reviving memories of that scene, with the dud oxygen cylinders piled against the cairn which was built to commemorate the seven porters killed two years ago'. It must have been a very uncomfortable moment, being reminded of all the guilt that he felt for the failure of the third attempt in 1922. This time, as he wrote in a letter to his sister Mary, 'It will be my job to get the party off the mountain in safety… No one, climber or porter, is going to get killed if I can help it.' But now, with the sun going down and the temperature dropping, he was under no illusions about how miserable the coming hours would be.

As soon as the Sherpas arrived, Mallory helped them pitch their tents and distributed Meta cookers to prepare hot food, before he and the other sahibs sorted out their own tents and sleeping bags. Their cook, Kami, got to work preparing a meal of mutton and vegetables, but when he checked their rations of cheese and jam, they were frozen solid. In 1922 John Noel had christened Camp 3 'Snowfield-camp', but though it might have looked picturesque, perched on the northern flank of a small tributary glacier that flowed down from the North Col into the main East Rongbuk glacier, it was a miserable spot, which usually lost the sun at around 5.00 p.m.

That night it was again bitingly cold. Irvine recorded in his diary how he slept soundly for a few hours before spending the rest of the night tossing and turning, trying vainly to get comfortable. Mallory lay awake thinking about how demoralized the Sherpas would be in the morning, before resolving to head back down the glacier at first light to collect the heavier sleeping bags, which were only supposed to be used above the North Col but were obviously needed now.

Mallory left Camp 3 at 7.00 a.m., shortly after the first rays of the sun had hit their tents. He wanted to get back down to Camp 2 before the next party of Sherpas left, but unbeknownst to him, they too had made an early start and did not realize that the heavier bedding was needed.

When eventually he met them, this new contingent of Sherpas told him that they had decided that, rather than sticking to plan and returning to Camp 2 after they had deposited their loads, they would spend the night at Camp 3. Mallory was aghast. There weren't enough tents higher up for more men, and without thicker sleeping bags the new arrivals would also spend a miserable night and end up just as demoralized as the first party.

Instead, he escorted them to a sheltered spot and told them to cache their loads before sending them back down the glacier. Feeling very tired and hungry, Mallory climbed back up to Camp 3. Nothing had improved. Half the Sherpas were still in their tents, suffering from headaches and exhaustion, and unable to go down to the dump to bring up the loads the other party had left. Mallory was utterly done in, but Irvine and Odell offered to take the four fittest down to the supply dump and bring up as much as possible from the latest batch of loads.

That night was the coldest so far, with the temperature dropping to −16 degrees at 5.00 p.m. and then plummeting to −30 overnight. The next morning, no one was in good shape, neither the sahibs nor the Sherpas, several of whom were now vomiting because of the altitude. Mallory dispatched Hazard with four men to intercept the next party at the dump, but none of the other Sherpas left in camp were in a fit state to do any work, so he decided to send them all down to recuperate in the slightly warmer and more comfortable confines of Camp 2.

It was a grim business getting everyone going. One Sherpa already showed signs of serious frostbite, his feet so badly swollen that he found it almost impossible to get them into his boots. Mallory helped him down for the first few hundred yards before instructing another Sherpa to take over while he returned to Camp 3 with Hazard and three of the second group of porters. Together, they managed to carry back seven loads from the dump to Camp 3, including a consignment of high-altitude sleeping bags, but Mallory was now getting very worried.

After just a few days, porter morale was 'shot to pieces'. If the weather didn't improve and if they couldn't make Snowfield camp a little bit more habitable, then they would never even reach the North Col, never mind get up the mountain. In theory, of course, the sahibs could have done their own carrying, but if they had, they would have been so exhausted by the time they reached the North Col, there would have been little chance at all of getting any further.

Back down at Base Camp, Norton had had no idea of all the problems, but as soon as he and Howard Somervell reached Camp 2 on 7 May, they realized how bad things were. The Sherpas sent down by Mallory were cheek by jowl with the second party who had tried and failed to get to Camp 3 – forty men crammed into shelters only designed to take twenty. As Norton wrote in his diary, they 'appeared dead beat and complained of great privations and hardships'. What had looked so easy on paper was much harder in the field. All he could do was issue extra food rations and blankets and hope that higher up it wasn't quite as bad as he feared.

On the next day Mallory came down himself, leaving Irvine at Camp 3 with Odell and Hazard. By comparison Camp 2, the Frozen Lake camp, was positively balmy, so hot that Mallory and Norton were able to eat breakfast 'al fresco' rather than shivering in their tents. There was no getting away from their problems, however. In 1922, parties of Sherpas had regularly gone up and down in a day between Camp 2 and Camp 3, but it was obvious to Mallory that this year the conditions were immeasurably worse. Instead, he suggested, one team should be based in the middle of the Rongbuk glacier at Camp 2, ferrying material up and down to the dump, while a second team of the strongest Sherpas should be permanently stationed at Camp 3, shuttling back and forth between the dump and their tents.

When Geoffrey Bruce arrived a few hours later, he too was shocked at the state of morale and readily agreed to the new scheme. Mallory and Norton hoped that Bruce's familiarity with the Sherpas and his ability to speak Nepali would steady the ship and re-energize everyone, so while Bruce settled in, Howard Somervell took the first party of fourteen porters back up the glacier, leaving Mallory to bask in the sun. 'A day of great relief this, with the responsibility shared or handed over,' he told Ruth. After so many fraught and uncomfortable nights he was only too glad to be able to relax, and for once he slept soundly.

The first few days had shown Mallory at his best, and his worst. If it weren't for his energy and drive, Camp 3 might not have been established and the porters would have suffered even more. Though he didn't really bond with the Sherpas, their welfare was never far from his thoughts. But he was also a man in a hurry, and woe betide anyone who couldn't keep up, whether a Sherpa or a sahib.

The next morning, Mallory was back in the fray, heading up the glacier with seven fresh men who had just arrived from Base Camp. He wanted to take them all the way to Camp 3 to spend a few days making the camp 'wonderful', but the weather gods had other ideas. As soon as they emerged from the Trough, Mallory's party was engulfed in a sudden blizzard which turned into a virtual white-out. It took a lot of cajoling just to get his men to the supply dump, and only when they were joined by Norton and the others did they manage to get all the way to Camp 3.

There was good news and bad news. On a positive note, Irvine had unpacked one of the expedition's 'roarer' cookers, a kind of super Primus stove which weighed over forty pounds and had been specially developed for the expedition. Though it guzzled fuel and initially terrified the camp cook, it was much faster to work with and soon its distinctively loud purr became a welcome sound to everyone.

The bad news was that, a day earlier, Odell and Hazard had failed in the expedition's first attempt to reach the North Col, the narrow strip of ground at 23,000 feet that linked Everest to Changtse, the North Peak, and was the starting point for any summit attempt. This was a real blow: before making any attempt on the summit, they would have to establish and fully stock a large camp on the col before heading up the North Ridge towards their goal. In 1921 and 1922, Mallory and Somervell had made it to the col on their first attempt, but because of the snow conditions Odell and Hazard only managed to reconnoitre halfway before they turned back after dumping their sacks full of wooden stakes and ropes.

For the moment, there was nothing Mallory or Norton could do but sit out the evening and wait hopefully for Kami to conjure up their evening meal. Even at the worst of times, the 1924 team displayed a remarkable *esprit de corps* and an ability to make the best of the most difficult circumstances. In a letter to Ruth, written several days later, Mallory described how he took off his boots and outer trousers, and donned the long footless socks that she had knitted for him two years earlier, some slippers and a pair of flannel pyjamas, before settling into his tent with Howard Somervell to play a few hands of piquet, a popular card game with a thirty-two-card pack. After reorganizing the tents so they were interlinked, Mallory produced his copy of *The Spirit of Man*, the anthology of poetry and prose produced in 1916 for the men in the trenches that he had taken on his previous expeditions. 'We all agreed that "Kubla Khan" was a good sort of poem,' Mallory told Ruth. 'Irvine was rather poetry shy but seemed to be favourably impressed by the Epitaph to Gray's "Elegy". Odell was much inclined to be interested and liked the last lines of "Prometheus Unbound". S [Somervell], who knows quite a lot of English literature, had never read a poem of Emily Bronte's and was happily introduced … And suddenly hot soup arrived.'

It was a quintessentially British scene, followed by a night that was quintessentially Everest. The temperature dropped to −12 degrees Celsius, the wind raged, and piles of spindrift blew into their tents, so that by the morning everything, inside and out, was covered in a thick layer of snow. It was obvious that there was no pointing in attempting the North Col again until the conditions improved.

Geoffrey Bruce was all for an immediate retreat to Base Camp, but Mallory wasn't quite so sure, arguing they should stay for another day. Norton agreed, before changing his mind when he realized how much fuel was being consumed. Even before they had got the roarer up and running a few days earlier, they had used a whole box of solid fuel as well as a lot of paraffin. To economize, Norton sent Mallory and Irvine down to Camp 2, to prepare the men there for a mass evacuation unless the weather suddenly improved.

Once again Irvine found it hard to keep up with Mallory. Just to get from Camp 3 to the top of the Trough left him panting with every step and occasionally staggering. To make things even harder, Mallory decided to scout a new route. In his diary Irvine recorded that he arrived at Camp 2 'very exhausted indeed. In one or two cases I collapsed almost completely after a little climb of ten or twenty feet.' Mallory commented to Ruth that both he and Irvine had suffered from 'glacier lassitude' caused by exposure to the sun and its harsh reflection off the snow and ice beneath them. It was a strange episode: was Mallory trying to prepare Irvine for the rigours to come when they made their summit attempt, or was he showing off his stamina with a little bit of 'competitive' marching, the kind which John Hunt and Edmund Hillary occasionally became involved in on the approach march to Everest in 1953, with the forty-three-year-old Hunt trying to prove himself the equal of his younger teammate? Or was Mallory simply oblivious to his young partner's discomfort?

In his letters home in 1924, it's striking how often Mallory commented on his fitness and the state of his health. Repeated declarations that he was the strongest member of the team and most likely to reach the top were interspersed with moments of doubt and uncertainty. In 1921, he had been one of the youngest members of the reconnaissance expedition, but now he was thirty-seven, soon to be thirty-eight – fifteen years Irvine's senior – and he occasionally felt his age. Mallory was periodically niggled by an old ankle injury, sustained in a climbing accident many years earlier, and during the march across Tibet he had suffered from acute stomach problems and severe sunburn. Perhaps the boasting about his fitness was to reassure his wife that all was well, but as Queen Gertrude said in *Hamlet*, there was a sense that he 'doth protest too much'.

Irvine, for his part, was in the prime of his life, but like a lot of first-timers in the Himalayas was taking time to adjust to the altitude. Fortunately, he was possessed of a young person's

powers of recovery and was instantly revived when they reached
Camp 2, where Bentley Beetham and John Noel awaited with
hot mugs of tea. Even better, that evening just after supper, a
porter turned up with no less than six letters from home, some
sent as long ago as February, two months earlier.

The next day, after another terrible night at Camp 3, Norton
decided that the time had come to take everyone off the Rongbuk
glacier until the conditions improved. 'All porters more or less
done in – Sahibs not improving much,' as he recorded in his
diary. On the way down he met some Sherpas with even more
bad news: two very sick men had been evacuated to Base Camp.
Sanglar, one of the Gurkhas, had severe bronchitis and the other,
Manbhadur the cobbler, had frostbite in both his feet. And that
wasn't all: a third man, Tam Ding, had slipped and broken his
leg on the glacier.

Fortunately, at the very moment when so many medical
emergencies were arising, the expedition doctor Richard
Hingston arrived at Base Camp in the late afternoon on 11
May after a very rapid twenty-day march across Tibet from
Kalimpong, where he had left the recovering General Bruce.
Before he got stuck in, that night his teammates cracked open the
champagne to celebrate his safe arrival – the very clean-shaven
and proper-looking doctor a stark contrast with the bearded
filthy men who sat opposite him.

Hingston was very glad to have arrived in time to play a
part, but it was very obvious that the expedition was not going
to plan. 'Things apparently are not satisfactory,' he commented
laconically in his diary, but the next day it went from bad to
worse with news that one of the Gurkha NCOs stationed at
Camp 1, Shamsher, was so ill that he could neither move nor
speak. Hingston went up to examine him and diagnosed a

potential cerebral haemorrhage. On 13 May, Hingston went up the glacier for a second time to evacuate him to Base Camp on an improvised stretcher, but though he made it most of the way, Shamsher died about half a mile from the camp.

It was now two weeks into the climb. According to Norton and Mallory's original plan, they should have been in position and poised to make an attempt on the summit in five days' time. Instead, the whole team had retreated to Base Camp, having not even succeeded in reaching the North Col. Though Norton and Mallory had no intention of taking any of the Sherpas on the final push to the summit, they were dependant on their ability to get supplies and equipment to a final camp at 26,000 or ideally 27,000 feet. Sherpa morale, however, was rock bottom, and even Mallory admitted to Ruth that he was 'going through a real hard time in a way I never did in '22'.

On both previous expeditions, the weather, as they now realized, had been relatively benign. There had been storms and blizzards, and high up on the mountain the climbers had been tormented by the vicious west wind, but the temperature had never been so consistently low on the Rongbuk glacier, and they had never suffered from really long periods of severe conditions. Their only option was to wait for the weather to improve, postpone their summit day to around 28 May, and hope that the monsoon didn't arrive early – or hadn't arrived already.

In his diary, Norton inscribed a quotation from the popular Australian poet and horseman Adam Lindsay Gordon:

> No game was ever worth a rap
> For a rational man to play
> Into which no accident, no mishap,
> Could possibly find its way.

The holder of a Military Cross and a Distinguished Service Order, Norton had seen enough action not to be phased by even serious setbacks – but, just in case, he decided on a change of plan. Before they went up the Rongbuk glacier again, they would seek some divine intervention.

7

Trapped

Despite its height, Everest has never been thought of as the most sacred mountain in Tibet. Far more important is the 21,778-foot Mount Kailash, which is held to be the centre of the world for Tibetan Buddhists; there are several other mountains that are also more revered. Nevertheless, the Rongbuk valley has long been considered a holy place and its monastery a very important institution. Though newer and smaller than some of the other monasteries the 1924 team had passed on the approach march, it was held in particularly high esteem by local Tibetans and the Sherpa community of the Solukhumbu, on the Nepali side of Everest.

The founder and head lama, Dzatrul Rinpoche, was a striking-looking figure who was said to be the reincarnation of Guru Rinpoche, the legendary Indian mystic who had introduced Buddhism to Tibet. In 1922 he'd blessed the British expedition on the way in and out of Everest, and though he and his monks were slightly sceptical about all the time and effort the strange Englishmen were willing to invest in climbing Everest, they tolerated what had become almost an annual invasion. Though Dzatrul Rinpoche had been ill a few weeks earlier, when he heard about Norton's problems on Everest in 1924, he welcomed the British team down and made himself available to see them.

The monastery was a three-mile walk towards the head of the valley, just past a small nunnery. Everyone, apart from Somervell and Beetham and three or four of the sickest Sherpas, joined the party. Initially the sahibs were ushered into an anteroom, where they were served buttered tea and a dish of noodles and mutton. Then, after about an hour and a half, everyone was led upstairs to meet the lama himself. He sat on a bed-shaped throne, surrounded by acolytes, dressed in dark robes and a pointed yellow hat embroidered with gold thread.

With great solemnity, Dzatrul Rinpoche blessed each of the sahibs by touching their foreheads with a small prayer wheel. The Sherpas then made an offering of two rupees each, given to them by the sahibs, and a white ceremonial scarf, before they too were blessed. When the ceremony was over, the head lama made a short speech in which he told everyone that in return for his prayers, they should obey the sahibs, while also calling on the sahibs not to do anything too risky. Norton presented him with a roll of elaborately stitched cloth and a watch, as well as a donation for the monastery. Then Dzatrul Rinpoche finished by leading the famous incantation 'Om mani padme hum' ('Hail the jewel in the lotus').

In their diaries that night, most of the sahibs wrote how impressed they had been by the head lama and his saintly air. The Sherpas too were much heartened by the meeting, and returned to Base Camp pleased that the ceremony had taken place. Mallory, however, did not mention the meeting at all in his letters back home to Ruth. As Howard-Bury, the leader of the

Everest reconnaissance expedition, had noticed in 1921, despite his interest in the arts and his passion for politics, Mallory barely paid any attention to the local culture. Most of the other climbers were fascinated by Tibet, but he only seemed to care about one thing: climbing its mountains, and most particularly reaching the summit of Everest. The next day, on 16 May, he headed back to the front line. 'I feel very strong for the battle,' he wrote to Ruth, 'but I know every ounce of strength will be wanted.'

Their second foray started well enough, with the weather holding for the next two days and most of the team leaving the comforts of Base Camp to head back up the Rongbuk glacier to re-establish Camp 3, at the foot of the North Col. Norton decided that the 'old gang' should be responsible for finding and fixing the route to the col itself, so on the morning of 20 May he left camp with Mallory, Somervell and Odell, along with one Sherpa, Lhakpa Tsering, to help carry the rope and wooden pickets.

They started confidently enough, but by the time they had slogged their way across deep snows to the foot of the main ice wall, Somervell was looking so unwell that Norton sent him back down. Above them towered a 1,500-foot icy slope, riven by crevasses – some small, some huge. In 1922, Mallory and the others had gone up and down several times, but after the avalanche that ended that expedition, they would not contemplate following the same route.

Instead, they headed further east to plot a new, slightly longer but hopefully safer approach. The main obstacle was a tall ice chimney about two-thirds of the way up. It was 200 feet high with hard icy sides and a wall of soft snow behind. The chimney took over an hour to climb, and as Mallory later wrote in a dispatch for *The Times*, was 'as steep and difficult as one could wish to find on any big mountain'. Today's climbers make swift work of the slopes up to the North Col, hauling themselves up fixed ropes installed by their Sherpas, and kicking their way into the ice with front-pointed crampons. In 1924 there were no pre-existing ropes and their crampons were crude and heavy, with only down-pointing spikes. Instead, Mallory swung his long-handled ice axe to chip steps in the ice wall when it got too steep. Occasionally it was so vertiginous that the only way for Mallory to make progress was to stand on the head of Norton's ice axe, which they had hammered into the slope. After several exhausting hours, at around 2.30 p.m. they finally reached the site of their old camp on a small ice shelf, a few hundred feet below the col.

It was a desolate spot. Nothing remained of the tents and equipment left there two years earlier; it had all been avalanched off or blown away. They lay in the snow and gobbled down a handful of sweets and snacks, before Mallory decided to carry on up to the col itself. He was so 'bust to the world' that he let Odell lead. Norton, equally done in, elected to stay back with Lhakpa to hammer in some wooden pickets and begin the rope-fixing.

It took half an hour for Mallory and Odell to climb the final hundred feet or so to the crest of the fabled North Col. It was as cold and windy as Mallory remembered – not the sort of place where anyone would want to spend any time at all. An hour later, they returned to Norton, looking even more shattered, and began their descent. It did not go well.

In spite of his exhaustion, Mallory decided to have a look at their old 1922 route, and went ahead, un-roped, with Norton close behind and Odell and Lhakpa tied together at the back.

Camp 4, just below the North Col or Chang La – a narrow strip of
land connecting Everest to Changtse, also known as the North Peak.

Before long Norton had a nasty slip which left him glissading down the slope until he managed to arrest his fall with his ice axe. Moments later Lhakpa also slipped, and to Norton and Odells's alarm discovered that he had not tied on correctly. If it hadn't been for a pile of snow in his path, he would have fallen much further.

Mallory raced ahead, oblivious, until he was stopped by a large, very deep crevasse. It was too big to jump so he tried crossing a snow bridge, only for it to collapse, sending him tumbling down, heading straight for the icy void below. By sheer luck, his ice axe caught on the side wall, arresting his fall. After a few nasty moments, he managed to wedge himself reasonably comfortably between the crevasse's icy walls, but when he called for help, no one replied or came to his rescue.

After several minutes' shouting, Mallory realized that they couldn't hear him, and the cavalry was most definitely not coming. Instead, he scooped out a hole in the ice and wormed his way up to the surface, only to discover that he was still on the upper side of the crevasse. The others were by then at least ten minutes below him. He had no alternative but to continue on down by himself, cutting new steps when necessary, until finally he reached a point where he could cross the crevasse and regain the lower slopes. By the time he reached the bottom to re-join the others, he felt utterly at the limit of his strength.

Getting to the North Col was a key moment in the expedition, but it hadn't been easy. Norton recovered from his exertions quickly, but he was still very concerned about the porters having to carry heavy loads on very steep terrain and was particularly worried about the ice chimney. Mallory and Bruce, his two strongest and most experienced climbers, both had a dry hacking cough. Irvine, who had arrived in Camp 3 on the same day, was suffering from severe diarrhoea after his trip to the Rongbuk monastery. Beetham was now in even worse shape: having recovered from his bout of dysentery, he had succumbed to a sudden attack of sciatica, leaving him unable to get out of his tent and unlikely to play any significant role in the remainder of the expedition.

The clear skies of a few days earlier were gone, replaced by high cloud and persistent snow. When on the following morning, Somervell led a party across the snowfield and then up the 1,500-foot ice wall to the top of the North Col with twelve porters, Irvine and Hazard, he found that most of the steps Mallory had so painstakingly cut a day earlier were now more or less invisible. It took them two and a half hours just to get all the porter loads up the ice chimney, with Irvine and Somervell at the top doing most of the hauling and Hazard directing operations from below. Higher up, they fixed more ropes at the most dangerous places, before stopping to allow Hazard and the Sherpa porters to traverse across the last 150 feet to the ice shelf just below the col, where they planned to re-establish Camp 4 and spend one night before climbing back down the following day.

When Somervell and Irvine turned around, it was the late afternoon and a blizzard had started in earnest. Fifteen-hundred feet below, Norton scanned the slopes above hoping to see the returning men, growing increasingly anxious when there was no sign. Irvine had a minor slip on the descent, and by the time they reached the foot of the slope, they were in the middle of a virtual white-out. It wasn't until 6.30 p.m. that Somervell and Irvine reached the tents of Camp 3, allowing Norton to breathe a little easier.

According to the next stage of Norton's revised plan, Hazard and his twelve porters would be relieved by Geoffrey Bruce and

Noel Odell and a larger party of seventeen Sherpas, with more tents and enough food and supplies to fully stock Camp 4, but the next morning it snowed so heavily no one could go up or down. That night was the coldest so far, with the temperature dropping to −31 degrees Celsius.

When on 23 May Bruce and Odell finally left Camp 3, a day behind schedule, with the second party of porters, the snow was so deep on the slopes leading to the North Col that they decided to dump everything halfway up, aiming to return on the following day to finish the job. Though it was too blustery to communicate, they saw Hazard and his party a few hundred feet higher, beginning their descent from the North Col. At 5.00 p.m., two hours after Bruce and Odell had returned, Hazard arrived at Camp 3. Everyone was much relieved to see him but there was a problem – he had only brought down eight of his twelve men.

Hazard told Norton that he had deliberately left his cook, Phu, behind, thinking that he would be of use to the next party. As for the other three, he didn't seem sure why they had stayed high, but one of them, Namgya, had badly frostbitten hands and there was very little food at Camp 4. Even the mild-mannered Norton was appalled – how could Hazard have left them there, with the weather clearly beginning to deteriorate and the monsoon almost upon them? There was no alternative but to go up the next day to bring down the marooned men, and then, if the weather didn't improve, to evacuate the whole line for a second time.

It was a ragtag rescue party that was due to set off the following morning. Norton was very worried about how they would fare and what they would find. The only men who he trusted to do the job were Mallory and Somervell, but they were both very tired and still suffering from sore throats and hacking coughs. After all the deaths in 1922, Norton and Mallory were utterly determined to bring the four Sherpas down safely, though they both agreed that the odds of being avalanched for a second time were two-to-one on. 'It is not all gain commanding an expedition of this sort,' Norton wrote in his diary with consummate understatement.

After waking up with a fit of coughing, Mallory led out at around 8.00 a.m. For the next three hours he stayed in front, ploughing his way through the snow and then slowly working his way up the icy face of the North Col before Somervell took over the lead. To their surprise, the snow conditions improved as they got higher, allowing them to climb more quickly. It was still exhausting work though, so Norton moved to the front, taking them up to the foot of the ice chimney. They had been going for five hours, so they paused for a brief rest before tackling the hardest part of the climb.

Two years earlier, Mallory and Somervell had been looking upwards towards the same camp just below the crest of the North Col, hoping to make a third attempt on the summit. Somervell tentatively went ahead to test the slope, which was blanketed in heavy snow after days of storm and blizzard. It looked possible, so he gave the signal for the others to follow. Then, a few minutes later, preceded by a dull boom, it seemed as if the whole slope had given way, engulfing the party of three climbers and fourteen porters in tons of thick white snow.

Somervell thought the end had come, but remarkably all the sahibs and the three nearest Sherpas managed to claw their way to the surface. The other nine Sherpas, however, had been swept over an ice cliff and thrown down towards the yawning mouth of a huge crevasse. Mallory and Somervell climbed down and vainly tried to extricate them with their bare hands, and though amazingly they managed to pull two men out alive, the seven others had died. Now, in 1924, Somervell and Mallory were wiser and warier, but that only made them realize even more keenly the huge risk they were taking.

Mallory was first up the ice chimney. He was very glad of the rope they had fixed a few days earlier, but all the steps he had cut were filled with snow. At the top, they switched roles again, Norton taking the lead up to a huge icy pinnacle, or serac, that marked the highest point of the climb. Once again they regrouped, before Somervell began traversing across the slope towards the tents where the four Sherpas were marooned. It was the most dangerous moment so far. He could just about make out Hazard's tracks, but moving horizontally across the slope was the most likely way to set off an avalanche. Mallory and Norton stayed back at the serac, holding the rope as Somervell edged his way closer until he was in shouting distance of the stricken men.

Down below, from a position on the East Rongbuk glacier, John Noel had his camera trained on the upper part of the slope. He was a mile and a quarter away and everything seemed to be happening in slow motion, but he couldn't keep his eyes off the events unfolding above.

In one of those strange moments of comedy that often seem to punctuate high drama, when Somervell called over the Sherpas thought he was asking if they were ready to go higher. He was not, Somervell explained. He was here to evacuate them. But there was a problem: the rope was not long enough to get all the way across. Somervell plunged his axe into the snow and then wrapped the end of the rope around it. Then he shouted and gestured to the Sherpas to move across the slope above him, aiming to catch them if they slipped.

The first two men, the cook Phu and the frostbitten Namgya, were in such a state that they slipped almost immediately. Somervell was unable to catch them and watched in horror as they slid down the slope, gathering speed until amazingly they stopped on a small ledge about fifteen feet below. As they clung on, terrified, Somervell kept on talking to calm them down. Then he called back to Mallory and Norton and got them to reset their belay to give him fifteen more feet of rope. He climbed down, but the rope just wasn't long enough, so he planted himself in the snow and stretched out his left hand, and hauled them up one after the other, before watching them traverse across to Mallory and Norton, using the rope as a handrail.

The last two Sherpas did not make the same mistake and managed to get to the rope without any problems, but one of them, Uchung, had frostbitten feet. As a precaution, Norton had brought up a portable stretcher, but they managed to get him down without having to use it. It was 4.30 p.m. and the sun was soon to start going down, making the situation even more fraught and uncomfortable, but fortunately there were no further mishaps. Norton was glad to have worn his crampons: several times he had to support the weight of Namgya as he helped him down the near-vertical ice chimney.

At 7.00 p.m. they finally reached the glacier and began wading through the snow towards their tents at Camp 3. As he would do several times later, Noel came out with Odell and a couple of Sherpas, carrying large thermoses of soup as well as blankets and dry gloves. They could not have been more welcome.

It had been a gruelling day and the night was no easier, with the temperature falling to −24 degrees Celsius. As Norton wrote in his diary, ultimately the mission had been a success, but they had come very close to disaster and were all utterly exhausted. The next morning, he ordered everyone to abandon Camp 3 and retreat down the glacier for a second time.

Back down at Base Camp, Hingston was suffering from too little rather than too much drama, confined to his post while all the action took place above him. Born in Ireland in 1887, he was an army doctor who had worked for the Indian Medical Service for the last fourteen years. Wiry and of medium height, he sported a small moustache and was invariably well turned out, whatever the conditions. Though he did not consider himself a mountaineer, he had taken part in an expedition to the Soviet Pamirs in 1913 before finding himself in the thick of the action in the First World War. He won a Military Cross for valour, campaigning in Africa, Europe and the Middle East.

Hingston's passion was for natural history, so he was pleased to be appointed the expedition naturalist as well as its doctor. By the time he reached Base Camp, he'd already collected over 2,000 specimens, mainly small insects. Besides the wildlife, he was intrigued by the physiological effects of altitude on the climbers and subjected them to regular tests during the approach march and on the glacier. In order to complete his programme, Hingston wanted desperately to climb up the glacier to Camp 3, but there was just too much to do.

His most needy patient was Manbhadur the cobbler, who had come down several days earlier with frostbitten feet. They had not improved, and to make things worse, he had developed bronchitis and was growing feverish. Hingston had a good medical kit with him, but he did not have the clot-busting drugs or antibiotics used to treat frostbite today.

In between ministering to Manbhadur and Beetham, who was still crippled by sciatica, Hingston explored the area around

Base Camp, setting a new personal altitude record by climbing to 19,100 feet on a nearby peak. He was particularly fascinated by the hermits who lived in roughly hewn cells nearby. Several of them were literally walled into tiny caves, where they were visited once a month by other monks passing food through tiny openings. One had been there for three years and planned to stay another two; the great Rongbuk Lama himself, Dzatrul Rinpoche, was said to have spent twelve years in self-imposed solitary confinement. As far as Hingston was concerned, it was a strange, miserable existence, but as he asked himself, was it any more absurd than the sahibs' obsession with Everest? Wouldn't the hermits see the whole expedition, as he mused in his diary, as 'futile and ridiculous'?

On 25 May, the same day that Norton ordered a retreat from Camp 3 to Base Camp, Manbhadur died. Hingston was phlegmatic: he had seen a lot of casualties during the war and had only just been told about the death of his own father, in a letter that arrived at Base Camp several weeks after he had passed away. 'It was better that he [Manbhadur] should do so,' Hingston wrote in his diary, 'for both feet would later have to be amputated above the ankle.' It was unthinkable, as far as Hingston was concerned, that this year's expedition would not get above the North Col, but there was no sign of their fortunes changing any time soon.

The following day, Hingston hiked up the glacier for the first time to Camp 1, where he'd been told Norton was holding a final 'council of war'. The news of Manbhadur's death was yet another blow to the expedition, but like Hingston, Norton thought it perhaps a merciful release rather than endure a double amputation.

Everyone could see they were a much-weakened party, with Geoffrey Bruce the only one who really looked fit. Mallory,

Norton and Somervell had recovered surprisingly well from their recent travails, but Beetham's sciatica showed no sign of improving, Odell was suffering with the altitude, and Hazard was 'in disgrace' for having left the porters on the col.

The other problem was lifting power. According to the two transport officers, Shebbeare and Geoffrey Bruce, only around fifteen out of their fifty-five Sherpas were fit enough to return to the North Col. The idea that they could get a large number of cylinders high up the mountain was now unthinkable, but without oxygen was there any real chance of success? The meeting broke up inconclusively, with Norton calling for another conference to be held the following day, when he hoped to reach a consensus.

On 27 May, a mail runner arrived in camp. Mallory wrote a long letter to Ruth, detailing the events of the last couple of weeks. Any sections where he seemed to be praising his own efforts, he warned, were for her own eyes only and should not be shared with anyone else. They were about to try again, he said, but everyone was worried that the monsoon was imminent. 'It is 50 to 1 against us', he wrote, 'but we'll have a whack yet and do ourselves proud.' In a dispatch that he helped Norton draft for *The Times*, Mallory tried to sound a little more optimistic but he was still far from confident: 'We expect no mercy from Everest. Yet perhaps it will be as well he should not deign to take much notice of the little group of busy ones on the great north side, or, at all events, that he should not observe among the scattered remnants he has half put to flight, the still existent will, perhaps power, to singe his very nose tip.'

That afternoon Norton held the second meeting, inviting all the climbers plus John Noel and Shebbeare to thrash out a final plan. Geoffrey Bruce proposed a simpler timetable in which two pairs of men would go in quick succession, climbing under their own steam and abandoning all thought of an oxygen-powered attempt. Shebbeare had the temerity to suggest that because some of the non-mountaineers were now in better condition than the climbers, they should be included in one of the parties, but as he wrote in his diary, 'Norton put his foot down very firmly on this suggestion.'

In the end, it was decided that on 29 May, after one more rest day, they would start up again to make two oxygen-less attempts. Mallory and Bruce would have the first crack at the summit, followed by Somervell and Norton. Irvine and Odell would act as reserves, stationed at Camp 4 on the North Col to support the climbing teams. Mallory was not entirely convinced – of his own fitness or the decision to go without any oxygen. 'All sound plans are now abandoned for two consecutive dashes without gas,' he wrote to his friend David Pye on 28 May. In his final letter to his mother he was even more circumspect: 'It will be a great adventure, if we get started before the monsoon hits us, with just a bare outside chance of success and a good many chances of a very bad time indeed. I shall take every care I can, you may be sure.'

A month after arriving on the Rongbuk glacier, with the monsoon fast approaching, it was time now to play their final hand. 'Action is only suspended before the more intense action of the climax,' Mallory wrote in *The Times*. 'The issue will shortly be decided. The third time we walk up East Rongbuk Glacier will be the last, for better or worse.'

8

There

In the autumn of 1916, when Mallory was stuck in a dugout in northern France, trying to stay alive and overcome the monotony of trench life, he set about recalling and reliving an adventure he'd had in the Alps five years earlier – climbing Mont Maudit, one of the satellite peaks of Mont Blanc, the highest mountain in Western Europe.

That attempt at recovering a cherished memory reappeared two years later in a celebrated article for the *Alpine Journal*. It was very different, though, from 'The Mountaineer as Artist', Mallory's climbing 'manifesto' which had been published a few years earlier. Whereas that had been an attempt to elevate mountaineering from a mere 'sport' into a complex aesthetic experience, 'Mont Blanc from the Col du Géant by the Eastern Buttress of Mont Maudit', as its title suggests, was a much more direct account of a climb and attempted to give an almost 'stream of consciousness' narrative, focusing on the emotions prompted by 'one splendid day' in the hills. Even though it had gone wrong in some ways, ultimately Mont Maudit left Mallory with a powerful set of memories which became what he called 'a friendly companion'.

The ascent had begun just before 4.00 a.m. on 18 August 1911, three years before the start of the Great War, when Mallory and two former companions from the Winchester Ice Club – Graham Irving, the schoolmaster who had taught Mallory how to climb, and Harry Tyndale, an old school friend – left the mountain hut on the Col du Géant to begin what they hoped would be another great day's climbing. They would be following a route pioneered twenty-four years earlier by Alexander Burgener, a legendary Swiss guide.

The snow was crisp and inviting and the weather perfect, but for much of the day Mallory was not in great shape, having drunk some bad wine the night before. He insisted on carrying on, but his stomach was in rebellion and his limbs leaden and uncomfortable. He fainted twice: the first time at breakfast, causing him to knock over the cooking pot; the second time during the climb itself, when he was supposed to be belaying Irving. Though his companions made light of it, he was hugely embarrassed.

As they continued upward, Mallory slowly started to feel like himself again, inspired by the 'wonderland' of icy peaks surrounding them. The climbing became exhilarating as he found himself moving rhythmically up the steep slopes, matching the speed of his friends, enjoying the thrill of the moment. Irving led a difficult, very exposed section up towards the summit, and suddenly, in the middle of the afternoon, they reached their goal. Rather than descending to the nearest hut, urged on by Mallory who now felt 'under the spell of a great Alpine adventure', they decided to go all the way to the summit of Mont Blanc itself, which they reached after several more hours of challenging climbing. 'We're not exultant,' Mallory finished the article, 'but delighted, joyful, soberly astonished... Have we vanquished an enemy? None but ourselves. Have we gained success? That word means nothing here. Have we won a kingdom? No... and yes.'

That day in August 1911 contained everything that Mallory loved about mountaineering: the special comradeship of climbing with friends; the sheer beauty of mountain landscape and the feeling of history; the thrill of risk, and the sense of fulfilment that came from pushing himself hard even when his body was calling on him to retire early.

Now, almost thirteen years later, he had swapped the Alps for the Himalayas, and the highest mountain in Western Europe for the highest mountain in the world. But everything was so different. Just before leaving England he had opened his heart to his friend Geoffrey Keynes. What they were about to face, as Keynes recalled Mallory telling him, 'would be more like war than adventure and that he did not believe that he would return alive'.

They were pessimistic words, but as the weeks had gone on, it had indeed begun to feel like a war of attrition. Two men – Shamsher the Gurkha NCO and Manbhadur the cobbler, who had been with them in 1922 – had died, and the ferocious winds and freezing-cold temperatures had forced them to beat a hasty retreat not once but twice.

Now, as the expedition came to a climax, Mallory was about to make the first attempt on the summit, but not in the way that he had wanted to and spent weeks arguing for. Instead of climbing with oxygen, he would be going under his own steam; and instead of partnering with Andrew Irvine, with whom he had developed a strong bond, or Howard Somervell, his great friend from 1922, he would be going with Geoffrey Bruce, someone he liked but barely knew and had hardly shared a rope with over the course of the last two expeditions.

He wasn't going to avoid his duty, though. The time had come for one final huge effort. He would make the first attempt with Bruce, and if they failed, Norton and Somervell would make the second. That was just how it was going to be.

And so, on Ascension Day, 29 May 1924, Mallory left Camp 1 on the Rongbuk glacier for what he hoped would be his last attempt. Hingston once again stayed back at Base Camp, but the two summit teams moved up together, accompanied by Irvine, Odell and Hazard. In spite of his sciatica, Bentley Beetham insisted on joining them, but it was obvious to everyone that he was in too much pain to do any difficult climbing.

The weather conditions were 'perfect', according to Norton. For the first time in several days, the streamer-like cloud that usually clung to the summit so defiantly had gone, leaving the top of the Everest silhouetted starkly against an azure sky.

Irvine confided to his diary that he was bitterly disappointed to be a 'bloody reserve' rather than a member of the first party, but, ever resourceful, he offered to build a rope ladder to help the heavily laden Sherpas get up the ice chimney below the North Col. Scavenging wood from wherever he could find it, he and Odell painstakingly assembled their Heath Robinson creation, with one wooden rung for every three fashioned from rope.

The next day, everyone moved up en masse to Camp 3. Though it started to grow cloudy again in the evening, during the day the good weather held and without the huge drifts of snow they had become used to, Camp 3 looked very different. The area was so bare that Mallory and Irvine had to root around to find a source of water. Back in Darjeeling, some tea planters had told them that, in some years, the first rains of the monsoon were followed by a few weeks of calmer conditions, before the real deluge started. Perhaps this was their 'weather window', and if so, now was the moment to make use of it.

For Geoffrey Bruce, it was the second time he had prepared for a summit attempt but this year it was very different. Like his uncle Charlie, he was a soldier who had fought in the mountains of the North-West Frontier, but prior to Everest he'd never done any 'sport' climbing. In 1922, he had been taken on initially as one of the expedition's transport officers and had never expected to go high. George Finch had only chosen him as a partner for his summit bid out of desperation because all the 'real' climbers had left Base Camp for the first attempt. In the event, they had done really well, reaching 27,300 feet before they were forced to turn back when Bruce's oxygen set malfunctioned.

As Bruce told Finch in a letter at the end of May 1923, when Hinks contacted him with the offer of a place on the 1924 expedition, he had signed up straight away: 'Did the duck swallow the bug? I said that any old capacity for this child would do. Transport, porters, latrines, any old thing.' Bruce had assumed that Finch would also be returning and was eternally grateful for all the support he'd given him in 1922. 'I can never thank you enough', he wrote, 'for electing to take me on the climb and the perfectly astonishing way you pulled me through it all. It was wonderful.'

Finch had not of course been invited in 1924, but Geoffrey had enjoyed this year's expedition so far. Early on, his main job had been to keep the porters happy and bolster their morale, but he hadn't been involved in any of the arduous carries up the Rongbuk glacier or the rescue of the trapped Sherpas. Perhaps because of this, Norton and Mallory thought him the fittest member of the team, so when two days earlier they had thrashed out their final plans, he was first choice to climb with Mallory. Now the moment had come to once again test his mettle.

It was another cold but promising morning on 31 May. 'Give us three more days of fine weather,' Norton declared to his diary, 'and we may do it yet.' At 8.45 a.m. he saw Mallory and Bruce off from Camp 3 with their support team, Odell and Irvine, and nine of the best porters. As they approached the slope leading up to the North Col, there was still plenty of snow about. In places, the hard crust gave way, plunging them into deep drifts, but they plugged on.

After an hour, they stopped to load up with some of the stores cached a week earlier. Then they moved up to the ice chimney to install the rope ladder that Irvine and Odell had so painstakingly constructed. It took two hours of hard work fixing it to the icy slope with wooden stakes, but it was immediately obvious that it would make life much easier for the Sherpas carrying supplies up to the North Col.

It was mid-afternoon when they reached Camp 4. They pitched a few more tents and then retired to their sleeping bags after enjoying a hearty meal of pea soup and tinned ox tongue, washed down with mugs of cocoa. Irvine had a sore throat, Mallory an inflamed eye, but so far there had been no serious mishap and, scanning the horizon, it looked as if the good weather would hold.

The next day Irvine and Odell were up at 4.30 a.m. to cook breakfast. It was a 'cold and disagreeable job', Irvine wrote in his diary, but having strong support parties to help the summit

The Summit
Pyramid

The Second Step
The First Step   28,250ft

The Shoulder   28,100ft

The North Ridge

The North-East Ridge

teams set off and receive them when they came back was an important part of Norton's thinking. Two years earlier, he'd climbed down into a deserted camp on the North Col with Mallory, Somervell and the frostbitten Henry Morshead, after their record-breaking ascent to 27,000 feet. They had hoped for a warm reception, but instead had discovered a deserted camp where they hadn't been able to find any stoves or other means to boil water. In the end they'd made do with a cold supper of strawberry jam mixed with snow and milk powder into an impromptu ice cream. This time, returning men could expect better treatment.

The sun hit their tents just after 5.00 a.m. but it took another three and a half hours of dressing and breakfasting and organizing before Mallory and Bruce led their porters out of camp up to the North Ridge, their highway to the summit. At high altitude everything seemed to take three or four hours longer than at sea level, almost as if the altitude had dulled their senses and made slow motion the norm. Irvine and Odell escorted them for the first few hundred feet before retiring back down to Camp 4.

As agreed with Norton, Mallory's aim was to set up two further camps, the first at 25,300 feet, near the spot where they had camped two years earlier, and the second as close as possible to 27,000 feet, leaving just 2,000 feet to the summit itself. The route was relatively straightforward – more of a slog than a climb up a steep ridge, with long stretches of rocky ground interspersed with large patches of snow. The skies remained clear and there was still no hint of monsoon clouds in the distance, but before long they were hit by a ferocious wind from the north-west. It chilled them to the bone, with gusts almost powerful enough to blow them over.

They all had windproof outer clothing, but soon the Sherpas started to flag. The sahibs were carrying light packs with spare clothing and a few personal items; the Sherpas each had a much heavier twenty-pound load, consisting of tents and bedding and supplies for the next two camps. Within a few hours, four of the porters had sat down, sure that they would not make it to the next camp.

Leaving them to find shelter, Mallory and Bruce struggled on, and at around 1.00 p.m. they reached the site for Camp 5, a small ledge just big enough for two tents on the eastern side of the North Ridge. Down below, Mallory could see the collapsed remains of his old tent where two years earlier he and Somervell had spent their last night before their failed attempt on the summit.

Four of their Sherpas did manage to join them at Camp 5, but with only half the required loads. So, while Mallory pitched and organized the tents, Bruce and Lobsang, the strongest Sherpa, made two trips down the mountain to collect the remaining supplies. Then, around mid-afternoon, one of the porters headed down to the four men who hadn't made it and escorted them down the ridge, leaving Mallory, Bruce and the last three Sherpas to cook a slender meal and spend a windy night preparing for the next stage of the battle.

Down below, Norton and Somervell were having a rather more comfortable time at Camp 4 on the North Col. They had come up in the afternoon with six more of their best Sherpas, now dubbed 'Tigers' to boost their morale, and thanks to the newly installed rope ladder had made a very rapid ascent. Odell and Irvine had greeted them at the top with warm food and a well-established camp, where they slept well. The next morning, they set off at 6.30 a.m. and continued up the North Ridge, carrying food and fuel and new tents for Camp 5, assuming Mallory and Bruce would have derigged everything and taken their tents and cooking equipment up to Camp 6. Mallory had left strips of ribbons attached to rocks to act as way-markers for anyone coming up or down, but as they scanned the slopes above them, there was no sign of any movement.

In fact, while Norton and Somervell were ascending the mountain, Mallory and Bruce were beginning their retreat. They had woken up to another clear morning and begun making breakfast, but even though he had tried several times, Geoffrey Bruce couldn't persuade the Sherpas to climb any higher. One man was fit but the other two said they were just too sick. To make things worse, Bruce had been seriously weakened by his exertions the previous day and would subsequently be diagnosed with a dilated heart. One Sherpa would not be able to carry all they required, and Mallory and Bruce knew that if they took on the porter loads as well as their own gear, they'd be so tired by the time they established Camp 6 that any attempt on the summit would be bound to fail. So, after a brief discussion, they decided to turn back.

It was another deceptive day. The sky was crystal blue and cloudless but the wind had not abated at all. For Norton it was the first real test of his Burberry windproof, but even though he was also wearing two sweaters, a flannel shirt, and a thick woollen vest, he still felt chilled to the bone. Ever the artist, Howard Somervell was determined to photograph the ridge, but it was so cold when he took out his Vest Pocket Kodak camera, he could not press the shutter. It took three attempts before he managed to take a photograph of the North-West Shoulder and the huge shadow of the nearby North Peak on the glacier below.

Six of the Tiger Sherpas who went highest on Everest: (from left to right) Bom, Narbu Yishé, Semchumbi, Lobsang, Lhakpa Chédé, Angtenjin.

The first inkling they had of Mallory and Bruce's problems came when they met Dorjay Pasang, one of their strongest Sherpas, coming down the ridge with a note. It was, as Norton later wrote with typical restraint, 'an unexpected and unwelcome sight'. Not long afterwards, they met Mallory and Bruce themselves and the remaining Sherpas. It was too windy to stop for anything but the briefest conversation, but clearly nothing had gone as planned.

The first summit attempt had been a damp squib; now the outcome of the expedition was entirely on Norton and Somervell and their porters. The only upside was that Mallory and Bruce had left everything intact at Camp 5, so Norton and Somervell did not have to re-pitch the tents. They moved in swiftly, got out their Primus stove, and began to cook a huge meal of ship's biscuits, bully beef and pemmican, washed down with lashings of coffee. Despite the feast on offer, Norton found that the altitude had killed his appetite, so he had to force himself to eat.

The prospects were not good for the following day. If Mallory and Geoffrey Bruce hadn't been able to get the best out of their Sherpas, would they fare any better? Would they too,

Somervell wondered, suffer from the 'high altitude torpor' that he remembered from 1922 – not panic, just a slowing-down of the thinking process and a dulling of all emotions?

To his surprise, he slept well. Mallory had done a very good job levelling the ground below the tents and neither he nor Norton had any trouble breathing. Their Sherpas were not so lucky. During the night, a rock came tumbling down the mountain, ripped through their tent canvas and crashed into two of the men leaving Lobsang Tashi with a nasty-looking head wound and Semchumbi's knee badly gashed.

When at 5.00 a.m. Norton tried to rouse them, it was obvious that Lobsang would not be able to carry on, but after a little persuasion the others, including the wounded Semchumbi, began making their breakfast and preparing the loads for the final camp. Norton wanted to stop at 27,000 feet, but as they made their way up, the climbing started to get harder. The treacherous layer of scree that covered the ridge seemed to become looser and looser with every hundred feet, causing everyone to occasionally slip and stumble. Between them the porters were carrying fifty pounds' worth of gear, far less than they had carried lower down but a real weight at this altitude.

Norton later wrote how, as they got higher and higher and the views got more and more staggering, they found themselves stopping frequently, justifying their moments of rest with the thought that they were really only pausing to take in the beauty of it all. Somervell tried his best to help Semchumbi with his burden, but he too was feeling worse and worse. None of the men who had rescued Hazard's Sherpas from the North Col had really recovered properly. In Somervell's case, his usual hacking cough had developed into a viciously sore throat that was becoming progressively more painful.

At 1.30 p.m. Norton called a halt at around 26,800 feet. It was a little short of what he had hoped for, but was still an amazing achievement for both the climbers and the Sherpas – a new world record for the highest camp ever pitched on a mountain. Not that it was in any way luxurious: a single tent, set precariously in a small dip in the ridge, which they hoped would be sheltered from any rockfall from above. There was no level ground, but the Sherpas spent an hour doing their best to build a small rocky platform before they retreated down the ridge, with a note from Norton praising their efforts and instructing everyone below to feed them especially well and let them go back to Base Camp straight away.

Again, though they immediately set the stove to boil water, Norton found it almost impossible to eat anything apart from a little soup and some coffee. In order to make an early start, they kept the stove going until they had filled two thermoses of tea and coffee for breakfast the following day. The weather remained calm, rewarding them with an incredible sunset and a vast panoramic view stretching from Kangchenjunga in the east to Gaurishankar in the far west, with many more mountains in between.

Down below, the rest of the team waited expectantly, but if anyone thought that Mallory was through with Everest, they were wrong. The previous day, almost as soon as he returned to the North Col, he had told Irvine to get ready to descend to Camp 3 to begin preparing for a third attempt, on oxygen, if Norton and Somervell were to fail.

Mallory never wrote anything about the first attempt and nor did Geoffrey Bruce. Though they both blamed the weather and thought that they had been let down by the Sherpas, there was something odd about the whole episode. If Mallory really believed it was his last chance, why hadn't he tried a little harder? Or was it that he never really thought it was going to work, and wanted to keep his strength for a last-minute oxygen-powered attempt with Irvine?

Irvine, however, was not in great shape. He too had a searingly painful throat and was severely sunburnt. 'My face was badly cut by the sun and wind on the Col,' he lamented in his diary, 'and my lips are cracked to bits which makes eating very unpleasant.' Nevertheless, he had always wanted a 'whack' at the summit, and readily descended with Mallory to Camp 3 where the oxygen equipment lay languishing in the snow.

John Noel, too, was down on the Rongbuk glacier with his specially picked camera porters. Having invested so much in the photographic rights, this was the moment when he hoped to get the shots that would make the film. He had established a camera position which he called 'The Eagles Nest' 1,000 feet up on Changtse, which offered an uninterrupted view of the summit. It was three miles away, but with his specially commissioned telephoto lens he could spot any movement against a snowy background. So far, the most impressive shots he had filmed were of Norton and Somervell heading upwards with a line of porters from Camp 5. If he could get more footage, showing them even closer to the summit, he would be very happy.

At dawn on 4 June 1924, Norton and Somervell were up at 5.00 a.m., hoping to make as early as possible a start, but almost immediately there was a problem: the cork had come out from one of their thermos flasks, soaking Norton's sleeping bag and robbing them of half of their liquid in one fell swoop. Norton was determined that they should be well hydrated when they left camp, remembering how desperately thirsty they had all become on their final climb in 1922, so even if it meant going through the painstaking process of melting more snow, he delayed their start.

Finally, at around 6.40 a.m., they were ready to leave, but rather than go all the way up the ridge as Mallory had intended, they traversed out onto the North Face about 600 feet below the summit ridge. Norton's plan was to move diagonally upwards until they reached a point where they could climb the summit pyramid more directly. They didn't bother roping up: the climbing looked relatively straightforward, and anyway, they reckoned, if one of them fell the other would not be strong enough to hold them.

The weather remained fine and relatively wind-less, but it was still bitterly cold. In spite of wearing several layers and whenever possible climbing in the sun, Norton just couldn't warm up. He found himself coughing so much that he thought he might be developing pneumonia. When they paused to get their breath back, he checked his heart rate and discovered that it was almost 50 per cent above normal.

Somervell started well, despite his still-painful throat, but as soon as they reached 27,000 feet he felt himself slowing down, with every step upwards requiring at least ten breaths. There was nothing heroic-looking about their progress, 'a couple of crocks slowly and breathlessly struggling up, with frequent rests and a lot of puffing and blowing and coughing', as Norton later recalled.

They were now climbing mainly on rock, following a series of ledges that ran across the North Face, hauling themselves up from one to the next. Norton took off his snow goggles thinking he didn't need them when climbing on rock, but he was soon seeing double. Every five or so minutes, both men were forced to stop and try to regain their breath, but Somervell's cough was going from bad to worse.

When they reached 28,000 feet at around midday, Somervell sat down on a ledge and accepted the inevitable. He just could not go on, and rather than slow Norton down, he signalled to him that he should carry on alone. Sheltering in the sun, he watched Norton climb slowly upwards and across. Now that he was no longer moving, Somervell found it remarkably easy to breathe. It was only when climbing, he realized, that the problems started. After a while, he even felt strong enough to take out his camera to record Norton's progress, taking several photographs to ensure that at least one came out.

On his own, Norton now found the climbing much tougher as he tried to cross a broad couloir, or channel, that ran vertically down the mountain. The rocky ledges had been replaced with sloping sheets that reminded him of large roof tiles. There were no easy handholds, and to make it even more dangerous, everything seemed to be covered in a layer of powdery snow that offered no grip. It was difficult to see ahead and work out the best route. Several times he had to turn around and retrace his steps when he ended up at an impassable position.

After an hour, Norton had gone around 800 feet horizontally, and made just over 120 feet of vertical ascent. High above he could see the easier-looking slopes leading up to the summit pyramid, but there was another 200 feet of difficult climbing before he got there. Even if he could struggle to the summit, he realized that it would be impossible to get back down again. Altitude dulls the senses and slows down the thinking process, but in a moment of clarity Norton realized that it would be futile to continue.

Down below, Somervell saw Norton stop for longer than usual and realized what was happening. 'We had always been willing to risk our lives,' he later wrote, 'but we did not believe

2 June 1924, c. 28,000 feet. Edward Norton climbs solo
towards the Great Couloir. Unable to continue, Howard
Somervell sits down to take this photograph.

in throwing them away.' Norton called for help while crossing the most precarious section, so Somervell struggled over to him and threw him a rope. By 2.00 p.m. they had regained Somervell's perch and were now beginning the descent proper. Going down should have been easier, but it didn't seem like it. It was still hard, breathless work which sent their pulses racing. The only compensation was the spectacle below: a clear line of sight stretching for over 200 miles into the distance over the Tibetan plain. For Somervell it was a God-like view, but he felt anything but divine. They were, he later recalled, 'the very epitome of human limitations'.

Though it remained clear, no one below had been able to pick out Norton and Somervell on the dark rock above. At Camp 3, Mallory was becoming increasingly nervous. Had they made it, or had something gone wrong? Would he ever get to make another attempt or would it turn out to be a rescue mission? As the hours ticked by, he grew more and more impatient, until finally in the middle of the afternoon he decided to go back up to the North Col with Irvine and two Sherpas. They retraced their now familiar steps, stopping briefly at the supply dump to collect several more oxygen bottles. The Sherpas climbed under their own steam, but Mallory and Irvine strapped on their sets before they resumed the ascent. It was the first time ever, apart from a few test sessions, that Mallory had climbed on oxygen, and he was pleased to find that it did make a difference, cutting their time to get to North Col from three hours to one and a half. When they reached Camp 4, though, there was still no news. Mallory scanned the summit and thought he saw some tracks around 700 feet below the top, but he couldn't be sure.

In fact, Norton and Somervell were still making their way down, but only in fits and starts. Somervell was so weary that he dropped his ice axe and watched it tumble down the North Face before spiralling off towards the Rongbuk glacier, never to be seen again. When they reached their tiny tent at Camp 6, they paused briefly to retrieve their sleeping bags and grab a tent pole for Somervell to use as a walking stick. The scree slope below seemed more treacherous than ever, so they un-roped. They were both so tired there would be absolutely no chance of holding someone if they fell.

Norton was no longer seeing double, so he moved into the lead and gave Somervell his ice axe. When they came to a long patch of snow, he even had the confidence, and the exhaustion, to slide down. Somervell did not follow. His breathing had become so laboured that he had to stop every few steps. The more he coughed, the sorer his throat became, and the harder it was to breathe. Convinced that he was about pass out, he flopped down.

By then Norton had slid so far below there was no chance that he would be able to hear him, even if Somervell could call out. He was all done in; if the end hadn't come, it would not be long. Then he remembered something: at medical school he had been taught that breathing involved both the chest and the diaphragm. He gave a mighty cough and simultaneously pressed on his abdomen, and watched with a strange mixture of horror and relief as a large bloody lump of flesh emerged from his mouth and flopped onto the snow in front of him.

Later he would identify this as part of the mucous membrane of his throat, which had probably been frostbitten for days, but for the moment, in spite of the gore, all that mattered was that he could breathe a little easier. He still wasn't confident enough to follow Norton's lead and slide down the snow snatch, so he stuck to the rock and climbed down slowly.

Norton was unaware of the drama taking place above. Later he said, with his tongue planted firmly in his cheek, that he had wondered if Somervell had stopped to sketch the view. Eventually reunited, they carried on down, using hand torches to illuminate the ridge and, more importantly, to let their comrades on the North Col know that they were still alive and on their way back. Norton gave a few hoarse shouts, thinking there was no chance that anyone would hear him, but it worked.

At around 9.00 p.m., someone at Camp 4 spotted beams of light 100 feet above. Leaving Irvine to prepare warm soup and drinks, Mallory and Odell rushed out of their tent – if rushing were possible at 22,000 feet – and came up with an oxygen set to give the returning men a boost. Forty-five years later, in an interview with the BBC, Somervell remembered the moment vividly: 'We saw two people and we thought "Splendid", we thought we saw a thermos but it was only an oxygen cylinder and a set, and I don't know what expletive we used but Norton shouted out, "Odell, we don't want the damned oxygen, we want drink, for goodness' sake we want food and drink!"'

Back in camp, Irvine plied the returning men with steaming mugs of soup, but however much he wanted to, Norton could barely eat anything. Later he would have his maximum altitude checked with a theodolite and realize he had reached 28,126 feet, but for the moment he stuck to 28,000, adding that they were both very disappointed not to have gone all the way to the very roof of the world. It was still an awesome achievement. Just three years after their first reconnaissance, a British team had got to within 1,000 feet of the summit of the world's highest mountain, setting a world record for climbing without oxygen that would stand for fifty-four years.

And then Mallory told him: he wanted to stage another attempt. With oxygen. With Irvine.

Norton was exhausted. Behind his eyes he could feel the pain growing: a sharp, searing sting that would leave him snow-blind for the next forty-eight hours and make any exposure to light an agony. But Irvine? Surely Odell would be a better partner? Though he had taken a long time to acclimatize, it was obvious to everyone that Odell had hit peak form. Over the last three days, he had ascended and descended from Camp 3 to Camp 4 no less than four times, without any apparent loss of fitness. If Mallory was really going to try again, wouldn't he be better off taking Odell rather than Irvine, the youngest and least experienced member of the team?

Mallory was adamant though: he had chosen his partner. No one knew the oxygen apparatus better than Irvine. He might not have the climbing experience, but Irvine had something equally important: guts.

In the 'official' expedition account, Norton would later write how much he admired Mallory and his spirit, but the fact that he also admitted questioning Mallory's choice of partner is telling. As in 1922, when against his better judgement General Bruce agreed to Mallory's request for a third attempt, now the exhausted Norton agreed to let him make what would undoubtedly be the last throw of the dice.

The next morning, Norton woke up totally blind and in excruciating pain. Then, as now, the best cure for snow blindness was to avoid light, but that wasn't so easy on the snow-covered North Col. The others covered his tent with sleeping bags to try to keep as much of the light out as possible, and then watched as Somervell climbed down by himself from Camp 4 to Camp 3, arriving voiceless and looking as rough as he felt.

Hingston, the expedition doctor, had been summoned by Norton a few days earlier to station himself at Camp 3 in case any of the returning men needed treatment. 'Another record is broken,' he wrote in his diary that night, 'and a fine feat performed.' Overstatement was never his style.

Hearing of Norton's agony, at dawn the next day Hingston left Camp 3 with two Sherpas, determined to bring him down. Almost two weeks earlier, Norton had led the party that had rescued the stranded Sherpas on the North Col, but now he was the casualty who needed help, still totally blind and very weak on his feet. Hingston checked his eyes and then, after a brief rest, strapped a pair of crampons onto Norton's boots and led him out of camp, with Hazard escorting them down the first stage and belaying Norton as he slowly descended the ice chimney. Hingston was indefatigable, guiding Norton's feet from rung to rung on the rope ladder and carefully placing them in the ice steps below.

Against the odds, they reached the foot of the slope without any accident and then Hingston sent one of the Sherpas ahead for a stretcher. Six porters returned, taking it in turns to carry Norton back to Camp 3. Close to camp they were met by Bruce and Noel, as ever greeting the returning men with thermoses of hot soup.

It took sixty hours of virtually total blindness before Norton started to regain his sight. When Hingston examined him properly, he discovered that Norton's heart was significantly dilated because of his efforts on 4 June. Having worried earlier that the whole expedition was in danger of returning to Britain having achieved nothing of note, Norton could now say that they had surpassed Finch's 1922 record by almost a thousand feet. There was still, however, a thousand more to go. Would

Mallory and Irvine be able to break through that final barrier and crown the expedition's success with the summit itself? On the morning of 6 June 1924, they strapped on their oxygen sets and left the North Col, intending to do just that.

9

The Boys from Birkenhead

About two years before George Mallory's father moved to the parish of St John's in Birkenhead, Andrew 'Sandy' Irvine was born in the town on 8 April 1902 in the rather more upmarket Park Road – the third child of William Fergusson Irvine. 'Willie' Irvine was a passionate amateur historian and a successful businessman with a growing family.

Sandy's early life was similar to Mallory's. After prep school in Birkenhead, he was sent first to Shrewsbury public school and then to Merton College, Oxford, to study engineering. Like Mallory he was athletically gifted – a powerful rower who represented his school and college before going on to join the Oxford team for 1922 and 1923, when they won the coveted Boat Race against Cambridge. In 1924 he might have captained the Oxford boat, if Everest hadn't intervened.

It all started with Noel Odell. In the spring of 1923, Odell had been invited to join a Merton College expedition to Spitsbergen, the huge island in the Arctic, as its geologist. He met Irvine in London with the other members of the rowing team, who were training on the Thames in Putney, and was immediately impressed by his strength and very positive attitude. Knowing that on Spitsbergen plenty of muscle would be needed to haul sleds across the ice, he offered Irvine a place on the team, and got a resounding yes.

In order to prepare, Odell invited Irvine to join him on a trip to North Wales, taking him to the classic crags and peaks where Mallory and his friends had done some of their first climbs. Odell was hugely impressed when Irvine led some difficult sections on the Great Gully on Craig yr Ysfa, a famous climbing route that was no mean feat for a complete novice.

Odell was equally pleased with Irvine's performance in Spitsbergen. Over the course of a month, the party made the first east–west crossing, mapping and surveying and climbing in the Chydenius and Stubendorff mountains, one of which was later named Irvinfjellet, or Mount Irvine. Sandy was always keen and willing and had the kind of calm and easy-going temperament that made him an ideal companion.

When later that year Odell was invited to join the forthcoming Everest expedition, he took it upon himself to engineer an invitation for Sandy. As Odell readily admitted, apart from those training climbs in Wales and some ski training in Switzerland at Christmas in 1923, Sandy had very little mountaineering experience, but he was full of promise and was an ideal candidate not just because of his stamina and strength, but because of his skills as a mechanic and his seeming ability to be able to mend almost everything.

From an early age, Irvine had been fascinated by machinery. When his father allowed him to use one room in the family home as his workshop, his fate was sealed as an inveterate tinkerer and taker-aparter. As a schoolboy inventor, he had written to the War Office with plans for a gyroscopic stabilizer for aeroplanes, and a specially designed gearing system that would allow a machine gun to fire through the blades of a propeller without damaging them.

There were questions about Irvine because of his lack of climbing experience, but eventually, as General Bruce wrote in *The Times*, the Committee decided to take him as the team's 'experiment'. 'His record at Spitsbergen last year and his really remarkable physique, to say nothing of his reputation as a general handy man, justify the experiment we are making in exposing one of his tender years to the rigours of Tibetan travel. We entertain no fears on this count.' When Irvine went for his medical with Dr Larkins of Harley Street on 13 November, he was pronounced 'in every way physically sound and fit', and a few days later duly signed up for the expedition. Before long he'd asked for an oxygen set and was taking it apart in his rooms in Oxford to figure out how it worked and how it could be improved, sketching out designs as he went.

Mallory had taken an instant liking to him, though admitted to Ruth in an early letter that Irvine could probably be relied upon for everything apart from 'good conversation'. While Mallory had spent his time at Cambridge talking art and literature with his fellow Bohemians and swans, Irvine had hung out with the roaring boys of the Myrmidon, Merton College's exclusive dining club, and courted various young women. Ultimately though, Mallory wasn't looking for a good conversationalist. He admired Irvine's physique and his

mechanical skills, but most of all he had two qualities that
Mallory thought of as essential on Everest: staying power
and 'guts'.

And so, on the morning of 6 June 1924, after a breakfast
of tinned sardines, ship's biscuits and tea, Mallory and Irvine
left the North Col with eight porters and enough supplies and
spare oxygen cylinders, they hoped, to get them all the way
to the top. Mallory's plan was to spend one night at Camp 5,
one night at Camp 6, and then climb the final 2,000 feet to the
summit on 8 June, and if everything went perfectly, get all the
way back down to the North Col on same day. In a way it was
everything that Mallory had always wanted: the scheme that
he had been discussing with Norton for almost two months,
the partner he had chosen, and the equipment he had selected.
Two boys from Birkenhead, about to write their names on the
summit. All they needed now was for the weather to hold.

6 June 1924, Camp 4, the last photograph of Mallory (left)
and Irvine (right). The photographer was Noel Odell.

Except... it wasn't quite like that. The grabbed 'snap' captured by Odell of the moment of their departure reveals a different truth. It is slightly off-kilter, an unusually candid moment from an expedition where most of the images were posed. Irvine is to the right, about to move off; Mallory's on the left, fiddling with something on his oxygen set. There are no beaming smiles or resolute jaws, no flags or pennants, no one else seems to be in camp. Norton, the expedition leader, is still stuck in his tent, stone-blind, and the Sherpas are nowhere to be seen.

They were leaving in a hurry. If Mallory wrote a last note to Ruth or any of his friends and family, it didn't survive. Irvine had decided not to risk taking his precious diary with him. He would have to fill it in later, when they got back down. If they got down.

The first news of their progress came at the end of the afternoon, and it was good. The Sherpas who Mallory had criticized early in the expedition had now hit top form and were climbing and carrying well. Mallory sent four back down from Camp 5, one of them with a brief note: 'There is no wind here, and things look hopeful'. Just five days earlier, the relentless wind had destroyed the morale of the porters and doomed Mallory and Bruce's attempt, but for the moment at least the conditions were ideal. Earlier that day, John Noel had even managed to shoot some moving film of Mallory and Irvine and their porters heading up to the snows of the North Ridge: they were just tiny dots, but it was another amazing shot from a camera stationed almost three miles away.

The next day, Mallory and Irvine moved up to Camp 6 and squeezed into the tiny two-man tent perched on the North Face at 26,800 feet. Down below, the others waited and watched, but the tension was palpable and, like Mallory a few days earlier, they could not sit still. John Noel left his position at the Eagle's Nest and climbed up to the North Col with his porters for no ostensible reason. He stayed for three hours and then descended.

Noel Odell went further, taking the last remaining Sherpa, Nema, and heading for Camp 5 with yet more supplies. On the way up he collected the oxygen set abandoned in the snow a few days earlier, when he and Mallory had rushed out to greet Norton and Somervell after their attempt. The mouthpiece was missing, presumably taken by Irvine as a spare, so the set was no use to him, but Odell carried it up anyway, hoping to find the missing part higher up.

When he reached Camp 5, Odell could see no sign of anyone above, but a short time later there was a small rockfall, heralding the return of Mallory's last four porters from Camp 6. Once again there was good news in the form of two notes. The first was addressed to Odell:

> We're awfully sorry to have left things in such a mess, our Unna Cooker rolled down the slope at the last moment. Be sure of getting back to IV tomorrow in time to evacuate before dark as I hope to. In the tent I must have left a compass – for the Lord's sake rescue it: we are here without. To here on 90 atmospheres for the two days, so we'll probably go on two cylinders but it's a bloody load for climbing. Perfect weather for the job!
> Yours ever,
> G. Mallory

The second note was shorter and addressed to John Noel:

We'll probably start early to-morrow (8th) in order
to have clear weather. It won't be too early to start
looking out for us either crossing the rock band
under the pyramid or going up skyline at 8.00 p.m.

    Yours ever

    G. Mallory

The notes were typical Mallory: very positive but with a hint
of chaos in the background. The good news was the weather was
continuing to hold, but the idea that Mallory and Irvine might
get to the summit and then back down to the North Col in the
same day was highly optimistic. The missing cooker and lost
compass would have been no surprise to Odell or anyone on
the team. The transport officer John Morris famously described
Mallory as 'the most absent-minded I have ever known' after
spending several months with him on the 1922 expedition. As
Morris recalled, team members took turns to check Mallory's
tent every time they broke camp to make sure that none of his
kit was left behind.

It's not absolutely clear what Mallory meant when he
said that they had used '90 atmospheres'. Their oxygen was
compressed to 120 atmospheres, and each cylinder held about
240 litres of oxygen. Probably he meant that they had used just
three-quarters of a cylinder each, a remarkably small amount
by today's standards – which can hardly have given them much
of a boost considering how heavy their sets were.

Clearly he made a mistake in his note to Noel, writing '8.00
p.m.' rather than '8.00 a.m.', as he certainly would not have been
visible at night. Surprisingly, he still wasn't absolutely sure whether
he was going to try to follow the North-East Ridge to the summit,
the route that he had always advocated, or traverse onto the North

Face following Norton's path; but either way, he was planning to start early on their summit day. Odell took heart – at the very least Mallory sounded confident and in good spirits. As his Sherpa, Nema, seemed to be suffering, Odell sent him down with Mallory's porters and prepared to spend the night alone.

After a slow start to the expedition, Odell was now thoroughly acclimatised and feeling supremely fit. The fact that he could carry up a heavy oxygen set from just above the North Col, and not use it at all, showed how strong he was. As a reward, he prepared himself a meal of tinned macaroni accompanied by cereal and jam. Then he hunkered down in two sleeping bags; if everything went according to Mallory's plan, this would also be his last night high on the mountain.

The next day, 8 June, was Whit Sunday: in pagan culture, the day to celebrate the arrival of summer; in Christianity, the day when the holy spirit descended on the Apostles, enabling them to speak in tongues. According to George Mallory's near-namesake, Sir Thomas Malory – the author of the fifteenth-century epic *Le Morte d'Arthur* – it was also the day when the Knights of the Round Table had a vision of the Holy Grail, inspiring their epic quest to find it. For George Mallory, the 'Galahad' of Everest, the moment of truth had come to achieve his destiny and reach the summit – the holy grail of British mountaineering.

There were signs, though, that the weather was changing. For the last couple of days, the thermometers positioned on the North Col had been showing record high temperatures, heralding a period of turbulence. When, at 8.00 a.m. that morning, John Noel trained his camera and his telescope on the ridge, as Mallory had asked him to, he could see nothing moving. Two hours later, the clouds rolled in and the view was obscured altogether.

At Camp 5, Odell had also enjoyed a clear start to the morning. He was up at 6.00 a.m., but as was typical at high altitude, it took him two hours to get out of camp. Mallory had not asked him to go any further, but Odell had decided to carry up a few provisions to Camp 6 in case he and Irvine decided to spend an extra night there on the way down. Though officially Odell wasn't allowed to do any geological work according to the British team's agreement with the Dalai Lama, it was too good an opportunity to be missed. Even if he didn't take anything away, Odell wanted to survey the different types of rock found high on Everest and look for fossils.

As he made his way up to Camp 6, the clouds rolled in until he could see nothing above. Odell was on his own, and the slab-like rocks were frequently covered with a layer of treacherous powdery snow. He took it slowly, traversing out onto the huge North Face, moving carefully upwards but rarely having to use his hands even as the ground grew steeper. At around 26,000 feet, he climbed a small crag about 100 feet high. He could have avoided it, but wanted to test his fitness.

When he reached the top, unexpectedly the clouds parted, revealing the summit of Everest and the North-East Ridge leading up to it. It was 12.50 p.m. If the timing on Mallory's note to Noel had been correct, he and Irvine should have been on the way down by now, but as Odell scanned the North-East Ridge he saw two small dots, so small that he couldn't really make them out properly, seemingly heading upwards at pace.

It was a moment that Odell would return to many times, as he was repeatedly asked precisely where on the North-East Ridge he had seen them, but that night his diary entry was short and simple: 'At 12.50 saw M & I on ridge nearing base of final pyramid. Had a little rock climbing at 26,000 ft at 2 on reaching tent at 27,000 waited [1] hr then out and whistled and shouted to give M&I direction. Blizzard cleared so decided to go back, reached IV c.6.45, no signs, lights on [ridge].'

When he finally reached Camp 6, Odell found a scene that was again typically Mallory, with clothes and food scattered inside the tent, and bits of oxygen equipment within and without. Odell wondered if they'd had problems with their sets or if Irvine had simply been tinkering, as was his wont, trying to get even more out of his rebuilt sets. There was no note or any other indication when precisely they had left, or what if anything had delayed them.

With a blizzard now raging all around him, Odell stayed in the tent for an hour, before venturing out aiming to catch sight of the summit party again. Visibility continued to be poor, so he shouted and yodelled and whistled, hoping that it might help them to descend, but he got no reply and saw nothing. Remembering Mallory's note from the afternoon before, and knowing that the tent was not big enough to hold three people should they return late, Odell turned back at around 4.30 p.m. and began his descent. As a parting gift, he left the compass that Mallory had misplaced at Camp 5, in case they should need it later.

Down at Camp 3, at the foot of the North Col, Norton's eyes were finally improving. He felt well enough to dictate another dispatch for *The Times* to Geoffrey Bruce. Most of it, detailing their record-breaking attempt a few days earlier, he left to Howard Somervell – who had by then made his way down to Base Camp – but in the opening sentences Norton captured the feeling of nervous anticipation that everyone shared:

> Above towers Everest, somewhat powdered with
> fresh snow, still and windless, and half-shrouded in
> that type of damp, sticky cloud which surely this time

presages the advent of the monsoon proper. Every eye
in camp is turned on the final pyramid. Expectation is
at its keenest, for somewhere there the final attempt,
as it must inevitably be, is at this moment deciding
the success or failure of the 1924 Expedition.

At the end of the day the skies cleared, but though they
remained on constant watch, they saw nothing on high – no
lights or flares; nothing apart from Odell returning to Camp 4.

The following morning, 9 June, there was still no sign of any
movement above. Initially everyone hoped that Mallory and Irvine
were at Camp 6, resting after their summit attempt the day before,
but as the minutes and then hours ticked by, they grew increasingly
nervous. The clouds came and went, first revealing then hiding the
summit, but neither through their binoculars nor their telescopes
could anyone see any hint of Mallory and Irvine. To make matters
worse, in the distance over the Rapui La – one of the passes leading
into Nepal – there were heavy clouds gathering, presaging the
imminent arrival of the long-feared monsoon.

At 11.10 a.m. , convinced that something had gone terribly
wrong, Norton dictated a note for Odell, telling him to keep a
close watch on the mountain for any distress signals but not to
go any higher than 27,000 feet and 'not to risk a single other
life English or Tibetan on the remote chance of retrieving the
inevitable'. Then, with a clatter, Edward Shebbeare broke the
tension, arriving at Camp 3 along with thirty porters, to begin
clearing the mountain. He had no idea that a third attempt was
taking place but could sense the anxiety in the air. After a few
hours' rest, Norton sent him back down, telling him to return
in two days, by which time everything would be settled – for
better or worse.

Up at Camp 4, Odell could not bear the tension any longer. At 12.10, three hours before Norton's note arrived, taking two porters and a mouthpiece for the oxygen set he'd found two days earlier, he headed back up the mountain, aiming to spend another night at Camp 5 and then climb back up to Camp 6. Before leaving, he agreed a set of visual signals with Hazard to tell him what he found: a single 'flea bag' in the snow if everything was 'all right'; two parallel sleeping bags if medical help was needed; two bags in the shape of a T if there was no trace. Hazard copied the signals out and then sent a porter down to Camp 3 with a parallel set of signals, to pass any message on to Norton.

High on the North Ridge, the conditions were no better. The wind had returned and so had the freezing temperatures. When Odell reached Camp 5, there was still no sign of Mallory and Irvine. Almost immediately, his porters curled down inside their tent, leaving Odell to cook a solitary meal before he too retired for the night. Even wrapped up in two sleeping bags with all his clothes on, it was so cold that he couldn't sleep.

Odell was up early next morning, 10 June, but it was obvious that the two porters, Nema and Mingma, were not fit to continue, so he told them to descend with a rucksack full of spare clothes. He sent a note down with them:

> No signs of M and I yet. There seems no particular
> advantage in getting, or trying to get, either of these
> to come on with me, so I am sending them down with
> this note. I'm going on to 6, and expect to return
> to 4 tonight – am sending down a few things in a
> green rucksack. Don't be certain of seeing signals
> from 6 but be on the look-out after 11.30, when I

shall probably reach there. The oxygen apparatus
here leaks badly but I have done what I can with it
and shall take it up to speed progress if possible. Too
boisterous last night to signal with fleabags [sleeping
bags], and there was nothing to report.

It was the first time that Odell had climbed on oxygen.
Initially he felt a little less tired, but after an hour he switched
off his oxygen and spat out the awkward and uncomfortable
mouthpiece. He didn't abandon the set quite yet, but ever the
scientist, he later noted that after turning off the gas, he didn't
suffer any of the catastrophic effects that had been predicted by
so many people back in London if oxygen were to be suddenly
removed at high altitude.

Camp 6 looked even more chaotic and bedraggled. Outside
was the same jumble of parts from oxygen sets, but a tent pole
had been collapsed by the wind. There was no indication that
Mallory and Irvine had been back, so Odell dumped his oxygen
set and went higher, trying to guess the route they might have
taken, hoping against hope that he might find them. It was
impossible, dangerous work which he knew was unlikely to get
him anywhere, but he had to try. After a few hours he abandoned
his search and retreated to the tent for a little respite from the
wind. Then, in a brief lull, he dragged the sleeping bags outside
and headed for a patch of snow above.

Down at Camp 4 on the North Col, the record heat of a few
days earlier had been replaced by a vicious wind and freezing
temperatures. Visibility was intermittent, but at 1.00 p.m. Hazard
spotted Odell at Camp 6. An hour later he watched him come out
and place two sleeping bags into the shape of a T. The wind had
picked up again, and Odell had to work hard to find loose rock to

weigh the bags down, but as Hazard recorded in the camp diary, the message was unmistakeable: 'No trace can be found – given up hope – Awaiting orders'. Five minutes later Hazard signalled back, 'All right return', and then at 2.25 p.m. he signalled down to Norton at Camp 3. Norton's reply to Hazard was equally stark: 'Abandon search – Return as soon as possible.'

Odell didn't need to be told. He took the compass that he'd left for Mallory two days earlier and the oxygen set, which he wanted to bring back but knew that he would never use, and began making his way down in the face of a bitter buffeting wind. Even though it took less effort to descend than it had to climb up, he moved slowly, taking a lot of care on the steep, slabby ground – dusted with snow and scree, making it even more hazardous.

At Camp 4, Hazard too was preparing to leave. He gathered up the possessions that Mallory and Irvine had left on the North Col, including Irvine's precious diary and a film camera left by Noel, and sent everything down with two Sherpas. After following Odell's descent through binoculars, Hazard sent the last remaining porter out to meet him at the foot of the ridge and escort him back to their tents.

Down below, Norton too had watched Odell's progress. Only after he finally reached Camp 4 did Norton set off back down the glacier towards Base Camp with John Noel and Geoffrey Bruce. Hingston and the cook Nursang stayed to await the return of the others, probably the next morning. The expedition doctor thought they should have abandoned Everest much earlier. Everyone had lost a lot of weight and no one looked in good shape. 'This is a bad ending and a serious loss to all in the expedition,' Hingston confided to his diary, 'It is certain to cause talk and criticism, though nobody is in the slightest to blame.'

On the morning of 11 June, Odell and Hazard left the North Col, abandoning most of the equipment and remaining supplies but carrying down the oxygen set and the stretcher, just in case they should be needed later on. Further down the mountain, Norton arrived at Base Camp in time to intercept the latest dispatch for *The Times*, detailing his own attempt a week earlier. He composed a telegram to send back to London with the news of Mallory and Irvine's disappearance and presumed death, and added a brief epilogue to his earlier dispatch, sketching out what had happened. 'The only likely explanation of the tragedy is that there was a mountaineering accident, unconnected with questions of weather or the use of oxygen. This is borne out by my own observations four days previously of the nature of the ground they were crossing when last seen.'

Somervell, who had formed a very close friendship with Mallory in 1922, was distraught but tried to keep a brave face. 'It is terrible,' he wrote in his diary. 'But there are few better deaths than to die in high endeavour, and Everest is the finest cenotaph in the world to a couple of the best of men.'

The following day they were joined by Odell and the remaining members of the team. Almost immediately Norton brought everyone together for a group discussion. When they returned to 'civilization' they would be bombarded with questions, but what exactly had happened? Norton thought they hadn't reached the top, others were not so sure, but most of them agreed that they had probably died in an accident. Having reached 28,100 feet himself and experienced the lethal ground near the top, Norton thought it was only too likely that one man had fallen and pulled the other off. After all, in 1922, when he and Mallory had climbed down from their record-breaking attempt with Somervell and Moreshead, there had been two slips, one very serious. Back then, Mallory had saved the day by holding everyone on the rope when Edward Norton took a misstep and pulled off the others, but it had been very close.

Odell disagreed. After seeing them so high, he thought that they probably had reached the top and most likely had been 'benighted' – forced to bivouac for the night on high – and died of exposure. Norton didn't like this idea, particularly the image of Mallory and Irvine freezing to death, but he was not the kind of leader who wanted to impose a collective version of the truth on everyone, and he recognized that Odell had been the last person to see them, so he agreed to disagree and let Odell write the dispatch dealing with Mallory and Irvine's attempt.

With Norton's telegram now on its way to the telegraph station at Phari, all that was left to do was wrap up Base Camp. Hingston gave the climbers a final examination. It made for sobering reading: everyone who had gone to the North Col or above – Norton, Somervell, Bruce, Odell and Hazard – still had a dilated or a slightly dilated heart. Norton had a frostbitten thumb and continued to suffer from residual snow-blindness. Somervell had laryngitis and Beetham still had sciatica. 'All of the above,' Hingston concluded with his usual understatement, 'are unfit to ascend the mountain.'

For the next two days Somervell worked on a large cairn to act as a memorial to all those who had died on the last three expeditions, carving out their names on pieces of rock: Alexander Kellas, the only fatality on the 1921 reconnaissance; Thankay, Sangay, Temba, Lhakpa, Pasang Namgyn, Norbu and Pema – the seven Sherpas and Bhotias who had died in the avalanche in 1922, now officially named for the first time; and Shamsher, Manbhadur, Mallory and Irvine, who had died this year.

June 1924, Base Camp on the Rongbuk glacier. The surviving
team members of the third British Everest expedition: (top,
left to right) Hazard, Hingston, Somervell, Beetham and
Shebbeare; (bottom) Bruce, Norton, unknown man and Odell.

Norton was equally busy composing the letters to Ruth
Mallory and Irvine's family that he had never thought he would
have to write. He told Ruth that George 'really was the best of
us' and that 'he simply would not accept defeat'; and he wrote
to Irvine's father Willie that his son might have started as an
'experiment' but had proved himself to be a very strong climber
and a real asset to the team. As for their final climb, he assured
him that Mallory had not been reckless. To both Ruth and Willie
Irvine, he insisted that whatever they read in the papers, he was
convinced that it would have been a sudden death in a regular
mountaineering accident, and they had not been benighted and
died slowly from exposure.

Norton felt the burden of defeat and loss intensely. He told Younghusband and Hinks, in a letter on 13 June, that he could not report success in any respect, 'for not only have we failed to establish a definite claim to have climbed the mountain – the point must always be in doubt – but Mallory and Irvine have been killed and two of our native establishment have died. I had determined that whether it succeeded or failed, the 1924 expedition should be free of casualties.'

In the official expedition book written much later, Norton wrote poignantly about how difficult it was to see Mallory and Irvine's empty tents at Base Camp and their unoccupied chairs at the mess table. He tried to stave off depression by keeping busy and revisiting the stoicism that had got him through previous campaigns. 'From the first,' he wrote, 'we accepted the loss of our comrades in that rational spirit which all of our generation had learnt in the Great War, and there was never any tendency to a morbid harping on the irrevocable... Death had taken its toll from the best, for they were indeed a splendid couple.'

On 15 June 1924, at midday, they finally abandoned Base Camp, moving off down the valley with 120 yaks carrying their baggage and any supplies they had chosen to take out with them. For the moment most of them were heading for the Rongshar valley, where they hoped to take a few weeks resting up before the long slog back to Darjeeling. After that they would once again go their separate ways – some back to England, others to the Middle East and South India.

As he stared back at Everest, Hingston – in some ways an outsider, in some ways one of the most acute observers of the drama – couldn't help but feel that Everest had won: 'The mountain looked magnificent as we retreated from it. It was half embraced in gentle cloud and seemed as though it gloated in its victory. In the foreground stood the cairn of stones... I wonder when the next attack will be made on the mountain. It never looked larger, more magnificent or more impregnable that when we turned our backs on it today.'

The 1924 expedition had come so close, but they were leaving Everest in disarray with four men dead, including the team's most totemic member. Right now, they were too shell-shocked to think of ever making another attempt, but Everest was still unfinished business. On the way down they said goodbye to the Rongbuk Lama, leaving a large pile of crampons and ice axes at the monastery. They imagined that another British party might be back next year to finish the job beyond all doubt – but what happened over the next few months would surprise everyone.

George and Ruth Mallory

Your Ever Loving George

W hen George met Ruth for the first time in the autumn of 1913, he was twenty-seven and she twenty-one. Within nine months they were married. They had their first child, daughter Clare, in 1915, followed two years later by Beridge and then John, 'a huge bumbling boy', in August 1920. By today's standards, domestic life was not difficult. They had a nanny – the indomitable Violet Meakin, or 'Vi' – a cook and a housemaid, as well as that luxury of luxuries, an automobile. As the family grew, George more often went with his friends on British climbing trips, but he and Ruth were still able to go on occasional holidays as a couple, leaving their children with Vi.

The biggest strains on their relationship were George's long absences and low income. As a schoolmaster he earned only a modest salary, so they needed a lot of support from Ruth's father to keep them going in the style they expected. The only way

Mallory could make any extra money was through lecturing and writing about his climbing exploits; Everest always required long absences.

And so Ruth became what George called the 'poor left-behind one', almost always in charge of their three young children. Each Everest trip took about six months, and in between expeditions he was the Committee's star lecturer, sent far and wide to preach the Everest gospel. When he returned from America in the summer of 1923, it seemed for a moment that things might have changed. For the first time in two years, he had a regular job that he really liked with a decent income and a bright future. He was so convinced that Cambridge was right for them that he persuaded Ruth to uproot their family from their home in Godalming and move halfway across England.

Then, at the very moment when the move was underway, he was asked to go back to Everest. The Mallorys enjoyed a fraught few months together, with George frequently busy or away for the night, and Ruth having to manage a new home that needed a lot of work. Inevitably there were tensions, but Ruth was a survivor, and by then used to having to look after the household. She settled into Cambridge and got on with domestic chores.

By the summer, Ruth had every hope that George himself would soon return and they would be able to start their new life together properly, but as he told her in his final letter on 27 May, she would probably hear the news first from *The Times* rather than directly from him. For Ruth and all the families and friends, letters from Everest were infrequent and sporadic. At the beginning of the expedition, members had been told to warn their families that it would take around twenty-seven days for the post to get from Tibet to England. *The Times* had organized dedicated couriers to take their dispatches back from Base Camp as quickly as possible, but all other mail went by regular runner.

In 1922, Arthur Hinks, the Everest Committee's joint secretary, had kept up an occasional correspondence with the 'expedition wives' – Charles Bruce's partner, the formidable Lady Finetta Madeline Julia Bruce, and Ruth – occasionally asking them to pass on titbits of expedition news and sometimes using them to scold or send less-than-subtle messages to their husbands, but in 1924 he was less frantic. Having secured £8,000 from Noel's *Explorer Films*, he didn't have the same financial worries. Hinks was not, however, entirely quiet. Even though the Everest Committee did not meet between January and June, he sent a stream of letters to Norton and Bruce asking about the progress of the expedition. Neither reciprocated. Norton was rarely at Base Camp, and was so busy with expedition business and dispatches for *The Times* that he didn't have time to reply. Bruce had plenty of leisure time but clearly found Hinks irritating.

Towards the end of May, Hinks's main preoccupation was organizing a grand meeting in London for the autumn, on the expedition's return. The plan was to take the Albert Hall if they returned in triumph, or the slightly smaller Westminster Hall if they came back not having reached the top. 'I do not think anyone will be disposed to have a Fourth Expedition,' he wrote to Norton on 27 May, 'so this meeting will be a winding up of the enterprise in a sense.'

On 31 May, *The Times* published Norton's third dispatch, in which he revealed their problems getting established on the Rongbuk glacier and the battle for the North Col. On 16 June, his next communiqué told the story of what the *Times* headline writer called the 'Second Check' – the rescue of the stranded porters from Camp 4. The odds of Hinks having to book the Albert Hall did not look good.

Then, on the afternoon of Thursday 19 June, a coded telegram arrived at the central station of the Eastern Telegraph Company at Tower Chambers in Moorgate. It was addressed to Obterras, the telegraphic signature of the Royal Geographical Society. When he arrived at his office the next morning, Hinks opened it.

MALLORY IRVINE NOVE REMAINDER ALCEDO

Hinks went to his code book to decipher it. His handwritten note was longer but equally stark:

> Mallory Irvine killed in action, remainder all in good order.

It was the message that no one wanted to hear: the expedition's most famous climber and its youngest member would not be coming back.

Hinks immediately went to see Norman Collie, the president of the Alpine Club, to discuss how to break the news. Above all, the two men decided, the families must not read about the deaths of their loved ones in the papers before they heard directly, so Hinks cabled Ruth at Herschel House in Cambridge and Mallory and Irvine's families in Birkenhead. Just in case the telegrams did not get through, *The Times* sent reporters to both homes to inform them face-to-face.

Hinks then sat down to write longer letters. He told Ruth and Mallory's father, Herbert, how he felt the loss of Mallory particularly, 'because it fell to me to secure him leave from his new appointment at Cambridge by pleading as earnestly as I could with Dr Cranage for him and for the Expedition'. It was harder to write to Irvine's parents because, as he admitted, he had only met their son once, but he felt sure, he told them, that Andrew 'seemed destined to play a great part in the conquest of Mount Everest'.

That Friday evening, Ruth was at home with her children. Shortly after 7.30 p.m. the telegram arrived from Hinks.

COMMITTEE DEEPLY REGRET RECEIVE BAD NEWS
EVEREST EXPEDITION TODAY NORTON CABLES YOUR
HUSBAND AND IRVINE KILLED LAST CLIMB REMAINDER
RETURNED SAFE PRESIDENT AND COMMITTEE OFFER
YOU AND FAMILY HEARTFELT SYMPATHY

Ruth decided not to tell the children straight away, but to wait until the following morning, when, gathering the three of them around her in bed, she explained that their father would not be coming home. They cried together.

Irvine's family was equally distraught. As his grandfather James Irvine later wrote with great directness and simplicity, 'Andrew was a splendid young fellow and had a great future ahead of him. We are broken hearted.'

On Saturday 21 June, *The Times* broke the news. At this stage, there were no details to report. Apart from the contents of the telegram, they had no information about where or how Mallory and Irvine had died, or the precise date of their passing. An editorial quoted Mallory's recent dispatch: 'The third time we walk up the East Rongbuk Glacier will be the last, for better or worse.' It was a line that would be repeated by several newspapers. *The Times* also included brief biographies, with Mallory described as 'one of the finest mountaineers that this or any other generation has produced' and Irvine praised for his prowess as a rower and his willingness to take huge risks to complete 'the great adventure in which he engaged'.

In 1924, *The Times* was still so determinedly sober and unsensational that it put small ads on its front page and kept headlines to a minimum. The other papers were not so low-key. The *Westminster Gazette* had the temerity to steal the *Times'* story and even sent a reporter round to interview the Chairman of the Everest Committee, Sir Francis Younghusband, on the night of 20 June. Their headline shouted out the story over four lines of capitalized text:

TRIUMPH FRUSTRATED BY DEATH

EVEREST EXPEDITION TO BE ABANDONED

TWO LIVES LOST

RECORD HEIGHTS REACHED BEFORE THE TRAGEDY

Younghusband didn't have any more information to pass on, apart from to comment on the severe weather conditions reported in the previous dispatch.

Most British newspapers led with a simple idea: that cruel Everest had 'won again', but although the deaths of Mallory and Irvine were a 'tragedy', the Everest expedition embodied essential British values – the same spirit that had 'led to the formation of the Empire itself'. They had paid 'the price of man's ascendancy over nature', and even though it was assumed that they had not reached the top, the expedition was, according to *The Star*, a 'Victorious Disaster'. Mallory and Irvine were elevated into the ranks of Britain's other lost explorers, Scott, Franklin and Livingstone, and praised as the incarnation of the spirit of adventure.

American newspapers took a similar, but less jingoistic line. The *New York Times* put Everest on its front page, with the headline 'Mallory and Irvine Killed in Attempt to Conquer Everest'. Back in 1923, it had covered Mallory's US lecture tour more comprehensively than any other paper, and now it returned to that coverage, quoting what would become Mallory's epithet – 'Because it's there' – and even reminding readers of the small nip of brandy that he had slugged on the way down from his attempt in 1922.

Several US newspapers also picked up the note of fatalism that had appeared in the British press, with the *New York Times* stating, on its second day of coverage, on 22 June, that there was 'no doubt that Mallory knew that he was leading a forlorn hope'. In Philadelphia, the city where Mallory had attracted the biggest audience on his American lecture tour, the local newspaper, *The Inquirer*, stuck to the theme of a tragedy, while the *Philadelphia Public Ledger* sought to rebut any criticism of the futility of mountaineering: 'It is not to the point for stay-at-homes to cast aspersions on the foolhardiness of those who feel and obey the lure of untrodden regions. Where the explorer goes, the long, deliberate train of civilisation one day follows.'

All the talk of heroism and the onward progress of 'civilization' did not heal Ruth's grief or that of Mallory's friends. In the days after the announcement, they wrote to her remembering George's companionship and charisma. Several of them echoed that feeling of inevitability reported in the press. Robert Graves remembered how George had told him one day, when out on Snowdon, that he hoped he would die climbing, and Maynard Keynes wrote, somewhat brutally, how he had known long ago that this was going to happen. Geoffrey Winthrop Young became one of Ruth's closest confidants, exchanging several letters with her. He was in France when the news broke and didn't contact her until he returned to England. The loss of his friend was 'unutterable', he wrote, and though he felt huge pride, it was tempered by 'a long numbness of pain'.

One of the most interesting commentaries came from George Finch. Much to Hinks's chagrin, in the months since he had been thrown off the team he had continued lecturing and had even published his climbing autobiography, *The Making of a Mountaineer*. Finch wrote a very detailed analysis of the mountaineering and physiological issues involved in attempting Everest for the *Daily News* on 23 June, dividing the mountain into three zones: the slog up the Rongbuk glacier, the climb up the ice slope to the North Col, and finally the ascent from the North Col to the summit.

Initially, when all that was known was the content of Norton's first telegraph, Finch guessed that Mallory and Irvine must have perished on the way up to the North Col on the avalanche-prone slopes that had killed the seven porters in 1922. He thought that Mallory was too good a climber to have died higher up the mountain, and that climbers of his calibre 'did not slip'.

When Norton's next dispatch reached London a week later, on 26 June, Finch was forced to revise his opinion. The largest part, written mainly by Howard Somervell, told the story of his and Norton's record-breaking attempt on the summit, but in a brief addendum Norton outlined the events before and after the disappearance of Mallory and Irvine. Norton had written it on 11 June, the day before he spoke to Odell, so it was not complete, but it contained the crucial detail that Mallory and Irvine had last been seen at around 28,000 feet, 'going strong for the top'. After that, he said, there had been no sign of them at all, even though they had come to Everest equipped with magnesium distress flares. Odell had visited their high camp twice, but with the weather deteriorating and no chance that they could have survived two nights out in the open, Norton had been forced to abandon the search and order everyone down.

This dispatch prompted another flurry of articles in the press, and an extraordinary official telegram from the Everest Committee to Norton, which was also released by Hinks for publication in *The Times*: 'The committee warmly congratulate the whole party on the heroic achievements published today. They specially appreciate the consummate leadership displayed. All are deeply moved by the glorious death of the lost climbers near the summit, and send best wishes for a speedy restoration to health of all surviving members.'

Not everyone approved. Douglas Freshfield, a prominent member of the Alpine Club, wrote to Hinks complaining about the triumphal tone, but he was unabashed. Hinks was impressed by Norton's achievements and his leadership but there was also some news management creeping in. Hinks felt that the earlier coverage in *The Times*, the only newspaper that he cared about, was too negative. Instead of treating the events as 'an unredeemed disaster', he wanted to emphasize that the expedition had been 'an heroic success in spite of the tragedy, and that it must be dealt with in this spirit'. Rather than present Mallory as a victim of Everest, he was a tragic hero who had died in battle with his young charge Sandy Irvine. There was no question now: Hinks would be booking the Albert Hall, not the Westminster.

Then, on 5 July, Odell's much more detailed account reached Britain. Norton prefaced it with a note in which he revised upwards Mallory and Irvine's final height. Their last sighting, he wrote, had now been properly established by theodolite, and it was not 28,000 feet but over 200 feet higher, at 28,227 feet – about 100 feet above Norton's own high point. It was a new world record, but Norton avoided any triumphalism, writing that 'the price is out of all proportion to the results'.

Odell's article was more expansive than his brief diary entry of 8 June which had simply recorded 'At 12.50 saw M&I on ridge nearing base of final pyramid'. He wrote:

> My eyes became fixed on one, tiny black spot
> silhouetted on a small snow-crest beneath a rock-step
> in the ridge, and the black spot moved. Another black
> spot became apparent and moved up the snow to
> join the other on the crest. The first then approached
> the great rock-step and shortly emerged at the top;
> the second did likewise. Then the whole fascinating
> vision vanished, enveloped in cloud once more.
> There was but one explanation. It was Mallory and
> his companion moving, as I could see even at that
> great distance, with considerable alacrity, realizing
> doubtless that they had none too many hours of
> daylight to reach the summit from their present
> position and return to Camp VI at nightfall.

He finished by agreeing with Norton that whether they had gone all the way to the top or turned back early would forever remain a mystery, but added, 'I personally am of [the] opinion that Mallory and Irvine must have reached the summit.'

This much more positive version of the story prompted another set of headlines in the British press, as the idea that Mallory and Irvine must have made the top began to take hold. Norman Collie wrote to the letters page of *The Times* that there was 'no reason why they should not have succeeded in attaining the summit'. Lord Martin Conway, a former president of the

Alpine Club, was more strident, arguing that Odell's article should have been entitled 'Victors of Everest' – and that with only 1,000 feet to go to the top they simply could not have turned back when they were so close. 'I think of them as somewhere very high aloft,' he finished his letter, 'still sitting on the rocks whence their spirits took flight.' A few days later, Geoffrey Winthrop Young wrote a further letter to *The Times* agreeing with Conway and declaring that, because of 'the exceptional mountaineering capacity and the temperament of the leader of the final party', they were most likely to have succeeded.

When George Finch was asked for a second time what he thought, he focused his attention on Norton and Somervell's attempt, praising their strength and tenacity and the modesty with which they had described their record-breaking climb. As for Mallory and Irvine, nothing, he wrote, could be known of their passing, but he was still in favour of using oxygen at high altitude.

The Everest Committee had been very careful not to reveal any of the problems encountered by the team with their equipment. When early on *The Times* had got wind of Odell's report from Kampa Dzong detailing the sorry state of the cylinders and the leaks in their apparatus, Hinks had only handed it over after they agreed not to reveal its contents. Finch, like everyone else, had no idea that things had been so bad.

Today it is hard to read his articles and not wonder what would have happened if he and Hinks had not been set on such a collision course. Finch didn't know the mountain as well as Mallory, but he had a forensic eye for a climb and a better grasp of the scientific and equipment issues than anyone else. If he had been in charge, it's unlikely that the oxygen sets would have been sent out in such a state.

Perhaps surprisingly, in view of how he had been treated, Finch seems to have endorsed the rhetoric of the organizers, praising the bravery of Mallory and Irvine and proclaiming that Britain owed her position in the world 'to the spirit of adventure with which her sons have always been imbued', regardless of whether or not they had reached the summit.

For the Committee the question was not just a theoretical one; there was a lot of money at stake. According to their agreement with The Times, if the expedition was successful and the summit was reached, they would get a second payment; otherwise they would get no more money apart from foreign royalties. A few days after Odell's dispatch, William Lints Smith, the manager at The Times who had negotiated the deal back in the autumn of 1923, wrote to Hinks. The paper, he said, was willing to act 'liberally' on the matter and would not require any further proof than a 'definitive ruling' from the Committee. If it confirmed that Mallory and Irvine had succeeded, not only would The Times hand over the promised 'summit bonus' of £1,000, but he also anticipated a further £3,000 or so from foreign rights, knowing that a more glorious story was likely to sell better overseas. 'I would personally much like to be able to take the view,' Lints Smith wrote, 'that the two brave men who sacrificed their lives did actually reach the summit.'

With up to £4,000 at stake, one-third of the cost of the 1924 expedition, it was a tempting offer, but the Committee did not succumb. After consulting with Sydney Spencer, his opposite number at the Alpine Club, Hinks wrote back to say that, though most of Mallory's friends thought he had succeeded and was 'probably lying on the summit', the Committee could not say this definitively. 'What happened to him and Irvine can, so far as I can see, not be known this year, and probably not at all.'

While all the letters were flying back and forth across London, back in Tibet, Norton and the remaining members of the team were in the Rongshar valley, five days' march away to the north-east of Everest, trying to recover from the rigours of the previous few months. It was not quite as verdant as the Kharta valley, which they had decamped to in 1922, but it was a lot warmer and more hospitable than Everest Base Camp.

By then fully recovered from his episode of snow blindness, in rapid succession Norton hammered out a series of dispatches for *The Times* on everything from the flora and fauna of the Everest region to the performance and habits of their Sherpas. He was very aware that after the deaths of Mallory and Irvine the drama had gone out of the expedition, but having only produced nine out of the promised sixteen dispatches he had plenty of column inches to make up. Inevitably though, Norton knew that they would all soon have to make the long journey back to 'civilization', and face a lot of questioning.

He met his first reporter, a local correspondent sent out by *The Times*, at Yatung, just a few miles from the Tibet–Sikkim border. After all the activity in the letters page, it wasn't long before he was asked about Mallory and Irvine's final altitude. Norton was tight-lipped, referring back to his earlier dispatch and maintaining that all that could be said for certain was that Mallory and Irvine had reached 28,227 feet – anything else was conjecture.

On 1 August, more than four months after they had left town, the British team returned to Darjeeling, where they were met by a large and enthusiastic crowd led by their former leader, General Bruce. He was now fully recovered and back to his usual ebullient form, complimenting everyone on how well they looked and planning a return match in which, as he wrote in

The Times, 'it is now almost certain that the conquest of Everest will be completed'. When a reporter spoke to the Sherpas, they described the expedition as a huge picnic and said they too would all be very glad to return.

For the next few days, Norton and Bruce dealt with the remaining expedition admin, paying off the porters and finalizing all the outstanding business. In February 1924, just before they left for India, the Olympic Committee had decided to award gold medals to the 1922 team, several of which had by then been sent to Darjeeling. In a small ceremony, Lady Lytton, the wife of the governor of Bengal, presented awards to Tejbir Bura, the Gurkha NCO who had accompanied Finch and Geoffrey Bruce two years previously, and to the Sherpas who had climbed highest in 1924. One of the other Gurkhas, Hurke, was given a commemorative watch for his sterling service, and several Sherpas who had performed well in 1924 were given extra baksheesh.

A week later, Norton reached Kolkata, and sat down for a longer and more detailed interview with *The Times*. He reiterated that, apart from Odell, most of the team did not think that Mallory and Irvine had reached the summit and instead had probably died in 'an ordinary mountaineering accident'. Asked why he didn't think they had made it, he argued that though Mallory was probably the most driven individual he had met, he was also a careful and responsible leader who would not have risked the life of his young partner. In the coming weeks, he stated, he was looking forward to a short holiday in the Alps before returning to England, but looking further ahead, he was already mooting a fourth expedition to ensure that 'Everest's very nose-tip be stung' in revenge for the deaths of Mallory and Irvine.

When the interview was published, Norton's verdict on Mallory and Irvine caused a small stir in England. Geoffrey Winthrop Young was very angry. He wrote to Douglas Freshfield that Norton was motivated by the desire to 'return to the attack', so therefore he needed to 'think the summit still unclimbed'. He, on the other hand, was sure that Mallory had succeeded. 'After nearly twenty years' knowledge of Mallory as a mountaineer, I can say... that difficult as it would have been for any mountaineer to turn back with the only difficulty passed – to Mallory it would have been an impossibility... the peak was first climbed because Mallory was Mallory.'

Ruth did not take part in any of the debates. As she told Young: 'Whether he got to the top of the mountain or did not, whether he lived or died, makes no difference to my admiration for him.' In spite of the comments from several of his friends, she denied that George was obsessed with Everest or that he had intended to risk everything. 'I don't think I do feel that his death makes me the least more proud of him. It is his life that I loved and love.' She did believe in the afterlife, however, and felt that George was still close to her.

As for Mallory's legacy, Ruth was already thinking about a potential biographer. The obvious candidate was Young, who had written five books and knew George well, but he was reluctant. He had been one of Mallory's closest friends; perhaps he was simply too close to him to spend months thinking and writing about nothing else.

Young did however write a very moving eulogy in *The Nation*, a liberal magazine that was the forerunner of the *New Statesman*, celebrating his young friend as the 'magical and adventurous spirit of youth personified'. He portrayed Mallory as a scholar and an idealist, but above all the consummate

George Mallory's friend and mentor, Geoffrey Winthrop Young.

mountaineer: 'From boyhood he belonged to mountains, as flame belongs to fire. He lived their romance, their simplicity, their open power, their unchanging loveliness.'

Though Young did not want to be his biographer, he was responsible for forging one of the most potent myths of Mallory: that of the chivalrous reincarnation of a bygone age. 'George Mallory – "Sir Galahad" always to his early friends,' he wrote in his piece for *The Nation*, 'gave back to the hills their life of inspiration, content. The greatest mountain upon earth is the monument to his clean and selfless use of his rare manhood.' Eventually, Ruth was able to persuade one of George's other friends, David Pye, to write the book, and handed over bundles of letters. It was published in 1927 – but there were two major events to commemorate the two lost mountaineers that took place much sooner.

The first was a memorial service at St Paul's Cathedral on 17 October – a significant public event, with both the families and the British establishment represented. George V had already sent his condolences to the Everest Committee. He did not appear in person because he was out of London at the time, but he and several other members of the royal family sent their representatives to sit alongside various ambassadors and the leadership of the Royal Geographical Society and the Alpine Club.

The bishop of Chester had already presided over a smaller service in Birkenhead, but he was asked to lead the service because both the dead men had come from his diocese. In his homily he portrayed Irvine as a gentle giant who was happy to use his strength to help others. Mallory, he said, was both modest and brilliant, and the whole enterprise had a spiritual aspect – with the mountaineers coming together for a common goal, displaying what he called 'splendid peaks of courage and unselfishness and cheerfulness'. Ultimately, he said to end his sermon, whether they succeeded or failed was not the only issue: 'The merciless mountain gives no reply. But that last ascent, with the beautiful mystery of its great enigma, stands for more than a heroic effort to climb a mountain, even though it be the highest in the world. *Sic itur ad astra* [thus is the way to the stars].'

Later that evening, many of the same family members, plus many more climbers from the Alpine Club and fellows of the RGS, crowded into the Albert Hall for a grand meeting that was both a eulogy to Mallory and Irvine and a celebration of the successes of the expedition. Norton spoke, along with Odell and Charles Bruce, who with his usual generosity praised Norton's leadership and his record-breaking climb with Somervell. 'Who would have thought four years ago that men could climb without oxygen to over 28,000 feet?' he boomed.

Norton then gave a graphic account of his climb with Somervell, revealing how in the last stages he had set himself a target of making twenty steps without stopping, but hadn't always achieved it. He talked about the moment when Mallory announced that he intended to make a further attempt, and though he would later reveal in the expedition book that he would have preferred Odell as Mallory's partner, he said that he had been 'entirely in favour of the plan, which now represented their last chance of success'.

Then Odell took the floor to repeat his account of his last sighting of Mallory and Irvine, 'moving expeditiously as if they were making up for lost time'. In front of the assembled masses, he was a little more cautious than he had been in *The Times*, now admitting that he wasn't quite sure if the second climber had managed to reach the top of the rock step before the mist rolled in and the two tiny dots were gone forever.

Odell did not repeat his opinion that Mallory had probably reached the summit, but perhaps this was not surprising in view of the opening address given by Lord Ronaldshay, the president of the Royal Geographical Society. He had made the now familiar invocation of the 'spirit of man' and insisted on the idealistic value of the expedition. But that wasn't all. 'Is the fight finished?' Ronaldshay asked. 'Is the possibility of climbing Mount Everest to be left in doubt? Neither the members of the expedition nor of the Mount Everest Committee are content to let the matter rest where it now stands, and it is our intention to apply immediately through the government of India for permission from the Tibetan government to make another attempt in 1926.'

As the spontaneous applause and cheering rang out across the hall, the Everest Committee could take understandable pride in what they had achieved. In three years, they had mapped most of the Everest region and dispatched two full-scale expeditions, both of which had been remarkably successful. All that remained was to make an undisputed ascent to the summit. On 5 November Hinks sat down to compose a rather pompous letter to the Undersecretary of State for India: 'I have the honour to inform you that at their last meeting the Mount Everest Committee received reports from the returned members of the expedition of 1924 and unanimously decided that the enterprise of climbing Everest could not be allowed to remain in its present almost successful but still incomplete state, and that application should immediately be made through the government of India to the Dalai Lama for permission to send a fourth expedition.'

While his request worked its way from Kensington Gore to Whitehall, and then across the water – first to Delhi, then Gangtok and finally Lhasa – there was one man for whom there was still plenty of work to do before the 1924 expedition could finally be put to bed: Captain John Noel, the photographer and director of the official expedition film, now entitled *The Epic of Everest*. He might have given up on his own ambitions to climb Everest a long time ago, but he had staked as much as anyone on the successful outcome of the 1924 expedition.

In the months before the expedition, Noel had sent the team members a memo, detailing his plans. 'The record that I hope to bring back of this tremendous feat will be a clean and well told story of what we hope to be the greatest exploit of British climbers and British explorers.' They would not, he assured, be asked to 'pose' for the camera or be photographed when they didn't want to be, and nor would the photographic party ever be a hindrance to the main effort.

Initially, as Noel revealed in an interview in 1969, Mallory had not been keen, telling him that he wanted to climb Everest, not be an actor in a film, but he was fond of Noel and by the end of the expedition was so keen to have his exploits immortalized on film that one of his last notes on the mountain was to Noel, telling him where to train his camera on the summit day.

Things had not gone to plan for Noel. On 8 June it had been too cloudy to capture any images of Mallory and Irvine on their way up the North-East Ridge, and though Noel had given Irvine a pocket movie camera to take high, it had never been used and had later been recovered by Hazard from Camp 4. Nevertheless, Noel had powerful images of the moment when Hazard made his sleeping bag signal to Norton from the North Col, announcing that Odell had given up on his search, as well as a lot of expedition footage and scene-setting sequences on Tibetan life which he was sure would fascinate audiences. After all the publicity over Mallory and Irvine's disappearance, Noel had every hope that *The Epic of Everest* would be a hit.

A natural showman, Noel had done everything he could to pique the public's interest and maximize the promotional value of the expedition. His most ambitious stunt was to arrange for a Citroën Kégresse tractor, the latest in automotive technology, to follow the expedition into Tibet. The plan was for it to make the first motorized crossing of the Jelep La, the 14,400-foot pass that marked the frontier between Sikkim and Tibet, before rolling on to ascend Chomolhari, the striking-looking mountain outside of Phari. The tractor and its drivers, Major Victor Haddick and two British soldiers, had arrived in Darjeeling in late March shortly after the climbers left town, and generated a lot of local headlines, carrying the governor's wife, Lady Lytton, and her daughters up nearby hills. Sadly, the Citroën didn't get much further, the dirt tracks of Sikkim proving more than a match for even the most rugged tractor available. Hinks and the Everest Committee were embarrassed by what they considered a stunt and tried to distance themselves as much as possible.

Noel's other 'side hustle' was a little more successful and leaves a legacy to this day. A few months before the expedition, he had announced that he planned to produce a special commemorative stamp, and that anyone who sent in their address and some regular postage stamps to cover costs would get a postcard sent to them all the way from Base Camp. In the end, thousands of people wrote in, prompting Noel to carry thousands of photographs in his baggage.

Noel had of course an ulterior motive, because each postcard – as well as bearing an image of Everest – was a publicity flyer for the forthcoming documentary. The first showing was scheduled for early December at the Scala cinema close to King's Cross station in London. Noel wasn't content just to project the film, however; to give the audience a real taste of Tibet, and garner yet more headlines, he decided to bring over a group of Tibetan lamas to perform their ritual music and dances on stage, before the lights went down and the film was shown.

In the nineteenth and early twentieth centuries, this kind of ethnographic 'human zoo' was not uncommon. There was a long history of indigenous men and women – from the Inuit of the high Arctic to the Botocudo of the Brazilian rainforest – being transported to Europe to be displayed at shows and museums. Even while the British team was attempting Everest, a huge Empire exhibition had opened at Wembley in London, featuring stands from fifty-six of Britain's fifty-eight colonial territories. There was a scale replica of Everest and numerous living exhibits, including a troop of Tibetan dancers.

Despite all the 'noise' generated by the Empire exhibition, Noel's group of eight lamas managed to garner a lot of headlines. They arrived in Britain on 1 December, eight days before the film was due to open, after being smuggled out of India disguised as bundles of fur in order to avoid detection by the Tibetan authorities, who might not have approved. When they arrived in London, accompanied by Lhakpa Tsering, one of the Sherpas who had been with Mallory and Bruce on their first attempt, and John MacDonald, the son of the trade agent at Yatung, they were spirited across the capital to their temporary home in Charlotte Street in Fitzrovia. According to contemporary reports, during the drive across central London they frantically waved peacock feathers in order to ward off evil spirits. Over the next couple of weeks, the lamas visited London Zoo, the Houses of Parliament and various department stores, prompting plenty of smiles and press reports wherever they went.

The lamas even accompanied Noel to the recently opened 2LO radio studio in Marconi House for a special broadcast. After they had performed on their instruments, Noel gave a talk on Everest, prophesying that one day the bodies of Mallory and Irvine would be found.

When the lamas finally appeared on stage at the Scala on 9 December, as the prologue to the film, reporters were less keen, most recording how bamboozled they were with the 'weird and wonderful' music performed on huge trumpets and horns made from human bones. According to one reviewer, it resembled the sound of 'a thousand distressed mooncalves calling for their mothers against the competition of a hundred foghorns'.

When it came to the film itself, the reviewers were much more positive, praising it for its photography and sense of scale. Prince Harry, according to one of George V's sons, was present, along with various members of high society and all the usual dignitaries from the Alpine Club and the RGS. It was a very strange, rather inauspicious first night though. London was blanketed in a dense cloud of fog, so all-encompassing that it even crept into the cinema itself, playing havoc with the projection.

Afterwards the fog was still so dense that when John Noel and his wife, Sybille, hailed a cab, the driver was so nervous about the 'pea-souper' that he refused to take them any further than Piccadilly, leaving them to walk the last three miles to their flat in Earl's Court. When they arrived, Sybille decided to have a bath and went into the kitchen to light the immersion heater. She didn't notice the smell of gas. A few minutes later, Noel found her collapsed on the floor. He dragged her away towards the front door, telephoned for a doctor and then promptly passed out. When the medic arrived, he found not one but two stricken victims. Noel recovered quickly, but Sybille remained unconscious for the next six hours. Later he told the *Evening News* that she had sat in seat number 13 at the Scala.

For all the fun and bravado of his film and the circus around it, *The Epic of Everest* did have one completely unforeseen and very damaging consequence that would affect Everest expeditions for years to come. The problems started in November, when Hinks received a cable from Major Frederick Bailey, the British political officer in Sikkim responsible for liaising with the Dalai Lama. He requested that Noel should cut out a scene from the film in which an elderly Tibetan was seen picking lice out of a child's hair and eating them. Before its release, excerpts from Noel's film had appeared in Pathé newsreels; the delousing scene was not well received by Tibetan officials. In earlier years, Major Bailey had been somewhat of an adventurer in his own right and was famous for his 'mission to Tashkent' in 1918 to spy on the Bolshevik government, but in 1924 his primary focus was on maintaining good relations with the Lhasa government.

Hinks passed the message on, but though Noel did some re-editing he did not remove the lice-picking scene in its entirety, arguing that the old man was killing the lice with his teeth rather than eating them. It was 'a fine distinction for the general public', as Hinks admitted in his reply to Bailey, but the Everest Committee, he said, were not in charge of the film and could not exert any editorial control over Noel.

When the Tibetan government also learned that eight monks had been taken from a monastery in Gyantse and were heading for London for the premiere, they were even more appalled. They had not liked the inclusion of Tibetan dancers at the Empire exhibition in Wembley, and were particularly concerned that nothing would be done to impugn their religion. Once again Bailey wrote to Hinks in London, requesting there must not be any suggestion that the lamas were performing religious dances. By the time the letter arrived in London, however, the curtain had already gone up and it was being widely reported that the monks were performing Tibetan 'Devil Dances', wearing religious masks and playing sacred instruments.

The film did well, with performances running into Christmas and large crowds attending, but nothing was heard from Tibet of the Everest Committee's request to stage another expedition in 1926. Then, in April 1927, L. D. Wakely, the Undersecretary of State for India, got back to Hinks, informing him that the Tibetan government had refused permission. Hinks immediately went on the offensive, claiming that it was all Bailey's fault and that he had displayed 'an exaggerated deference to the more reactionary side of Tibetan feeling'. He told Wakely that to accept the Tibetan government's refusal would be a 'serious rebuff to Britain's prestige', but it was to no avail.

Over the next few months of extended correspondence, it emerged that the Tibetan government had a whole list of complaints against the British team. First and foremost, whatever Noel maintained, the lamas had never been given official permission to leave their monastery, and at one stage had also been refused passports by the Indian government. The former abbot of the Gyantse monastery, Hinks was told, had been summoned to Lhasa to be punished, and if the lamas ever returned to Tibet they too would face the same fate.

After the initial London run ended in the early spring of 1925, the Tibetan monks went on tour with the film, visiting Wales and the Midlands and even venturing as far as Belfast and Berlin. Later that year they were released from their duties and sent back to India, only to find themselves stranded in Colombo when Explorer Films went bankrupt, after *The Epic of Everest* failed to get cinema distribution in the US. 'I have lost everything myself,' Noel wrote plaintively to Hinks in December, 'in consequence of this unfortunate company and the general affairs of the expedition.' Even though they had previously refused to take responsibility for anything to do with the film, the Everest Committee was forced to send money out to Colombo to pay for the hapless monks' onward travel to India and Sikkim.

In addition to their complaints about the lamas and the content of the film, the Tibetan government was unhappy about what it said was an unauthorized expedition to Lhatse to the north of Everest, undertaken by John de Vars Hazard at the end of the expedition. Ever the loner, he had not headed for the Rongshar valley to recuperate with the rest of the team, but instead had gone back up the Rongbuk valley to lead a survey party, and then had made a second surveying trip to Lhatse, a settlement on the Tsangpo river.

Hazard and Norton replied that they had in fact obtained permission from the governor of Shekar Dzong, but the Tibetan authorities maintained that the excursion violated the terms of their official passport. More generally, as Bailey had written to Hinks in June 1925, the Tibetan government were backtracking on their original permission, saying that they had only allowed the British teams to enter Tibet as an act of kindness and were not keen on another expedition, feeling themselves 'in some degree responsible for the deaths of the people who lost their lives on Everest'.

To add to Hinks's discomfiture, there were persistent rumours that climbers from Germany and America were intending to apply for permission – and, horror of horrors, that his old enemy, George Finch, might even be planning to return to Everest at the head of a Swiss team! None of the rumours turned out to be true, but Hinks did ask his contact at *The Times* to keep a particularly close eye out for any more information on the 'member of the 1922 expedition who was not taken in 1924 who had formed the project of cutting in on his own account'.

While Hinks fretted and schemed at his office in Kensington Gore, the families of Mallory and Irvine struggled to adapt to life without their loved ones. Towards the end of 1924, both their estates were wound up: Mallory had left £1,706; Irvine significantly more, at £3,598. Ruth moved out of Herschel House and went back home to Godalming. Initially she saw it as a temporary relocation, but she never returned and before long the house was sold.

In early 1925 there were reports that a British aviator, Alan Cobham, was planning to make an aerial survey of Everest, but he didn't get above 16,000 feet before his photographer fell ill with altitude sickness. With no prospect of another expedition in the near future, it looked very unlikely that anyone would solve the mystery of how high Mallory and Irvine had been on the mountain and where they now lay.

Not that Ruth wanted her husband's final resting place to be violated. When a former Indian army officer called Barwell offered to go to Everest and bring back his body, she firmly rejected the suggestion: 'I would so much rather my husband's body lay where it does, though I do not know where that is, at least I know that it is in clear clean pure snow and as near to God as he could get on this earth. That he would like it to stay there undisturbed I have no doubt.' It was a sincere and heartfelt wish, but the idea that her husband's body would never be disturbed would turn out to be a forlorn hope.

The urge to solve the mystery and figure out whether Mallory and Irvine were in fact the first men to reach the highest point on earth would not go away, and would lure many subsequent mountaineers to the slopes of Everest. The next attempt to resolve that question came from somewhere entirely different, however: a small house in Paris that briefly became a portal into the spirit world.

The Searchers

It came completely out of the blue.

A package containing a book and a letter from Sir Oliver Lodge, the celebrated physicist, sent to Willie Irvine in Birkenhead in the spring of 1928. 'I'm writing to you on the assumption (I hope not a mistaken one) that you are the father of the young Irvine who heroically lost his life in the Himalayas.' Lodge clearly wasn't absolutely sure of the recipient, but he went on to explain that his new book would include the story of Andrew Irvine's disappearance on Everest.

His was not another Himalayan history, though. As well as being a famous scientist who had made millions on radio patents, Lodge was a paranormal investigator and a prominent member of the Society for Psychical Research. His most famous work, *Raymond: Or Life and Death*, was the story of how he and his wife had used a medium to communicate with their youngest son, Raymond, who was killed in the First World War. In his latest book, a proof copy of which he had included, he was going to narrate a series of further encounters with the recently departed, including Andrew Irvine.

The story began with his friend and fellow spiritualist, the poet Frederic Myers. According to Lodge, in early May 1924 Myers had been in Paris when he heard a message via two psychic friends that danger was 'impending' on Everest. Later that year, Lodge encountered Sir Arnold Lunn, the famous skier, in Switzerland. Lunn had met Irvine in 1923, a few months before he left for Everest, and had been so impressed that he had invited him to join the Alpine Ski Club.

According to Sir Oliver, during the autumn of 1924 he was sent several messages from Irvine to be passed on to Lunn, after a series of seances – some in Paris, some in Bath. They told how Mallory and Irvine had reached the summit and planted a flag but had died on the way down, frozen to death on a narrow ledge 100 feet below. 'After the cold, cold so intense that none of you can grasp what I mean,' Irvine's spirit said, 'came drowsiness and peace; and after that freedom, but some call it death.'

Lodge had passed the messages on to Lunn, who he admitted had been rather sceptical but had nevertheless agreed to allow his name to be included in the book. Lodge wasn't asking for Willie Irvine's permission to include the story, he wrote, as the book was just about to go to print, but he did want to give him advance notice of its publication.

Willie was having none of it. He didn't think any of the messages sounded like his son and told Lodge that he did not approve. Sir Oliver relented, and a few weeks later wrote back to say that the publishers had agreed to remove the passages concerning Everest and that his son's story would not be included.

Lodge was not the first psychic to claim that he had been in touch with Mallory and Irvine, and he would not be the last.

In the 1920s there was a lot of interest in the paranormal, and previous explorers – such as John Franklin, who had disappeared searching for the Northwest Passage in 1845, and Robert Falcon Scott, who had more recently died on his way back from the South Pole – had also allegedly been contacted in the spirit world.

In truth, whatever he claimed, Lodge's story was an embroidered rehash of Odell's version of events. Lodge had added some picturesque details and some purple prose, but essentially he too wanted to believe that Mallory and Irvine had conquered Everest and died of exposure on the descent, rather than in an accident on the way up or down.

It was a theory mooted in, but not entirely endorsed by, a number of books published after 1924, maintaining interest in the story of Everest and the mystery of Mallory and Irvine's disappearance. Even if there still seemed little chance that British mountaineers would return to Everest itself anytime soon, the Everest Committee were keen that Britain's claim to the mountain should not be forgotten.

The official expedition account, *The Fight for Everest*, was published in November 1925. Edward Norton was the lead author, but several other members of the team had also contributed, with Odell writing the chapter on Mallory and Irvine's final climb. Though Norton disagreed, and maintained elsewhere in the book that it was a case of 'not proven', once again he allowed Odell to put forward his theory that there was a 'strong probability that Mallory and Irvine succeeded'.

The Fight for Everest sold reasonably well, but after three official books in four years, it was not the success that everyone had hoped for. This didn't stop the publishers asking for another one a few years later; entitled like the film, *The Epic of Everest*, it was a digest of the previous three official accounts put together by Sir Francis Younghusband. Though the Everest Committee had not paid any of the previous contributors, even when Mallory had asked directly, they awarded Younghusband an honorarium of £100 for his trouble. Younghusband stuck to his by-now familiar theme of Everest as a mystical quest. 'Man, the spiritual,' he declared loftily, 'means to make himself supreme over the mightiest of what is material... The mountain may be high. But he will show that his spirit is higher.'

As to whether Mallory and Irvine had reached the summit, Younghusband sat firmly on the fence: his natural instinct might have been to agree with Martin Conway and Geoffrey Winthrop Young, but mindful of the possibility of a fourth expedition, he didn't want to present Everest as if it had already been climbed. He did argue though with Norton's contention that if Mallory and Irvine had not died in a fall, they would undoubtedly have used their distress flares or torches to call for help on the way down, arguing that they might not have done so for the sake of 'chivalry', knowing that if Odell had seen something, he would have been forced to try to rescue them and put his own life at risk.

In 1927, David Pye published Mallory's first biography, *George Leigh Mallory: A Memoir.* Its aim was to present George in the round, taking him from his days as a schoolboy who had terrified his parents by climbing church towers, to the thoughtful but adventurous student, the valiant soldier and the idealistic school teacher. Pye was not entirely uncritical, being candid about Mallory's impatience and impulsiveness, but he portrayed him as an aesthete, drawn to the mountains for their beauty and their spiritual qualities. 'It is well for us to try to see Everest as Mallory saw it,' Pye wrote. 'To him the attempt was not just an adventure, still less was it an opportunity for record-breaking.

The climbing of the mountain was an inspiration because it signified the transcendence of mind over matter.' Pye did not spend a lot of time speculating on how and where Mallory and Irvine had died, but he did conjure up the image of his friend driving himself relentlessly upwards, propelled by sheer nervous energy until it deserted him right at the end.

Pye's book was well received, but the reviewer for *The Times* concluded that Mallory himself might have contributed to the tragic end of the 1924 expedition. Acknowledging his guilt over the deaths of the seven porters on the North Col in 1922, the reviewer asked 'if both it [1922] and the culminating disaster in which he and Irvine perished, was attributable to his impatience' – though adding in mitigation that Mallory's single-minded pursuit of victory was essential for all human progress, because 'to him and his kind are due the gaining by man of painful inches'.

Dr Gustav Lammer, who reviewed the German edition of *The Fight for Everest*, was more direct in his criticism, focusing in particular on Mallory's choice of Irvine as a climbing partner. 'Why did he select this 22-year-old athlete and oarsman who had accomplished no mountaineering expeditions worthy of mention and was suffering from throat trouble?' Instead, Lammer argued, Mallory should have taken Odell, who 'had brilliantly passed the altitude test'.

Lammer's criticisms were newsworthy enough to be picked up by the *New York Times*, prompting a reply from Colonel Strutt, the climbing leader on the 1922 Everest expedition who had become the editor of the *Alpine Journal*, and Douglas Freshfield, the former president of the Alpine Club. They defended Mallory, arguing that Irvine was no more ill than anyone else on the team, and that Odell had not distinguished himself until right at the end. They did admit, though, 'there are few mountaineers who will not agree, in theory at any rate, with Dr Lammer's stern reasoning. Many of us, including those who know the mountain, are inclined to believe that Mallory and Odell would have achieved the summit and returned.'

Direct criticism from the continent was not the only issue to contend with. Though none of the rumours of a German Everest expedition had proved true, by the end of the 1920s German mountaineers were making the running in the Himalayas. In 1929, a former army officer, Paul Bauer, led a very strong party of Bavarian climbers to Kangchenjunga, the world's third-highest mountain. His young team did not get very high, stopping at 24,300 feet – about 4,000 feet below the summit – but their heroic efforts brought them attention all around the world, with Strutt writing in the *Alpine Journal* that the attempt was a feat 'beyond parallel in the annals of mountaineering'.

The following year, a second, much larger expedition attempted Kangchenjunga. This time it was led by Günter Oscar Dyhrenfurth, the climber known as G.O.D. to his friends. He was another German, though no friend of Bauer's, and he billed the attempt as an 'International Expedition', with climbers from Germany, Austria, Switzerland and Italy – and, from Great Britain, Frank Smythe, the young climber who had been turned down for Everest in 1924 after Howard Somervell judged him a 'bad mountaineer' and an 'intolerable companion'.

Dyhrenfurth's team approached Kangchenjunga from the Nepali side, and though they did not get higher than Bauer, they generated huge amounts of press and publicity. *The Times* sponsored the expedition, with Smythe writing on-the-spot dispatches which he later turned into a very successful book, *The Kangchenjunga Adventure*.

The following year, Bauer returned, this time with an even stronger all-German team. They advanced a little further along the North-East Spur, but once again stopped short of the summit. Though one German and one Sherpa died early on in the attempt, once again Bauer's expedition was hailed as a triumph of guts and tenacity and mountaineering skill. Strutt even managed to exceed his earlier praise in the *Alpine Journal*, declaring that 'for skill, endurance, cold-blooded courage and especially for judgement, the expedition will stand as the classical model for all time'.

While all this activity was taking place in the Himalayas, British requests for a return to Everest were still falling on deaf ears. In 1925, John Noel had laid the blame on the British political officer, Major Bailey, but Bailey left his post in 1928 and nothing changed. Then in March 1931, with renewed rumours of both German and American interest in Everest, the Everest Committee reconvened for the first time in five years. Now sounding a little desperate, Sir Francis Younghusband suggested writing once more to the Dalai Lama to plead their case. 'This country should have a priority,' the Committee minutes recorded, 'in view among [other] things that her Countrymen lay at or near the top.'

Younghusband's reference to Mallory and Irvine's sacrifice was not enough to convince the India Office. They didn't think the Tibetan government would allow anyone else in, and remained 'decidedly against' a further British expedition. They even suggested approaching the Nepali government, after it had allowed the Bauer and Dyhrenfurth teams to enter their territory for their attempts on Kangchenjunga.

There was a big difference, though: Kangchenjunga lay in a remote, underpopulated region in the far east corner of Nepal, very close to the border with Sikkim. Everest, by contrast, was on Nepal's northern frontier, and no one really believed that the Kathmandu government would allow a large British party to travel through the country's heartland. Besides which, after Mallory had popped his head over the West Ridge of Everest in 1921 and seen the icy carnage of the Khumbu Icefall, it seemed unlikely that Everest was climbable from the Nepali side.

In July 1931, Frederick Williamson, the latest political officer, wrote to Hinks, pouring cold water on any notion of an early return to Tibet. It was all Noel's fault, he repeated, for the 'travesties of religious dances' performed on stage in London at his instigation. They had been featured in weekly picture magazines, which had been seen by the Dalai Lama himself as 'an affront to the religion of which he is head'. Noel's unfortunate lamas, he told Hinks, had not yet returned to Tibet, for fear of arrest and punishment, and were currently in exile in Darjeeling and Kalimpong, eking out a meagre existence. Williamson didn't deny the possibility of another British Everest expedition at some point, but he didn't want to push too hard in case a refusal set a precedent for the future.

In October, the India Office further dampened spirits with an official letter in which they announced that they would not bother applying to the Nepali government because informal soundings had convinced them the answer would be negative. It didn't look as if the mystery of what had happened to Mallory and Irvine would be cleared up anytime soon. The Everest Committee still had £5,000 in the bank from royalties and the residue of the last expedition, but with no prospect of a new expedition imminently they began discussing where to invest it for the long term.

Then, utterly out of blue, the India Office wrote to Hinks in August 1932 to announce that their latest political officer,

Colonel Weir, had managed to obtain consent for a fourth British Everest expedition in the following year. An official letter followed from the Dalai Lama reminding everyone of the religious significance of Tibet's mountains and warning any newcomers not to 'give unnecessary trouble to the people of Tibet'. But he had agreed to the expedition, he said, 'in deference to the wishes of the British Government and in order that the friendly relations may not be ruptured'.

With no obvious reason for the Dalai Lama to have changed his mind, it was an astonishing turn of events which surprised everyone in London – but time was of the essence. The Committee had enough money to get things under way and were confident they would get sponsorship from *The Times* or another British newspaper. All they needed was a new team and a leader.

Top of the list was Edward Norton, followed, amazingly, by the now sixty-six-year-old Charles Bruce, but neither man was able to go. After ten years' hard work in an Indian hospital, Howard Somervell didn't feel up to another major expedition either, and Geoffrey Bruce couldn't get out of his army commitments. Noel Odell and Edward Shebbeare were available, as was Colin 'Ferdie' Crawford – one of the climbers from 1922 – but none of them were considered suitable for the leadership role, though Odell was invited to join the climbing team.

Instead, the Committee turned to Hugh Ruttledge, a former civil servant and archetypal 'old Indian hand' who had done a lot of mountaineering in the Kumaun Himalayas of Uttarakhand in north-west India. Aged forty-eight, he was not considered a leading mountaineer, but around him the Committee assembled a very powerful and dynamic group of young climbers, including Percy Wyn-Harris and Jack Longland and four members of the team that had just made the first ascent of 25,000-foot Kamet in India, the highest peak yet to be climbed: Eric Shipton, Dr Raymond Greene, Bill Birnie, and the redoubtable Frank Smythe.

Though very different in background and style, Smythe was in some respects the new George Mallory – a handsome, charismatic public speaker and talented author who was fast becoming the poster boy for British mountaineering. As a climber he had proved himself in the Alps and could claim to be the most experienced high-altitude climber in Britain. A year earlier, he'd even had the temerity to apply directly to the India Office to make a private attempt on Everest when it looked as if the Committee would get nowhere with their grand official expeditions.

The 1933 team's goal was to build on the experience and success of 1924, and to go that extra 1,000 feet to the summit. It was not lost on British newspapers that this would be the first opportunity to work out what had happened to Mallory and Irvine. After all the problems in 1924, there was very little enthusiasm for supplementary oxygen, and Norton and Somervell's record-breaking ascent to 28,000 feet had convinced Smythe and the others that it would be possible to reach the top under their own steam and discover what had really happened in 1924. In November, Noel Odell announced that, because of business commitments, he would not be able to take part. It was a blow to the expedition, but his replacement, Lawrence Wager, was another strong young mountaineer.

Before they left London, Ruttledge spent a lot of time consulting with Norton, developing a plan to acclimatize slowly on the way in; and then, after setting a high camp at around 27,000 feet, to go for the summit. A few oxygen sets would be brought along for use above the North Col 'as a last resort', but it was hoped they would not be needed.

Once again, the great unknown was the weather, but Ruttledge's team did have two advantages in the perennial race against the monsoon: they set off much earlier, leaving Darjeeling in early March, and this time they were equipped with a powerful radio which could both send and receive messages and weather reports. For once *The Times* did not publish expedition dispatches, the *Daily Telegraph* having bid higher for the exclusive rights.

They arrived at Base Camp on 17 April, twelve days earlier than in 1922. Ruttledge had hired seventy-two Sherpas and Bhotias as high-altitude porters, and recruited a contingent of Gurkhas to guard the expedition cash box and organize the camps. Very quickly, as they advanced up the Rongbuk glacier, they began finding evidence of the previous expeditions. The stone huts, or sangars, that had been erected at the first camp way back in 1921 were still standing, and once they reached the Trough – the huge depression in the glacier between the second and third camps – they found old oxygen bottles and broken crampons. Strangely, the cairn built by Howard Somervell in 1924 to commemorate all those who had died on Everest expeditions had gone, but whether it had simply been cannibalized by lamas or yak herders to build shelters, or had been deliberately destroyed was impossible to tell.

Like Norton's expedition nine years earlier, the 1933 team struggled to get from Camp 3 to Camp 4 on the North Col, but this time the topography was as much the problem as the weather. The route taken in 1924 was now a very steeply angled ice wall and was clearly too dangerous to use. Instead, they took a chance and reverted to the 1922 route, but spent a full two weeks putting up fixed ropes and ladders to make it easier and safer for the porters to carry up their loads. At the top, there was nothing to see. The old ledge on which Mallory and Norton had pitched Camp 4 had disappeared, blown away in its entirety by storms and avalanches. Instead, they found another small shelf to pitch their tents, about 250 feet from the crest of the col.

For a week, bad weather and arguments over strategy kept them stuck in their tents, but on 22 May they started up again, aiming to find a site for Camp 5 and then Camp 6, from which they hoped to launch their summit bids. They found no other signs of Mallory and Irvine until further up the North Ridge, where expedition doctor Raymond Greene, the brother of Graham Greene, spotted a pile of about a dozen oxygen cylinders – and a little higher, George Finch's tent from 1922. Cold and exhausted, Greene opened the valve on one of the bottles and was given an instant boost as the oxygen hissed out.

More intriguingly, Greene found a roll of film, which he assumed had been taken by Finch. In 1922, some of his critics had questioned whether Finch really had got as high as he claimed, citing the lack of photos as proof that he was exaggerating, but Finch simply replied that he and Bruce had been too busy getting on with the job of climbing to stop to take photographs.

A three-day storm halted progress, but on 29 May, the British climbers headed back up to establish a new Camp 6 at 27,400 feet – in the middle of the 'Yellow Band', the prominent strip of limestone that ran along the face below the North-East Ridge. Wager, the last-minute replacement for Noel Odell, proved to be such a strong climber that he was chosen to be part of the first summit pair with Wyn-Harris. Longland, another Lakeland climber, went up with them in support, leading a team of porters to their high camp; on the way down, he spotted Mallory and Irvine's Camp 6, last visited by Odell nine years earlier. Inside what was left of their tent he solved one small mystery, finding a working lever torch and a folding candle lantern. Mallory and Irvine must have started off in daylight on 8 June 1924 and either left them behind to save weight, or simply forgotten them; either way it would have been impossible to make any light signals had they been benighted.

The most important discovery came on 30 May, the day of the first summit attempt, by Wager and Wyn-Harris. They set off at 5.30 a.m., planning to roughly follow Mallory's route along the ridge. After about an hour, to his astonishment, Wyn-Harris spotted something a few feet above him: an ice axe in such good condition that it might have been put down the day before. The head was polished, the wooden handle still intact with barely any damage. It lay on a ledge about sixty feet below the ridge crest and 200 yards away from the First Step, the small cliff that interrupted the North-East Ridge as it rose toward the summit.

Wager and Wyn-Harris had other business to complete, so leaving the axe where it lay, they carried on up towards the First Step and, after a quick scout, managed to find a way to traverse around rather than having to scale it directly. When they reached the Second Step, the higher and more formidable interruption to the ridge a few hundred yards further on, they were forced to stop. They could not see a way to regain the ridge without tackling the Second Step head on, but at 28,200 feet it was just too difficult – even for two strong mountaineers. Instead, they changed course and headed for Norton's lower route, aiming for the broad channel – the Great Couloir – that split the face high up.

At around 12.30 p.m. they reached 28,100 feet – Norton's high point in 1924 – but again they found the rock slabs in the couloir covered in loose powdery snow. Even if they could have gone further, it was already too late to get to the summit and back in a day. The next summit party, Shipton and Smythe, were probably already on their way up, and would want to occupy the small, two-man tent at Camp 6. If they came back late, with or without the summit, there would simply be no room.

Wager and Wyn-Harris decided to return to the Second Step to confirm they had not been too hasty in dismissing it. They had a good look around, but once again decided that it was simply too difficult to overcome at that altitude. On the way back down, while Wyn-Harris headed for the First Step to swap his ice axe for the one he had found earlier, Wager climbed up to the crest of the North-East Ridge and looked over onto the 'stupendous, ice-clad' South-East Face. Like Mallory, who'd photographed the East Face on the 1921 reconnaissance and stated that 'other men less wise might attempt this way if they would, but emphatically it was not for us,' Wager did not like what he saw.

Meanwhile, Shipton and Smythe had climbed up as planned to stage a second attempt the following day. On the way up, they thought they saw Wyn-Harris and Wager in the far distance on the North-East Ridge, only to realize later that they had been fooled by the play of light on the rocks. When the two summit pairs met briefly at Camp 6, Wyn-Harris advised Shipton and Smythe to take the Norton route but said that Mallory's ridge route couldn't quite be ruled out.

The two men endured an uncomfortable night and woke to find a storm brewing, which soon became so violent that they had to spend the whole of the next day confined to their tents, fantasizing about the food that they didn't have. The weather improved enough by dawn for them to brave an ascent, but even as they broke camp Shipton was complaining of stomach problems.

He made it past the First Step, but then got slower and slower until he was forced to turn back, leaving Smythe to carry on alone towards the Great Couloir. Smythe was disappointed for Shipton's sake, but he was unphased. He made it across the couloir but, like Wyn-Harris and Wager, he stopped at around 28,100 feet, realizing that the snow conditions made any prospect of progress impossible. It was 11.00 a.m. but he was sure that he couldn't overcome all the difficulties that lay ahead and return safely. 'I remember glancing up at the summit,' he later wrote. 'How pitilessly indifferent, how utterly aloof and detached from my futile graspings and strugglings it appeared!'

It had been an amazing solo effort on Smythe's part, but as he climbed back down towards Camp 6, he felt so oxygen-starved that he developed the strange sensation that someone was climbing down with him. At one stage, he saw mysterious cylindrical objects in the air above – 'Frank's floating teapots', as they were later dubbed. Shipton was there waiting for him, but Smythe was so exhausted that he elected to spend another night at Camp 6 on his own before descending the following day.

Back down on the North Col, as soon as he heard about Wyn-Harris and Wager's first attempt and their surprise discovery of the ice axe, Ruttledge sent a message to the *Daily Telegraph*. Whereas in 1924 it had taken about a week to get news of Mallory and Irvine's disappearance back to London by runner and telegram, Ruttledge's message was published just three days later – telephoned from the North Col to Camp 3, then radioed down to Base Camp before being transmitted onwards to Delhi and then by undersea cable to the *Telegraph*'s offices in Fleet Street.

The sensational discovery of the ice axe was all over the press, prompting renewed speculation over the fate of Mallory and Irvine. Here at last was concrete proof that they had reached

16 April 1933. The men who found the ice
axe in 1933 on the North-East Ridge.

the North-East Ridge, but had they dropped the axe on the way up, or the way down?

The debate played out in the letters pages of the national newspapers, with the bestselling novelist E. F. Benson writing to the *Daily Telegraph*, with slightly tortuous logic, that the position of the axe proved that they must have been going strongly for the top because they couldn't possibly have reached the Second Step climbing with just one ice axe. Therefore, he argued, they must have reached the summit, turned back when it was growing dark, and then made a fatal slip where the axe was found, while groping around for shelter. Another letter-writer in the *Observer* countered that it was more likely to have belonged to Somervell, who had dropped his ice axe on the way down from his attempt with Norton.

On 7 June, in a further demonstration of modern communication technology, the governor of Bengal spoke directly to Frank Smythe at Everest Base Camp by radio from his official residence in Darjeeling. Asked about the axe, Smythe replied that they all thought it was Mallory's because it was stamped with a maker's mark, Willisch of Täsch – a well-known company based in Switzerland, where Mallory had climbed before the 1924 expedition.

It wasn't long before members of the 1924 expedition became directly involved in the debate. Noel Odell, then at Clare College in Cambridge, tried to dampen down the speculation, arguing that the position of the ice axe indicated nothing about where the climbers had died. That it was in such good condition implied that it might not have been involved in an accident at all. Mallory and Irvine might have deliberately left it there on the way up, he wrote, realizing that with very little snow on the rocks above, a second ice axe would not be needed. As to where he had last seen them, Odell admitted that he still could not be sure whether it was the First or Second Step, 'owing to the similar form of these steps in foreshortened profile', but he now believed that it was more likely that he had seen them on the First Step, because the Second Step would have been obscured by projecting rocks.

A month later, in July 1933, Howard Somervell joined the fray. He had been away in Kashmir and had only just heard the story of the ice axe, which had been widely reported in the Indian press. Remembering how he had 'disgraced' himself in 1924 by losing his axe, he said that it was 'almost certainly' his, though he awaited further information on its precise position.

Back on Everest, Ruttledge had brought everyone down the mountain to Base Camp to recuperate. Raymond Greene examined the climbers and pronounced them good to go again, so they trooped back up the Rongbuk glacier; but when they had a look at the slopes leading up to the North Col, they found all the ropes they had fixed so carefully were now buried in snow, perfect conditions for another avalanche – or another retreat. They chose the latter, but Ruttledge then proposed to do what the Everest Committee had always wanted: to stay on into the autumn to make a further attempt after the monsoon. To his great surprise, the Committee declined the offer, telling him that there wasn't enough money left in the kitty to support an extension.

As the team headed back, the *Daily Telegraph* published longer and more detailed reports of Wyn-Harris and Smythe's attempts, along with their own interpretation of the significance of the ice axe and their theory of what had happened to Mallory and Irvine. Wyn-Harris reiterated that most of the climbers thought the axe marked the scene of an accident, and discounted Odell's idea that it had been left there deliberately – on the grounds that no climber would have abandoned his ice axe, especially when it would have been obvious that steps needed to be cut on the way to the summit. Besides, he argued, perched above steep rocky slabs there would be no guarantee it would be there when they returned. As to the slightly more wayward suggestion from Lord Martin Conway – now aged seventy-seven and one of the grand, grand old men of British mountaineering – that the ice axe might have been taken to the summit by Mallory and then been blown off in a storm, only to land 800 feet along the ridge, Wyn-Harris considered it simply absurd.

After communicating directly with the team, Somervell wrote to the *Daily Telegraph* for a second time, now declaring that contrary to what he had said in his first letter, he was certain it was not his ice axe. Apart from the fact that it was far to the east of where he had dropped his, the brand was wrong. As for Hugh Ruttledge, though he had tremendous respect for

Mallory and Irvine, and admitted in the expedition book that he would have *liked* to think they had reached the summit, he had come away convinced that they could not have done it, after hearing descriptions from the climbing team of the dangers of the North-East Ridge, and in particular the virtual impossibility of climbing the Second Step, which Wager and Wyn-Harris had said resembled the prow of a huge ship.

Odell, however, still stuck to his theory that they had made it. When someone proposed that, like Shipton and Smythe, he might have confused the play of light on the rocks for the two climbers or even mistaken them for a pair of Himalayan birds, he reacted with irritation, insisting that he had been the last person to see Mallory and Irvine in 1924. It might have been the First Step not the Second as he had originally thought, but he was sure that it had been them.

The discovery of the ice axe was an important new piece of information which indicated that at very least Mallory and Irvine had got high on the mountain, but the ensuing debate proved how complicated it was to interpret any 'clues' and how difficult it was to be definitive. Mallory and Irvine clearly had been very high, but it was still impossible to say whether they had dropped the axe on the way up or on the way down. As to its provenance, almost everyone continued to assume that it was Mallory's, and the Alpine Club even fixed a brass plate on it to say so, but when Odell saw it, he noticed something: two-thirds of the way up the wooden shaft there were three parallel notches, similar to markings used by Sandy Irvine to identify his equipment.

One of Irvine's relatives dug out an officer's 'swagger stick' owned by Sandy when he was in the cadet force at Shrewsbury School which had almost exactly the same pattern. Further investigation of the archives revealed that the organizers of the 1924 expedition had bought a batch of Willisch ice axes to be used as general expedition equipment, so it looked as if Irvine had taken one of them and marked it up to identify which was his. The brass plate was subsequently removed.

Of course, whether the axe belonged to Mallory or Irvine did not settle the arguments as to why exactly it had ended up on some rocks below the North-East Ridge. More information was needed to decide how and when any accident might have taken place. Fortunately, the Tibetan government kept the door open.

In 1935, Eric Shipton led what was billed as a reconnaissance rather than a full expedition. Though hailed as one of the stars of British mountaineering, his approach was profoundly at odds with that of the Everest 'establishment'. Instead of huge teams laying siege to a mountain, he was much more comfortable keeping everything small and low-key, living off local food rather than luxury goods from Fortnum and Mason.

Though Shipton encountered remarkably good weather and a mountain relatively free of snow, he chose to spend most of his time mapping the area around Everest and reconnoitring possible new routes, rather than making an all-out attack on the summit. His expedition was the first to include Tenzing Norgay, who made his debut aged twenty-one as a high-altitude porter, but Shipton did not try to get very far up Everest, only reaching the North Col in mid-July – by which time the upper slopes of Everest were plastered with snow and unclimbable. Shipton's party returned to Britain without any guilt, though: they had made twenty-six first ascents of peaks over 20,000 feet, even if they'd made no headway on Everest.

Shipton had found nothing new pertaining to Mallory and Irvine, but he did make one shocking discovery: the body of

Maurice Wilson, the traumatized British veteran of the First World War who had made an illicit solo attempt on Everest in 1934. Wilson was an aviator who had flown all the way to India before hiring a small group of Sherpas in Darjeeling and crossing into Tibet disguised as a monk. Though he had no mountaineering experience, he had managed to get up the Rongbuk glacier to Camp 3 at the foot of the North Col.

At this point, Wilson had left his Sherpas and was never seen again.

Shipton's party found his dead body in the snow, next to the tattered remains of a tent, ironically just a few hundred yards away from a cache of food left by Ruttledge's 1933 expedition. Shipton recovered Wilson's diary and then helped bury him in a crevasse, wrapped in the remains of his tent.

The following year Shipton was back, with a huge new British expedition, led once again by Hugh Ruttledge. For the second time, he had assembled a very powerful climbing party, which included several members of the 1933 team as well as John Morris, the transport officer from 1922, but even though they managed to get dozens of Sherpas up to the North Col, the early arrival of the monsoon put paid to any hope of getting high on the mountain.

In the British press, George Finch vented his fury at yet another failed Everest expedition, telling the *Morning Post*, 'We are beginning to make ourselves look very ridiculous.' Finch put the blame squarely on the now even more elderly Everest Committee, arguing that the RGS should have nothing more to do with organizing expeditions or selecting teams. 'Everest is now a climbing job,' he declared, 'and that job should be in the hands of climbers.' His words fell on deaf ears. In 1938 the Everest Committee organized another expedition, this time led by Eric Shipton's friend and regular climbing partner, Bill Tilman. They did a little better than the 1936 party, reaching 27,200 feet, but again did not get high enough to make an attempt on the summit and did not come back with any new information about Mallory and Irvine's last hours.

Not that Ruth Mallory minded. She treasured George's memory but, save the odd letter to Hinks, she had not really kept in touch with the mountaineering world in the years after her husband's death, though she had stayed part of his Cambridge friendship circle. She continued to live with her father in Godalming, bringing up her three children in the spirit of which George would have approved. They skinny-dipped in local rivers, learned to climb, first on trees then at the seaside and later in Snowdonia, and eventually all went to Cambridge – Clare to study history, Beridge to take natural sciences, and John Mallory to follow his father to Magdalene College.

In 1939, after fifteen years on her own, Ruth was remarried to Will Arnold Foster, a family friend and member of the Bloomsbury Group who had been close to George. They spent three happy years together until tragically Ruth developed cancer. Mallory's friend Geoffrey Keynes, by then an eminent surgeon, operated on her, but though the tumour did not seem to have spread, she died on 1 June 1942, just nine days before her fifty-first birthday, from what Keynes called 'an obscure secondary cause'.

Five years later, another severe blow was dealt to the Mallory family when George's younger brother, Trafford, died in an air crash in the French Alps. After learning to fly in the Great War, he had risen through the ranks of the Royal Air Force, to become acting air chief marshal, one of its most senior ranks. In November 1944, Trafford was on his way to South-East

Asia to take up a new command along with his wife and closest aides, when in very bad weather his plane crashed into a peak close to Grenoble. Initially no wreckage was found and it was feared that, like George, his body might never be recovered. But seven months later, in June 1945, melting snow revealed the wreckage of the plane, along with Trafford and his wife and eight others. They were subsequently buried in a village cemetery in the nearby mountains.

As for finding George Mallory's body, there seemed even less chance of that. In 1939, Himalayan mountaineering had stopped when Germany invaded Poland. The Second World War was as brutal and all-consuming as the first. Both India and China were dragged into the conflict, and apart from Heinrich Harrer and Peter Aufschnaiter, members of the 1939 Austro-German expedition to Nanga Parbat, who both spent most of the war exiled in Lhasa, European and American climbers stayed away from the Himalayas.

Eventually, Himalayan climbing began again, but there was one major difference. After the invasion of Tibet by China in 1950, the northern approach to Everest, and all the other peaks that straddled the border, was closed off to the West. There would be no further British climbers on the North-East Ridge for decades to come.

At the same time, fearing invasion by either China or its other new neighbour, the Republic of India, the Nepali government reversed its age-old policy and for the first time opened its border to outsiders. Within a few years an American party had visited the southern side of Everest, followed shortly by Eric Shipton, by then the British public's new 'Mr Everest', who made the first proper reconnaissance of the southern side and the infamous Khumbu Icefall, first seen and photographed by George Mallory in 1921. Despite Mallory's very negative assessment of its viability as a climbing route, Shipton and his team managed to get almost all the way through the icefall to the edge of the Western Cwm before they were stopped by a huge crevasse.

They planned to come back to explore further, but later that year the British climbing establishment – who had re-established the old Everest Committee as the Joint Himalayan Committee – got a rude shock when the Nepali government gave permission for not one but two Swiss expeditions to Everest in 1952. The first, in the spring, almost succeeded in getting to the top, with Raymond Lambert and Tenzing Norgay reaching 28,200 feet on the South-East Ridge, just higher than Edward Norton's pre-war record on the other side of the mountain. The second attempt in the autumn was less successful, but it was clear that Britain's monopoly was over.

When the ninth official British Everest expedition set off for Kathmandu in early 1953, its leader, John Hunt, knew that if his team didn't reach the summit that year, there were rival parties from France, Switzerland and the US queuing up to have a crack at the world's highest mountain.

In the end, Hunt's expedition succeeded, with the New Zealander Ed Hillary and Tenzing Norgay reaching the summit on 29 May 1953. Hillary, a great student of Himalayan history who had read all the books about the pre-war British expeditions and been inspired by Mallory, immediately started to look for evidence that Mallory and Irvine might have preceded him to the summit, but he found nothing. He took photographs in all directions and peered down over the North-East Ridge, before concluding that Mallory's route looked much tougher than the ridge that he and Tenzing had just taken to the top.

In the following years there was a succession of Everest expeditions from the Nepali side, but with China barring entry to Tibet there seemed to be no hope that anything more would be discovered about the fate of Mallory and Irvine. Then, in 1960, to widespread surprise in the West, the Chinese government announced that a large half-Tibetan, half-Chinese team had just reached the summit following Mallory's route, climbing the Second Step and, after a heroic effort, reaching the top on 25 May. According to official sources the Chinese climbers left a bust of Mao Zedong, a flag and a note, but there was no mention of finding any trace of Mallory or Irvine on the summit or anywhere else along the route. The Chinese claim was greeted with considerable scepticism by British mountaineers. In 1952, there had been a flood of rumours that a Russian team had made a similar ascent from the Tibetan side, leaving a statue of Stalin on the summit snows. Their claim had been widely dismissed, and so too was that of the Chinese, especially because they offered very little photographic evidence to back it up.

By the end of the sixties, Everest had been climbed thirty-three times, and Nepal had become a go-to destination for Western tourists. Some of them stuck to Kathmandu but a growing number were joining organized treks in the Himalayas, even as far as Everest Base Camp. Tenzing Norgay was running a travel company and Ed Hillary had built the first schools and medical centres under the auspices of the Himalayan Trust. Theirs were the two names most associated with Everest, and with no sign that the 'Jade Curtain' between Tibet and Nepal would come down any time soon, there was little interest in the pre-war expeditions.

Then, in October 1970, there was a sudden flurry of press when the BBC broadcast a new documentary, *The Mystery*

of Mallory and Irvine, based around interviews with three of
the remaining members of the 1924 team: Howard Somervell,
John Noel and Noel Odell. It was the first TV documentary
to review the early Everest expeditions, and as well as long,
detailed interviews there was archive film from John Noel's *Epic
of Everest* which had not been seen for many years.

Odell repeated his account of spotting the two climbers for
the final time, pushing on towards the summit. 'I have even
thought at times they reached the top of Everest,' he said, slightly
cagily. Noel remembered Mallory writing letter after letter in
his tent to his friends and family, but said that 'he knew that the
mountain would get him in the end'. Recalling his own summit
bid, Somervell admitted wryly that they ultimately failed because
'we were two ordinary mortals and could not do any better',
before going on to say that he had never quite understood why
Mallory chose to take Irvine – but suspected that it was because
of a 'half promise' made at the beginning of the expedition. Noel
agreed that by the end Odell was probably the best-acclimatized
member of the team, and continued his fatalistic theme that
Mallory had pushed on towards the summit on 8 June 1924,
even though he had known that to do so would mean never
coming back.

As the film wound to a conclusion, Somervell repeated the
idea that the ice axe found in 1933 had marked the site of the
final fatal slip, and finished by declaring that all worthwhile
adventures had an element of risk attached and that 'death in
battle against a mountain is a far finer and nobler thing than
death in battle against an enemy whom you are trying to kill'.

This was a powerful end to the documentary, but there was
a far more throwaway remark from Somervell earlier in the film
that would have greater significance and kick-start a renewed

push to find out what had really happened to Mallory and Irvine. Over archival footage of the mountain, Somervell recalled how he had loaned his camera to Mallory but that it had never come back. 'If ever Mallory's body was found,' he said, 'I wonder if the camera will still be in his pocket, and development of the film preserved in ice for perhaps 100 or 200 years will be capable of producing any pictures. If so, we may find out whether or not he reached the top.'

Somervell didn't realise it at the time, but he had just fired the starting gun on a new race to find out exactly what had happened high on Everest on 8 June 1924.

The Vest Pocket Kodak. Introduced in 1912, it stayed in production until 1935, by which time more than 2 million units had been sold.

12

A Tale of Two Photos

In the summer of 1930, a Norwegian sealing ship, the *Bratvaag*, stopped at Kvitøya, a remote, desolate island in the Svalbard archipelago. Usually encircled by a thick band of ice and shrouded in dense fog, it had only been visited a handful of times. Two hunters went ashore to search for walrus, while a party of scientists, the other element of the expedition, remained aboard the ship.

The hunters were kept busy, but at the end of the day the captain returned with some astonishing news: not only were the hunters coming back with several carcasses, they had also found something truly unexpected – the last resting place of the Swedish explorer Salomon August Andrée and his two companions, photographer Nils Strindberg, the second cousin of the famous playwright, and an engineer named Knut Fraenkel.

Thirty-three years earlier, in July 1897, the three Swedes had flown off from Danes Island in the far north of Spitsbergen in a huge hydrogen balloon, the *Svea*, aiming to become the first men to reach the North Pole; but after a flight that lasted just under 300 miles, they came down on the pack ice. Lacking any way to reinflate the balloon, they abandoned the *Svea* and began man-hauling their equipment across the ice in a small boat, heading for an emergency food cache that had been deposited on Franz Josef Land. They didn't reach it and were never seen again. Despite intense press speculation and countless rumours and apocryphal tales of homing pigeons carrying messages back to Sweden, nothing was found of them until 1930.

When news of the *Bratvaag*'s remarkable discovery reached Sweden, it was front-page news and soon became a huge international story. Interest in polar exploration was at its height, after recent attempts by aviators from America and Europe to fly to the North Pole in planes and airships. What made this story truly remarkable was that, as well the bodies and a lot of equipment, they had also found a diary and several cameras and rolls of film.

Initially, no one held out any hope that the images could be salvaged from film that had expired three decades earlier, but working with Hasselblad, the famous manufacturer that had supplied the expedition with state-of-the-art cameras, Swedish technicians were able to develop the exposed stock and produce an extraordinarily good set of prints from photographs taken by Andrée and his team, chronicling the end of the expedition and their desperate trip across the ice. Colour stock deteriorates quickly, but because black-and-white film is so much cruder in chemical terms, it has much greater longevity.

When in 1933 Raymond Greene found a tin of film high on Everest near an old camp previously occupied by George Finch, he wondered if it could be another 'Andrée moment' and if this relic might also reveal some amazing secret about the 1922 or even the 1924 expedition. It was not to be. When the film was developed there was nothing on it, but the idea that there might be some abandoned piece of equipment high on Everest – or, even better, the camera Howard Somervell told the BBC he had loaned to Mallory – did offer the possibility that, in similar fashion, the 'mystery of Mallory and Irvine' might one day be solved.

Not that finding the missing camera was ever going to be easy. Unlike the large format cameras carried by the Swedish balloonists, Somervell's Vest Pocket Kodak was tiny, built for soldiers and adventurers and designed, as the name suggested, to take up the minimum amount of space. Somervell had used it in 1922 and 1924 before lending it to Mallory, and had come back with memorable photographs of Edward Norton and George Mallory high on the mountain; but even if the camera was still there, the problem remained of getting access to the north side of Everest.

When the BBC transmitted *The Mystery of Mallory and Irvine* in 1970, China was still closed to the West, so there was no immediate prospect of anyone chasing down Somervell's camera. This didn't kill interest in the story, though. In the spring of 1971, the journal *Mountain* published an article by an American computer engineer called Tom Holzel. He was a self-confessed 'light-duty' climber who had become interested in Everest after reading a long travel piece on Nepal in the *New Yorker* magazine by the travel writer Jeremy Bernstein. The article focused on the nascent trekking industry but included a resumé of Everest's climbing history and the intriguing tale of Mallory's disappearance and the discovery of the ice axe in 1933.

Holzel had never been to Everest, but he was smitten and consumed every book he could lay his hands on before coming up with a radical new version of what might have happened on that fateful day in June 1924, if Mallory and Irvine had

separated. It was speculative, he admitted, but backed up by
a lot of historical analysis, as well as a review of more recent
developments in high-altitude mountaineering – and in particular
the impact of oxygen on climbing rates.

According to Holzel, after reaching the top of the Second
Step, Mallory and Irvine had faced a moment of crisis. They
didn't have enough oxygen to reach the summit, so instead they
either pressed on, knowing that it would probably run out, or
decided to separate – Irvine heading back down towards the
safety of their final camp, and Mallory carrying on alone, having
somehow shared Irvine's remaining oxygen. This enabled him
to reach the top and achieve his ambition, but both he and
Irvine died on the descent: Irvine in the vicinity of where the
ice axe was found, Mallory either on the summit pyramid itself
or lower down.

Holzel maintained that, after the expedition, Norton and
the British climbing establishment had downplayed the chances
that Mallory could have succeeded, because it diminished their
own achievements and also proved the case for oxygen.

It was a provocative piece, which simultaneously presented
Mallory as a victim whose triumph on Everest had been denied
by the British climbing establishment because of their 'almost
universal prejudice against the use of oxygen', and a villain
who had left Irvine to climb down alone because he was so
fixated on getting to the top. Subsequently, Holzel qualified his
theory, arguing that Mallory's might have decided to separate for
Irvine's own good – taking him out of danger– and pointing out
that there were plenty of examples of British climbers splitting
forces high on Everest. It prompted a fierce rebuttal from Percy
Wyn-Harris, now Sir Percy – the man who had found Irvine's
ice axe in 1933.

In his reply, published in a subsequent edition of *Mountain* in 1972, Wyn-Harris argued that Holzel had misunderstood and misconstrued the motives and behaviour of both Norton and Mallory, and that a lot of his calculations and assumptions on climbing rates and oxygen equipment were simply wrong. As for the idea that Mallory could have left the inexperienced Irvine to descend on his own, it was utterly inconceivable. 'At this point, Mr Editor, you will be glad to know words fail me,' he wrote starkly at the end of his article.

Holzel refused to back down and almost seemed to relish the battle with the 'Old Guard' and 'anti-oxygenists'. At the very least, he had put the story back into the public eye. He began corresponding with Audrey Salkeld, a leading British mountaineering historian and picture researcher. They didn't always agree, but together they amassed a huge body of biographical information relating to Mallory, much of it unpublished, and wrote a book together, also called *The Mystery of Mallory and Irvine*. But Holzel was not interested in just building a paper mountain; he felt the only way to resolve the mystery was to go to Everest and stage a dedicated research expedition, which would systematically comb the mountain for artefacts and, crucially, find definitive photographic evidence.

In 1953, after taking his famous image of Tenzing on the summit, Ed Hillary had turned his camera on Makalu, the nearby 8,000-metre peak that he hoped would be his next conquest. If Holzel could find Mallory's camera, and if it contained a similar image of Makalu – or another high shot that could only have been taken from the summit – it would prove that Mallory had got there first. If he found Irvine's camera, he hoped that it might include an image of Mallory at the top of the Second Step, heading for the summit.

While Tom Holzel dreamed and schemed about a future research expedition, back in Britain a very different kind of photographic evidence was being discussed from an even more obscure though not totally unexpected quarter: the spirit world. In 1974, Clement Williamson, like Sir Oliver Lodge a member of the Society for Psychical Research, wrote to Noel Odell to say that a medium called Walter Gray had recently received some messages from Andrew Irvine concerning his climb with Mallory.

Gray's psychically inspired version of events was much more familiar than Holzel's theory. He told Odell that, on 8 June 1924, Mallory and Irvine had endured a lot of problems with their oxygen sets at the beginning of the day, but had reached the summit together at 2.30 p.m. Mallory had indeed taken some images at the summit, and additionally he had left a photograph of a woman – his wife Ruth, Walter Gray assumed – at the top. Then, on the way down, Mallory had slipped when he was un-roped, and had fallen down a huge couloir, leaving Irvine to carry on alone until he eventually sat down and fell asleep, only to wake up again with Mallory's spirit looking down on him.

Williamson asked for photographs and any mementos that might help channel Irvine's spirit in future seances, so Odell got in touch with John Noel, who obliged with a studio portrait of Mallory and an image of Irvine in Spitsbergen in 1923. Neither Noel nor Odell dismissed the story, but when they contacted Howard Somervell, he was less impressed. Irvine's brother Kenneth, who met Odell in Perth, was not convinced either, scorning any messages from 'across the Styx'. There was nothing in Williamson's story that was new, apart from one detail: the idea that Mallory had left a photograph of Ruth at the summit. In the admittedly unlikely event that it was found there, it would offer a different kind of photographic evidence of Mallory and Irvine's triumph.

The problem remained getting into Tibet. Holzel contacted George H. W. Bush, then the chief US liaison officer in Bejing, to ask him to intercede. The only help he could offer was a few words of encouragement: 'Don't give up!' Holzel got so frustrated that he even devised a plan to get a permit to attempt nearby Makalu and then secretly cross the border into Tibet. In 1975 the permit came through, but the complicated political situation at the time led him to pull out of his undercover expedition.

It was a good thing too, for in the same a year an enormous Chinese expedition arrived on the Rongbuk glacier with a small army of 410 climbers and Sherpas. After spending weeks hacking their way up the mountain, the nine-strong summit team reached the top via Mallory's ridge route, but this time they brought a metal ladder which they installed on the Second Step, at the most difficult section at the top. In order to squash any scepticism from the West, they didn't just photograph themselves; they left a tall survey tripod which was so prominent that it was soon appearing in everyone's summit photographs.

Some European climbers thought that the whole thing was excessive in scale and the ascent had not been made in the correct 'style', but there was at least one unexpected development: in 1979, the Chinese government reopened the north side of Everest to outsiders, starting with a joint Chinese-Japanese reconnaissance expedition to be followed by a full-scale attempt in 1980. Tom Holzel immediately wrote to the Japanese Alpine Club, to ask them to keep a lookout for a body and a camera on a snow terrace he had identified from photographs and maps at around 27,000 feet. Positioned more or less directly in the fall line of the ice axe found in 1933, the terrace seemed a likely location for where Mallory or Irvine might have landed after an accident higher up.

Unfortunately, the 1979 Everest expedition hit the familiar problem of severe weather and was called off after an avalanche on the North Col claimed the lives of three Chinese climbers and almost killed the Japanese climbing leader, a Buddhist monk called Ryoten Hasegawa, who was left with five broken ribs. They found no new pieces of equipment or evidence of Mallory and Irvine, but Hasegawa returned to Japan with something almost as dramatic: an extraordinary story about one of the Chinese climbers who had died below the North Col.

That Chinese climber was called Wang Hongbao and he had also been part of the successful 1975 expedition. On the day before he died, Hasegawa had been quizzing him about the body of Maurice Wilson, the maverick British climber who had perished close to Camp 3 in 1934. His body had been found a year later by Eric Shipton and buried in a crevasse, but Hasegawa had heard that his remains had somehow come to the surface and been spotted by the Chinese team. Was it true? Wang confirmed that it was, and that he had seen the bones himself – but, to Hasegawa's amazement, added that he had also seen the body of another 'English dead' much higher up the mountain, at between 26,500 and 27,000 feet, sitting upright with a prominent gash on his cheek. Wang recalled that when he had touched the tattered clothing, 'it flew into pieces and they danced on his breath'.

When Hasegawa told this to Japan's *Asahi* newspaper, there was a huge amount of publicity which led to offers of significant sponsorship for the follow-up expedition in 1980. The only English climbers who had died high on Everest in any of the pre-war expeditions were Mallory and Irvine, so it had to be one of them. If Tom Holzel was right, and Mallory had perished close to the summit, then most likely Wang Hongbao had seen

Irvine's body lower down, especially if it was anywhere near the fall line from the ice axe found in 1933.

It was impossible to confirm the sighting or get any more details, because Wang left no diary or written notes, but a few months later, in the winter of 1980, the Japanese expedition set off for Tibet. With a reported budget of $4 million according to the *New York Times* it was the most expensive undertaking in mountaineering history, its aim to lay siege to Everest and find 'the most famous of all climbers'. Eastman Kodak had been contacted and had confirmed that if the Japanese climbers found any film, they would probably be able to develop it.

Not everyone approved. Bernard Levin, the respected British critic, wrote a piece for *The Times* in which he argued that however well-meaning the expedition organizers, Mallory and Irvine should be left to rest in peace, undisturbed. The expedition went ahead anyway, arriving at Base Camp on the Rongbuk glacier via an improved Chinese road, with twenty-five tons of supplies and seven cameras attached to the latest video-tape recorders. They managed to put four team members on the summit – two via the North-East Ridge route and two via the North Face – but they did not find the bodies of either Mallory or Irvine, nor any Vest Pocket Kodaks.

The failure of the Japanese expedition did not deter Tom Holzel. He contacted several subsequent expeditions to the north side to ask if he might join them until, after many years of thinking and planning, he finally got permission to stage his own dedicated search expedition in 1986. As well as Audrey Salkeld, he recruited David Breashears, an award-winning cameraman who specialized in high-altitude photography, and Andy Harvard, a very strong mountaineer and veteran of three attempts on Everest's very difficult and dangerous Kangshung Face.

It was a complicated and expensive business to stage an Everest expedition in 1986, so by the time they arrived on the mountain, their team had swollen to include a BBC documentary producer, Alistair Macdonald, and three top female climbers who were aiming to become the first American women to reach the summit. The plan was to make not one but three new documentaries: one for the BBC, which would include fresh interviews with Odell and Noel as well as Ed Hillary; one for the US network ABC, focusing on the women; and one by David Breashears and Andy Harvard's company, Arcturus Films, for general distribution.

Once again, the proposed search prompted controversy, with both Hillary and the British mountaineering writer Jim Perrin arguing in the press that Mallory and Irvine should be left in peace. A transatlantic schism was developing, which would linger for the next few decades, with Americans criticizing a lack of curiosity on the British side, and British climbers arguing that it was more important not to disturb the bodies than to attempt to solve the 'mystery' of Mallory and Irvine.

It's worth remembering that if Holzel or the Japanese team had succeeded, Mallory and Irvine would not have been the first explorers to be have been disturbed posthumously. As Levin admitted in 1980, at one point there had been a plan to retrieve Francis Drake's body, which had been buried at sea off Portobelo in Panama. That plan had been abandoned, but in 1968 Chauncey C. Loomis, the American academic, travelled to a remote corner of Greenland to exhume the body of the Arctic explorer Charles Francis Hall, in an attempt to prove his theory that Hall had been poisoned by the crew of his ship. Afterwards, forensic analysis of his hair and fingernails did find traces of arsenic, but there was no conclusive evidence as to how it had got there.

Holzel didn't expect to have to do anything so invasive, but he hoped that if he found Irvine or Mallory, there might be a camera nearby or somewhere in their clothing. Now renamed the Mount Everest North Face Research Expedition (MENFREE), its members arrived on the Rongbuk glacier at the end of August 1986 to find themselves sharing Everest Base Camp with a small Chilean student team, in disarray after one of its climbers had died, and a larger British team who were trying to climb the Pinnacles, a notoriously difficult feature close to the point where the North Ridge meets the North-East Ridge.

Initially conditions were good and confidence was high. Holzel had come equipped with a specially calibrated metal detector set up to identify a Vest Pocket Kodak, and a patent oxygen system that he hoped would enable him to spend a long time on the snow terrace at 27,000 feet where he thought any bodies were most likely to be. He spent several days at Advance Base Camp and got an early boost when he found two oxygen bottles from the 1922 expedition, but ultimately his expedition foundered due to the familiar story of bad weather and heavy snowfall. Just as Holzel was about to leave for the expedition's high camps, a Sherpa, Dawa Neru, was killed in an avalanche while descending from the North Col. After that, with the weather continuing to deteriorate and morale low, the expedition broke up and everyone went their separate ways – Audrey Salkeld to work on the BBC documentary, which eventually reached the screens as an episode of *Wideworld* in 1988, and Tom Holzel to return to his computer business in America.

After so many years thinking about Everest, it was deeply frustrating, but there was one small compensation at the end of his trip when Holzel stopped off in Bejing to interview a climber called Zhang Junyan, who had shared a tent with Wang Hangbao in 1975. Zhang was tall by Chinese standards and a tough-looking customer, but Holzel got straight to the point: had Wang also told him about finding the 'English dead' all those years ago? Zhang had not seen anything himself, and had been in his sleeping bag when Wang went out for twenty minutes, but he was able to confirm the story, saying that Wang had found a body and told other Chinese climbers. It was fulfilling to hear Hasegawa's story corroborated, but having spent so much time and money on what had proved to be a fruitless search, Holzel was not about to return to Everest any time soon. His books and his tenacity, however, would have a long-lasting and significant impact.

Over the next decade there were no more dedicated searches, though there were several further climbing expeditions to the North side. Mallory's grandson, George Mallory II, reached the summit in 1995 with an American team, and left a photograph of Ruth and George there – to fulfil a promise made many years earlier, he told the *Otago Daily Times*. Occasionally climbers did encounter traces of previous expeditions, with a pair of ancient-looking oxygen cylinders spotted by an American mountain guide, Eric Simonson, in 1991, below the crest of the North-East Ridge, but there were no other significant discoveries. British television continued to be fascinated by Everest, with the actor Brian Blessed starring in a lavish documentary feature on Mallory, *Galahad of Everest*, in 1991, and a follow-up made in 1995 in which he attempted to climb Everest at the age of sixty, but most of the BBC's Everest programming from this period focused on Hillary and Tenzing's ascent in 1953.

On the mountain, things were changing with a new type of expedition appearing at base camps on both sides of Everest, in which climbers paid around $50,000 to join ad hoc teams put together by commercial climbing companies. Gone were the days when the Nepali government only allowed attempts by one or two 'national' teams every year. Instead, more and more permits were issued, so that in any season there might be several different teams on the mountain simultaneously. The elite climbers who had taken part in the climbs of the 1970s and 1980s were replaced by a new type of 'client' who paid their way onto expeditions.

For some, this represented a democratization of Himalayan climbing, along the lines of what had happened in the Alps in the late nineteenth century. For others it was a desecration of the world's ultimate peak, and brought with it mountains of trash and inexperienced climbers with inevitable consequences. This era was brilliantly captured in 1996 by the American writer Jon Krakauer, who was commissioned to write an article about the new Everest 'business' for the magazine *Outside*, joining a team led by the New Zealand climber and expedition leader Rob Hall. Krakauer managed to get to the top, but the 1996 Everest season was one of the deadliest on record, with a total of eight climbers dying in the spring – including Hall and a very experienced mountain leader from the US, Scott Fischer.

Into Thin Air, the book chronicling his experience that Krakauer published the following year, was a huge international success. Its sensational stories of abandoned bodies and rich socialites hiring Sherpas to haul their laptops up Everest's slopes might have appeared to be a cautionary tale, exposing the risks of the new era of Himalayan climbing, but it had the opposite effect. Commercial climbing companies were inundated with enquiries from potential clients wanting to take on Everest.

Previously, America's press and media had never been that interested in mountaineering, but following the success of *Into Thin Air* and all the other publicity around the events of 1996, suddenly they woke up to Everest. As more and more people began to learn of its early history, interest grew in George Mallory and his pioneering expeditions. The idea that without sat-phones, down clothing and all the paraphernalia of high-tech modern climbing, he and Irvine could have reached the summit back in 1924 seemed ever more attractive in an increasingly complicated and technologized world.

Paradoxically, this renewed interest in Everest's early history coincided with the rise of something absolutely new: the world wide web. Initially only a small number of people had access to the home computers needed to ride the 'information superhighway', but by the mid-1990s mountaineering was being drawn into the digital age, with websites like EverestNews.com and MountainZone.com that specialized in high-altitude climbing. Most of their coverage was contemporary, but they also became a forum for discussing historical questions such as the fate of Mallory and Irvine. In 1998, by some act of mountaineering serendipity, three history buffs, who had never met before, came together with one aim in mind: to renew the search for photographic evidence and solve the mystery of what precisely had happened in 1924.

It started with an American amateur climber and marketing director, Larry Johnson. In 1998, he began corresponding with a young German geology student, Jochen Hemmleb. Inspired by the work of Audrey Salkeld and Tom Holzel, Hemmleb had become fascinated by the Mallory and Irvine story, and was now sharing his theories on EverestNews.com. He had amassed a large collection of photographs, in an attempt to precisely identify where the 'English dead' discovered by Wang Hangbao might be located. Like Holzel, he realized that the only way to solve the mystery was to go to Everest and hunt for physical evidence, but as an impecunious student he thought it unlikely that he would ever be able to follow up his theories in the field.

At the same time, over in England, another Everest aficionado was trying to get an Everest search expedition off the ground. Graham Hoyland was a BBC sound recordist who had worked on Brian Blessed's *Galahad of Everest* documentary, and had also climbed Everest in 1993, becoming the fifteenth Briton to reach the summit. But that wasn't all: he was a relative of Howard Somervell and had heard directly his story about loaning a camera to Mallory the day before he left for his summit attempt in 1924.

The BBC had regularly made anniversary films to commemorate Hillary and Tenzing's ascent, but Hoyland tried to persuade his bosses to commission a film for 1999, on the seventy-fifth anniversary of Mallory and Irvine's disappearance, that would help fund a proposed new search expedition. Eventually, after a lot of complicated negotiations, it was agreed the BBC team of Hoyland and Peter Firstbrook, a very experienced producer, would join forces with Johnson and Hemmleb and use an American company, International Mountain Guides (IMG), to organize and run a joint research expedition.

It wasn't easy to get the money together for the documentary or the expedition itself. Having recently paid for several other Everest films, and knowing from previous expeditions that the odds of finding anything were low, BBC commissioning editors dragged their heels over what would inevitably be an expensive project. They were not willing to cover the cost of the film in its entirety, so eventually Firstbrook put together a consortium of broadcasters – including the BBC, BBC Worldwide, the German channel ZDF, and the American channel PBS, who for many years had broadcast a very successful science series, *Nova*, which had recently made several Everest films.

Meanwhile, over in the US, Eric Simonson – one of the founders of IMG, and the same guide who had found the ancient-looking oxygen bottle on Everest in 1991 – had taken charge of the mountaineering aspects of the search expedition and recruited a strong team of climbers. It included some previous Everest summiteers and some younger members with a lot of promise, most notably Conrad Anker, who was widely regarded as the most exciting prospect of his generation. With the TV money only covering part of the costs of the expedition, estimated at $300,000 (about $550,000 in today's money), the American team approached several companies for sponsorship, ranging from Lincoln cars to mountaineering equipment manufacturers such as Mountain Hardwear and Lowe Alpine. They also cut a deal with the website MountainZone.com, who agreed to put a substantial sum of money into the expedition in return for exclusive coverage.

It was the first expedition since Tom Holzel's to have the specific purpose of searching for evidence of the 1924 expedition, but there was some scepticism about the odds of anything being found. As the well-known American mountaineering author David Roberts later wrote, 'most observers however viewed the expedition as something of a boondoggle – one more stratagem to finance an expensive outing on the world's highest mountain'.

Simonson's biggest worry was money. Bureaucratic and contractual delays had held up initial payments from the BBC and *Nova*, and this was having a knock-on effect on some sponsors whose funding would only come in once all the TV money had been paid. Things got so tense, as Simonson later admitted, that when Firstbrook and the BBC film crew arrived in Kathmandu to join the climbers for the journey into Tibet, he threatened not to take them on the bus if the BBC did not wire the rest of the payment. Eventually he relented, and a few days later the final payment came through, but it was not an auspicious start to the expedition. Over the coming weeks, the tension between the two men would not go away.

Six days later, after a long drive through Nepal and then Tibet, the team reached the Rongbuk glacier. They were the first in that year and quickly began fixing ropes up to the North Col and beyond. The plan was to work their way up to a sixth camp at roughly 27,000 feet and, once established, concentrate their searches around the area identified by Hemmleb, the expedition researcher, as the most likely spot where the bodies lay.

Nothing went perfectly. Hoyland suffered a suspected transient ischaemic attack (a minor stroke) and had to return to the UK, and Simonson had to turn back at 24,950 feet because of acclimatization issues, but the weather held and for once the upper slopes of Everest were relatively free of snow.

On 1 May, after a month of hard work, the search team were in position at 25,600 feet and finally ready to begin their work. Dave Hahn was the climbing leader, with Conrad Anker, Andy Politz, Jake Norton and Tap Richards making up the remainder of the party. If the weather remained stable, they planned to stay high for up to a week, systematically exploring the terrace close to the area where Hemmleb believed the Chinese camp had been placed back in 1975, about 1,000 feet below the spot where Irvine's ice axe had been found in 1933.

That morning they woke early and brewed a hot drink before breaking camp at around 5.00 a.m. It was a tough start to the day, with a bitter wind blowing across the ridge. Thom Pollard, the expedition's high-altitude cameraman, filmed the search team leaving, but before long his oxygen set developed a problem and he was forced to turn back. The others carried on going until five hours later they reached the site of their next camp, at around 27,000 feet.

After a brief pause to unload their tents and equipment, they moved off across the huge North Face. Down below, at Base Camp, Hemmleb watched and waited, focusing his high-powered telescope on the search zone. He had given everyone in the party an eight-page spiral notebook, detailing the terrain and telling them where he thought it would be best to look, but high on the mountain, each of the climbers appeared to have their own idea of where a body was most likely to be. It was their first outing, more of a recce than a full-on working day. The key was to get familiar with the terrain before taking a more methodical approach over the next week. It was a challenge, with the search area covering about the size of twelve football pitches – with an average slope of around thirty degrees and plenty of treacherously loose scree everywhere that had to be crossed with care. On a more positive note, much of the rock remained free of snow.

The climbers carried radios whose range went all the way down to Base Camp, but they were very aware that other expeditions might be listening in on their messages, so they had agreed a few code phrases to be used if they found something. To add a more chaotic element, they discovered that their bandwidth had been breached by cell phone calls from all over Nepal, filling the airwaves with intermittent babble. The whole thing was a little surreal: five young American mountaineers, searching for the bodies of two British climbers who had disappeared seventy-five years earlier, based on the testimony of a Chinese climber who had died the day after he told his story to a Japanese monk. The odds were not good.

It was not long before the past started to invade the present. Jake Norton, the youngest member of the team, found first an old wooden-handled piton hammer and then a more recent Chinese oxygen cylinder, flecked with blue paint. Then Conrad Anker encountered two bodies in quick succession – the first dressed in a purple suit, the second in a faded blue-grey outfit. They were too modern-looking to match Wang Hangbao's description, and both looked as if they had fallen from high up on the mountain. Goraks, a type of Himalayan raven that can fly up to 29,000 feet, had taken their fill of the first climber and both bodies were twisted and contorted.

Anker had strayed so far outside the initial search area that he was told off by one of the other climbers, but with experience of mountain rescue work he followed his instincts, trying to guess where Wang Hangbao might have reached twenty-four years earlier when he'd found his 'English dead', and looking for the points on the mountain where the topography would tend to funnel any bodies.

Initially he concentrated on a lower area where the slope ran down to some much more vertical-looking cliffs, but at around 11.45 a.m. he stopped to remove his crampons before moving back upwards. Then he spotted something: a piece of blue and yellow tent fabric. It looked modern-day, but as he moved up to investigate it, he noticed something else: a patch of white that he later said 'was whiter than the rock around it and whiter than the snow'.

As he traversed the slope to get a closer look, he suddenly realized that it was another body, but this time the clothing was much older and there was much more flesh exposed. 'The last time I went bouldering in my hobnail boots I fell off,' he called into his radio. 'Boulder' was code for a body, but initially none of the others seemed to pay any attention so he tried again: 'Why don't you come down for tea and Snickers.' Still no one, apart from Jake Norton. Then Anker became much more explicit: 'I'm calling a mandatory group meeting right now.' This time they came.

It was something that none of them had ever expected to see, especially on their first day: an ancient body almost frozen into Everest, its head partially buried in the scree, arms stretching upwards, strong-looking shoulders and hands, part of the back and buttocks exposed and seemingly turned to marble. Some pieces of the clothing had been shredded by the wind; other layers appeared remarkably intact. One boot was in very good condition, the other reduced to little more than a tongue of leather.

At first no one was sure what to do. They took photographs but should they, could they, touch the body? They were carrying zip-lock transparent bags in case they found the camera or any other pieces of physical evidence, but the idea that they would come across a body so quickly was almost inconceivable. Jake Norton began scratching out a memorial stone recording the last resting place of 'Andrew Irvine: 1902–1924', but no one was sure what they should do next. Then someone took a closer look at the remains of a shirt. It was labelled 'G. Mallory'. Why, they wondered, was Irvine wearing his climbing partner's shirt? Everyone had assumed that because the body lay roughly in the fall-line from the ice axe found in 1933, that it must be that of Sandy Irvine. Then they saw a second label: G. Leigh Mallory. Slowly it dawned on them that this was not Andrew Irvine, but the legendary George Mallory, a climber with mythical status in their eyes.

For Dave Hahn, this was an extraordinary humbling moment. Here they were, professional mountain guides, dressed in the latest climbing equipment, with temperature-resistant plastic boots and voluminous down clothing, staring at the body of an amateur climber who appeared to be wearing little more than they would on a cold day at home in America. If he'd ever doubted the toughness and determination of the British pioneers of the twenties, here was the evidence right in front of him. A decision had to be made: either leave George Mallory's body where it was, or search his clothing for the camera or any evidence that could prove that he and Irvine were the first men to summit Everest.

It was a question that would lead to a lot of debate after the expedition, but they were at 27,000 feet on Everest and had to make a decision. Here was one of the great figures from the history of mountaineering, the central character in one of the great mysteries; the best way to honour him, they decided, was to do a thorough search of his clothing before formally burying him.

The problem, and the blessing, was that Mallory was face down. This meant that his pockets had been protected from the elements and the scavenging Goraks – but in order to examine those pockets, first they had to break into the ice that glued his body to the mountain face. It was very hard work but gradually they were able to remove enough of it; initially chipping away with their ice axes and then using penknives to scrape away the remains of ice when they got closer.

Finally, they were able to access his pockets and a small bag under his right arm. From the outside it felt promising – a hard, metallic-sounding shape, around the size of a small camera, but when they cut the cloth, inside there was nothing more than a tin of beef lozenges. In another pocket there was an altimeter, calibrated to 30,000 feet, but the hands and the glass were broken.

Over the next couple of hours, they extracted a collection of objects and paperwork and packed each item away in its own plastic bag. Though they were sure that this was Mallory's body, Anker took a small patch of skin from Mallory's arm to provide a DNA sample. As for the main object of the search – Mallory's camera – there was no sign of it, or of any rolls of film. After about two hours, all that remained to do was to bury Mallory as best they could. There was very little loose rock nearby but eventually they formed a line and scavenged enough to cover the body.

A few months earlier, the BBC producer Peter Firstbrook had approached the bishop of Bristol and asked him for a committal prayer, which he'd then had printed up and given to the climbers. Andy Politz, one of the older team members, read it aloud, and then they moved off down the mountain. Conrad Anker, Mallory's discoverer, lingered to leave a small Buddhist-style offering of a candy bar, like the sweets that Tenzing left on the summit of Everest in 1953. Then they were gone, with the words of Psalm 103 hanging in the air: 'As for man, his days are as grass; as a flower of the field, so he flourisheth, for the wind passes over it, and it is gone.'

Back at Base Camp, Jochen Hemmleb and the others had been trying to follow the action through his telescope, but as the afternoon wore on hazy clouds drifted in and obscured their view. After Anker's call for a mandatory group meeting, there had been no further radio transmissions. Everyone guessed that something had been found, but they had no idea what it was or who it belonged to. All they could do was sit it out and wait.

Then, at the end of the evening, Dave Hahn came on the radio with an intriguing message: 'Jochen, you will be a happy man now.' Hemmleb knew that it must be something significant. He walked out onto the glacier and fell onto his knees, overwhelmed by emotion and a sense of gratitude. After so many years thinking about Mallory and Everest, at last his team had found something.

Liesl Clark, the young American producer employed by *Nova*, had come to Everest equipped with two laptops and a satellite phone. As well as working with Firstbrook and the BBC crew, she was busy taking and uploading digital photographs and writing dispatches for the *Nova* website and occasional reports for the *Boston Globe*. That night, Clark's dispatch, entitled 'Waiting in Silence', chronicled the early part of the day and the discovery of the first two bodies. One had been tentatively identified by Hemmleb as a Chinese climber who had fallen from the First Step in 1975, the other he thought was probably a Russian. As for what had happened later in the afternoon, all she could report was a series of messages that appeared to be in code, followed by radio silence. It looked as if Conrad Anker had found something, she reported, but all they knew was what they had been told: 'Jochen Hemmleb would be happy'.

The next day, the climbing team came down the mountain to Advance Base Camp at the foot of the North Col, where the expedition leader, Eric Simonson, was stationed. He'd been part of the previous night's radio conversation but had no more information than anyone else. All he knew was that his climbing team had had a tough but fruitful first day and had probably found something interesting.

Once Thom Pollard had filmed them walking into camp, they told him. It was an amazing moment. After so many months of preparation, and so much tension, this team with personnel from America, Britain and Germany had succeeded spectacularly. For seventy-five years there had been endless speculation about

George Mallory's fate. Had he died on the summit? Had he fallen off the North Ridge onto the Rongbuk glacier or the Kangshung Face on the other side of Everest? Now they had the answer – or at least part of it.

That night, Simonson switched on his sat-phone to call his partner Erin Copland back in Washington state, only to hear that the story was already partially out. The *Nova* dispatch of 1 May had sent interest in the expedition skyrocketing, even though no one really knew exactly what they had found. Simonson and Hahn would break the news that night of the discovery of George Mallory's body, with two long detailed dispatches to MountainZone.com, which would turn the expedition into a global news phenomenon.

It was one of the biggest stories to have been broken via the internet and the team at MountainZone could not believe their luck. Their site was an internet start-up created in the early days of the dot-com boom. Initially it had concentrated on skiing and snowboarding, but their coverage of the 1996 Everest disaster, including pieces by John Krakauer and the Russian guide Anatoli Boukreev, had given them a huge boost.

After that, straight climbing stories had taken centre stage, with MountainZone pioneering the use of satellite phones for live reporting. They had risked $50,000 on the 1999 search expedition, knowing that it would be a big story for them whether or not anything was found. Today it's commonplace for expeditions to report their progress live, but in the late 1990s this was something radically new and different – supercharging media interest.

In 1924, it had taken ten days for the news of Mallory and Irvine's disappearance to get from Camp 3 to *The Times*. In 1953, it had taken four days for the story of Hillary and Tenzing's first ascent to get from the Western Cwm to London on the day before the Coronation. Now, in 1999, a telephone dispatch recorded at 8.00 p.m. local time in Tibet was converted into text in Seattle and posted on the internet almost immediately. Before long there was even a digital photograph of George Mallory's weather-bleached body on their site. America had been indifferent to Mallory on his lecture tour in 1923, but in May 1999, as MountainZone's Peter Potterfield would later write, 'The world went nuts.'

By the morning of 3 May, the site was receiving millions of hits per hour and thousands of emails. Soon afterwards, the story broke in the conventional American press, and later in the evening editions of British newspapers. In 1999 the internet was still not part of many people's lives, but hundreds of thousands of people all around the world heard interviews with Ed Hillary and Mallory's seventy-year-old son, John, responding to the news on BBC radio, or read extracts from Hahn and Simonson's dispatches in the press.

By 4 May the news was all over Britain's daily newspapers. The *Guardian* called it 'an extraordinary breach in the fabric of time' and referred back to Mallory's famous quotation: '"Because it's there" remains the best explanation, not just for climbing. It's the doggedness of just wanting to find out, to get to the top or bottom for the sake of curiosity.' The *Daily Telegraph* featured an interview with Graham Hoyland, then back in Britain, recalling how he had heard about Howard Somervell's Vest Pocket Kodak at the age of fourteen. When Chris Bonington, Britain's most famous climber, was asked to comment, he repeated the idea that finding that camera was the critical thing. 'Photographic evidence', he said, 'is the usual way to prove that you have been to a summit.'

George Mallory was back on the front pages, and the possibility that he and Irvine were the first climbers to reach the summit of Everest was once again being widely aired. The 1999 expedition hadn't actually produced any evidence yet that would confirm or deny this, but there was a growing sense of momentum around the idea that the camera would be discovered and finally provide positive proof. Ed Hillary was very gracious when interviewed, telling reporters that Mallory had been an inspiration to him and that he would be very pleased if he had reached the summit in 1924, though he did add wryly that, in his view, making the first ascent of a mountain required a climber to get *down* as well as up.

John Mallory gave an interview to the BBC that was widely disseminated, but his response to the discovery of his father's body was sombre and had none of the triumphalism present in some of the press coverage. 'My guess is that they probably did make the summit, but probably not until very late in the day,' he told a reporter. 'Most people who don't make the summit until somewhere near sunset don't get down. To me the only way to achieve a summit is to come back alive: the job's half done if you don't come down again.'

The 1999 expedition was a welcome distraction from the main news stories of the day, most of which concerned the brutal war in Kosovo. Here was a good story from the past, a reminder of man's capacity to achieve amazing things. Most of the media coverage was very positive, though the *Daily Star* did cheekily run a picture of a Mallory, buck naked except for his hat and knapsack after a quick Tibetan skinny dip, with the headline: 'Was nude Brit the first to conquer Everest?'

Then, just a few days later, with interest still running high, a huge storm blew up over the publication of the photographs of Mallory's body. Though an image had already been on the MountainZone website for several days, when it was published in newspapers and magazines around the world – along with others including a close-up of Mallory's broken leg – the 1999 team found themselves in the eye of the storm.

Press interest had been intense, prompting the team to send their pictures to a commercial photo agency, who auctioned them off. In Britain, the *Daily Mail* won the bidding war, printing them in their Sunday edition on 9 May. On same day, the *Observer* published an article denouncing the massive profits being made from the photographs, and the lengths to which the expedition's agents had gone to extract the maximum value. When reporters went back for comments from Ed Hillary and Chris Bonington, their tone was markedly different from earlier in the week. 'I'm absolutely appalled by this,' Bonington told the *Observer*. 'Words can't express how disgusted I am. It's a disgrace, these people don't deserve to be called climbers.' Hillary agreed, saying that he too was appalled that they should have 'flogged off' photographs, while John Mallory told an interviewer that publishing them for profit was a breach of good faith.

The outrage that he and the British climbing establishment felt was genuine, but it was also a classic 'hero to zero' press storm: one week the team members were intrepid climbers bringing history to life, the next week they were greedy opportunists, making money out of someone else's tragedy. In 1930, when Salomon Andrée's body was found on Kvitøya, there had been no question of publishing any photographs of his grizzly remains. Nor had photos been published of Maurice Wilson's body when it was found in 1935, but sixty-four years later, the media landscape had changed. Eventually the photographs were also published by *The Sun* and the *Daily Telegraph* in Britain,

Newsweek in the US and *Stern* in Germany. The papers who bought the images avoided the controversy, while those who hadn't led the condemnation, though occasionally reproducing the photographs for the very purpose of criticizing their sale.

Back on the mountain, all the publicity and global attention did have a destabilizing effect. Nobody was prepared for the massive press attention and all the enquiries and offers coming in from outside. Peter Firstbrook had left to take the DNA sample and his film rushes back to the UK, but there was still tension in the air, with Eric Simonson furious over Liesl Clark's dispatch for *Nova* of 1 May, which he thought had upstaged MountainZone's coverage.

In many ways this was nothing new. Throughout the 1924 expedition Hinks had struggled hard to keep a very tight lid on the news coverage in order to preserve his exclusive contract with *The Times*. In 1953, reporters from rival newspapers had stalked the British team in Nepal and repeatedly tried to scoop the story of Hillary and Tenzing's first ascent. The *Times* correspondent attached to the British team, Jan Morris, had to fight tooth and nail to keep rivals at bay.

What was different this time was the speed with which information was being mediated. In 1924, the *Times* coverage had lagged roughly two to three weeks behind events on the mountain, with photographs taking even longer to be published. By 1999, news from Everest was being relayed almost instantaneously. There was little time for anyone to stop and consider what to publish and what not to – the world's media was hungry for 'content', the main issue was how to get over the time difference.

On 12 May, the search team headed back up the mountain for a second time. Over the previous ten days they had rested and helped bring down a stricken Ukrainian climber. Now they split into two parties, aiming to solve two very different questions. The first was whether Mallory and Irvine could have got up the Second Step in 1924.

By 1999, it had been climbed several times by climbers from previous expeditions, but they had all used ropes and modern safety devices, and availed themselves of the ladder installed by the Chinese team. Conrad Anker wanted to attempt the step in the same way that Mallory and Irvine would have had to in 1924, free-climbing the rock and studiously avoiding the ladder and all the fixed ropes that had been left in position.

The second question was less dangerous to answer, but in its own way just as tough. Thom Pollard and Andy Politz would return to the search area to look for Andrew Irvine's body, in the unlikely hope that they could repeat the success of 1 May. They were all aware that the position and state of Mallory's body did not match the description given by Wang Hangbao in 1979. His 'English dead' was seated and had a noticeable hole in his cheek, unlike Mallory who had been found facing into the mountain. Could Hangbao have actually seen Irvine, and if so, was his body nearby? It was a long shot, but there was still time to look.

The weather, however, was not on their side. Almost two weeks after the initial search, there was now much more snow on the mountain, so they changed plan and instead of looking for Irvine decided to return to Mallory's grave for a second look, just in case they had missed the elusive camera the first time round. Even though Politz had been part of the initial search, it still took him almost two hours to find the site.

Once they had relocated his body, Pollard and Politz unpacked their metal detector and began removing the stones that had been placed on top of him, to examine Mallory's body for a second time. There was still no sign, or sound, of the camera, but in a pocket they did find Mallory's watch, which had been previously overlooked. The glass was broken and the second hand was missing, but there was no indication when the damage had occurred. Though on 1 May the first search team had made a conscious decision not to disturb Mallory's head, this time Pollard worked his way under the body to stare Mallory straight in the face. His eyes were closed and there was a small but perfectly formed hole just above his left eye, as if he had been hit by a rock. Mindful of all the arguments about the publication of the first images, he did not photograph his face. Before they left, they covered Mallory's body with stones once again and read the committal prayer for a second time.

Higher up the mountain, the climbing party was struggling up the North-East Ridge towards the Second Step. Two of the four American climbers turned back, as did their Sherpas, but Conrad Anker and Dave Hahn pushed on. Hahn was a veteran of three previous Everest attempts. Twice he had been forced back at 28,000 feet before reaching the top for the first time in 1994, only to find himself benighted and having to bivouac close to the First Step. This time he was planning to do the high-altitude camerawork, filming Anker as he attempted to free-climb the Second Step.

Both men were on oxygen, but when they reached the crux of the Second Step, Anker took his set off to be as unencumbered as possible. Hahn kept his set running to make sure he was alert, but at the very moment when he was about to film Anker's historic free climb, his camera began to play up. It was Murphy's law at 28,250 feet, but there was nothing they could do about it; and besides, there was plenty of other work to get on with.

Belayed by Hahn, Anker continued his ascent, scanning above for a feasible way to reach the top without using the Chinese ladder. There were two possible cracks in the rock that might provide a route up – one looked lethal, the other just doable, so stopping only once to put in a tiny 'cam', a spring-loaded protection device to which he attached his rope, Conrad started up. He almost made it, but just before the end he rested his foot on one of the ladder's metal rungs and cursed himself for compromising his otherwise free ascent.

Once he reached the top, Anker hauled up his pack and then belayed Dave Hahn as he climbed up. Ahead of them was what should have been a fairly straightforward slog up to the summit, but suddenly about sixty feet below the top, out of nowhere, Dave Hahn became violently ill. It was about the worst place for it to happen, but rather than turn around, they struggled on, finally reaching the summit at 2.50 p.m.

It had been a brave and tenacious ascent from both men, but it left neither thinking that Mallory could have reached the summit. For Anker, the technical difficulties of climbing the Second Step with the kind of equipment available would have been just too great in 1924, however good a climber Mallory was. Dave Hahn wasn't quite so ready to rule it out, but he thought it would have been virtually impossible for Mallory and Irvine to have got *up* the Second Step, and then, after reaching the summit, climbed *down* again with hardly any climbing rope and no pitons or any other protection devices.

Two days later, the whole team was reunited at Base Camp to celebrate the end of the expedition. As well as all the items found on Mallory's body, they had also retrieved one of the oxygen cylinders that Eric Simonson had seen below the North-East Ridge in 1991. It turned out to be an important discovery, with

Jochen Hemmleb identifying it as a 1924 bottle which could only have been left there by Mallory and Irvine. Lying close to the site where the ice axe was found in 1933, it was another confirmation that at the very least they must have reached the crest of the North-East Ridge; and to add further proof, it had a number printed on it that corresponded with some handwritten notes found on the back of an envelope in Mallory's pocket.

After a rapid derig of Base Camp, they all headed back to Kathmandu, and on 25 May held a press conference at the Yak & Yeti Hotel to show reporters from all over the world the items brought back from the mountain. Eric Simonson and Conrad Anker announced that they would be donating their shares of the proceeds of the photographs to various local charities. 'We are mountaineers not treasure hunters,' Simonson told reporters. 'Nobody expected to get rich from this.'

As for the question of whether the photographs should have been released to the press in the first instance, Simonson was unrepentant, later telling *Newsday* in November 1999, 'It's not a story that could not be shared. And sharing meant showing the photos.' He continued in exasperated tones, 'The British, those who complain about this, I've got to say, he was their guy. Why the hell didn't they ever go look for him? They had 75 years. They're just upset that a bunch of Americans found him.'

There were disagreements too about the clothing and equipment brought back from Mallory's body: what the search team referred to as 'artefacts', George Mallory II regarded as his grandfather's *possessions*. When the team returned to the US, the items were exhibited at the National Geographic Society in Washington, where Mallory had spoken in 1923, and at a museum in Washington state. Only later were they returned to the family, who sent them to England to be first displayed at the

National Mountaineering Centre in Cumbria and then taken into the care of the Royal Geographical Society in London.

To see them today, it's hard not to be simultaneously awed and appalled. Put into position on a table by a white gloved archivist, the scraps of clothing and equipment have the aura of religious relics. Some items are remarkably well preserved: a box of Swan matches that looks as if it could have been bought yesterday; a tiny pair of nail scissors and a beautiful silk handkerchief, both in perfect condition, next to Mallory's broken altimeter and wristwatch, its glass face missing and hands long gone. Equally you do wonder why it was necessary to strip Mallory of so much of his clothing. What was it like to remove his boot, how easily did it come off? If the purpose of the search was to look for the camera, why was quite so much taken from his body?

One answer, of course, is that these items are clues to a mystery. In the years since Mallory's body was found, the significance of these objects and the other evidence found on Everest has been endlessly debated by researchers and historians trying to create a narrative of that final fateful day on 8 June 1924. Some items are fascinating to look at but don't reveal anything significant: the penknife, the pencil, the matches, the safety pin, the tin of beef cubes were the kind of things that you might expect any climber from the period to carry. Others, from the monogrammed silk handkerchief to the elegant pair of nail scissors and their leather case, reveal a little bit more about Mallory and the social class from which he came, but don't offer any new insights into the events of his final day.

Mallory's altimeter and wristwatch were greeted initially as exciting discoveries, but neither quite delivered as much as they promised. The altimeter would have once registered the final

29,028ft   *The Summit Pyramid*

The Second Step

The First Step

The Shoulder

Ice Axe
27,720ft

Oxygen Bottle
27,800ft

Mallory
26,760ft

Found On Everest 1933 and 1999

Discoveries on the mountain

height Mallory reached, but unlike modern digital versions it didn't contain any kind of recording device or give any other indication of what that high point was. Briefly there was a lot of interest in Mallory's watch: did rust stains on the face made by the missing hands indicate the precise time when Mallory fell? It was a tantalizing possibility but ultimately the evidence was too ambivalent. The fact that the watch was discovered in his pocket and not on his wrist implied that it had been broken prior to the final accident which killed him, and on examination the stains on the face didn't line up with the broken ends of the hands.

For some, the tinted snow goggles in his jacket pocket seemed like an important clue: had Mallory taken them off as he came down in the dark after a long day of climbing, which by implication meant that he got very high? Again the evidence was ambivalent: Mallory might simply have taken them off earlier in the day, as Edward Norton had on his attempt on 4 June when he came off the snow onto the rockier sections of the North Face.

The torn rope was more significant. Contrary to some theories, it showed that Mallory and Irvine had been together before one of them slipped, pulling the other off. The rope didn't indicate who had made the slip or where Irvine might have ended up, however. The physical damage to Mallory's body observed on the mountain was again complicated to interpret: if the accident had occurred just below the crest of the North-East Ridge at 27,760 feet, where the ice axe was found in 1933, then Mallory would have fallen approximately 1,000 feet, enough of a drop for him to have broken several limbs. Yet, apart from his fractured right leg and some bruising still visible around his waist, his body was remarkably intact, suggesting that he fell from much lower down. So could he in fact have come off twice? The first time higher up, at the site where the ice axe was found – accounting for the broken watch in his pocket and possibly the bruising – and then a second time, much lower down, when he sustained the broken leg? The puncture wound on his forehead that Thom Pollard saw on the second search of the body in 1999 might have been caused by a falling rock, and would have undoubtedly caused him to fall.

For Jochen Hemmleb, the young German researcher who had spent so many years thinking about the story, the most interesting discoveries were some of the smallest and flimsiest: the handwritten notes found in his pocket. They contained lists of supplies and equipment to be taken up the mountain, and most intriguingly indicated that Mallory and Irvine might have carried a lot more oxygen than had initially been assumed. As well as the bottles on their pack-frames when they left camp on the North Col, the notes suggested that the porters might have carried up between six and eight more bottles. The more oxygen available on the final day, the further they could have gone, even perhaps all the way to the summit.

The other important piece of evidence was the 1924 cylinder, spotted first by Eric Simonson in 1991 and then recovered in 1999. It was found at roughly 27,900 feet, a few hundred feet further west from where the ice axe had been discovered. It proved unequivocally that Mallory and Irvine must have been using oxygen on their final day, and from its location, implied that at the very least they had got very close to the First Step.

Any evidence to do with oxygen though has to be treated cautiously: in the first instance, as Odell revealed in his report on 24 April 1924, midway through their approach march, the 1924 sets were dogged with manufacturing faults. Irvine did his best to repair and modify them, but both the cylinders and the apparatuses leaked, and as the climbers went higher and the air pressure decreased, the stress on the valves and joints would have increased – making them more likely to malfunction. Secondly, compared to modern oxygen sets, they delivered very little oxygen. Their maximum output was 2.5 litres/minute, hardly anything when compared to the sets carried by Hillary and Tenzing in 1953, which could deliver up to 4 litres/minute, or modern sets which can provide 6 litres/minute and are much lighter.

Part of the debate over whether or not to use oxygen for high-altitude climbing has always been a cost-benefit analysis: does the boost given by breathing in more oxygen compensate for the considerable weight and discomfort of carrying an oxygen set? Even when they were trying hard to economise, Hillary and Tenzing ran their oxygen sets at 3 litres/minute on their summit day in 1953. When in 1955, the British climber Joe Brown climbed a difficult rock pitch at around 28,150 feet just below the summit of Kangchenjunga, he cranked his set up to 6 litres/minute to maximize his chances of success. It's hard to imagine that when confronted with the Second Step, the toughest obstacle on the North-East Ridge, the 2.5 litres/minute of oxygen available to Mallory would have helped him much at all.

In the end, the problem with all the evidence found in 1999 was that though it was fascinating and added significantly to the picture of their final day, there was nothing that clinched it, nothing to prove absolutely where or why the accident happened – or whether Mallory or Irvine had gone all the way to the summit. The 1999 team had come looking for the camera, hoping that it would provide definitive evidence, but they had not found it.

One further and very different sort of photographic evidence was suggested by Clare, Mallory's eldest daughter, shortly after the 1999 search team discovered her father's body. She was then living in northern California, having married an American, Glenn Millikan, in 1938. Tragically, he had also died in a mountaineering accident, leaving her, like Ruth, to bring up her children alone. Aged eighty-four, Clare's feelings were mixed about the discovery of her father's body. She did add one new and intriguing detail though, remembering how her father had promised to leave a photograph of her mother on the summit. If no photograph of Ruth had been found on his body, did that mean he must have left it at the top?

It was a curious story. In his Everest letters from 1924, Mallory had asked for some family photographs, but though Ruth did send a picture of the children, he had to ask her twice for a photograph of herself, and there is no reference anywhere to his having received it. When a year earlier he had been asked by an American reporter whether he or his teammates had left anything at their high point on the 1922 expedition, Mallory had dismissed it as a rather silly question: 'Why, nothing at all. Why should we?' So where did the family story of leaving a photograph of Ruth on the summit come from?

It is possible that the suggestion originated with the psychic Walter Gray, the details of whose supernatural encounter with George had been passed on to Clare by Noel Odell in the late 1970s, but even if this was not the case and it was an older family story, the idea that the *absence* of a photograph proved that he had reached the summit was not as convincing as finding a camera with images of Mallory or Irvine taken at 29,029 feet. But would that elusive Vest Pocket Kodak or any other camera ever be retrieved?

With media interest remaining high, new expeditions were announced and organized. In 2000, Graham Hoyland went back, supported by the BBC, to continue the search for Irvine's body, but bad weather prevented him from finding anything. The following year, Eric Simonson announced that he was planning to return, with a large party that included several members of the 1999 team.

At this point Irvine's family intervened. There had been a lot of anger and disquiet in Britain over the graphic descriptions in the search team's books of how Mallory's body had to be hacked out of the ice, like digging into a frozen driveway, and then levered up rigid in order for his pockets to be examined. The fact that his body had been disturbed not just once but twice, even after a burial service, was deeply upsetting to many. So, in early 2000, members of Irvine's family sent an open letter to Simonson 'amid fears', as they told *The Times*, 'that his remains will be desecrated, and photos of his corpse sold for profit'.

John Irvine, one of Sandy Irvine's descendants, described the treatment of Mallory's body as 'scandalous', and other family members were equally upset by the sale of the photographs. 'We can't stop them,' John told a reporter. 'But we are asking them to treat the body with respect and to return any artefacts to us.' Doug Scott, the president of the Alpine Club, added further weight to their request, writing an article for the International Climbing and Mountaineering Federation's bulletin with a set of guidelines for any historical investigation, detailing what he considered 'appropriate conduct' should a body be found. Scott had been particularly angered by the second search of Mallory's body, and asked for Irvine's body, if found, to be committed and covered with stones. 'The body should thereafter remain untouched. In Britain and many other countries it is illegal to disinter a body without a Court Order. This practice should be respected in the mountains.'

With the arguments escalating, Eric Simonson told the *News Tribune*, that he was on the side of history, and of Mallory and Irvine: 'Ultimately I think George and Andrew would have wanted the world to know what happened to them. I just keep thinking that if I was the guy lying up there dying, I know I would have been thinking, "God I hope someday somebody figures out what happened."' He hit out at the nephews and nieces of Irvine. 'All of a sudden people realize, "Hmmm maybe they do have a chance, so we better get a pre-emptive foot in the door to stake our claim…" They've claimed the camera. They've claimed the photos. Any photos we take, they want. Anything that we find, they want. They've claimed the right to all news releases. They've basically claimed everything.'

In the end, perhaps fortuitously considering all the rancour and controversy, the 2001 Mallory and Irvine expedition did not find Andrew Irvine's body or any other significant further traces of the 1924 expedition, save one of Norton's socks and an unlabelled mitten on the North-East Ridge, close to where the ice axe had been found in 1933.

Hemmleb and Simonson weren't quite finished, though. Some months later, in August 2001, they flew to Bejing hoping to interview several veteran Chinese climbers. Like Tom Holzel in 1986, they met Zhang Junyan. the tent-mate of Wang Hangbao, the climber from the 1975 expedition who had encountered his famous 'English dead'. Though his description of a seated corpse with a prominent gash on one cheek did not match what they had found in 1999, Hemmleb and Simonson came away convinced that Wang probably had seen Mallory's body. More intriguingly, they also met a member of the 1960 Chinese team,

Xu Jing, who said that he too had found a body – but about 700 feet or so higher, at around 27,230 feet, wrapped in a sleeping bag, most of which had rotted away. Was it Irvine? Would the whole circus start again?

In the decade that followed, there were several more search expeditions conducted by Graham Hoyland and various members of the 1999 US team, but none was on as large a scale as 1999 or 2001, and none found anything of real significance.

One interesting thing that did emerge in this period was a previously unpublished letter written by Frank Smythe to Edward Norton in 1937, which was included in *My Father Frank*, a biography written by his son Tony, published in 2013. After all the comments about British climbers being uninterested in the fate of Mallory and Irvine, the letter revealed that in 1936 Smythe had actually spotted what he thought might be the remains of a body, after scanning the North Face of Everest through a high-powered telescope.

Smythe, who'd some years earlier taken part in a grim search for dead bodies on Mont Blanc, had noticed an unusual-shaped object in a gully below the Yellow Band which he was sure was not a rock. He had not investigated further after terrible weather brought a premature halt to the 1936 expedition, but he had hoped that future expeditions would be able to examine the site properly. At the time, he told Norton, he had not reported what he had seen publicly, for fear that the press would sensationalize the story.

Smythe's historic letter did not immediately set off any further search teams, but interest in Mallory and Irvine continued, fed by reports that a Hollywood movie was about to go into production, with either Tom Hardy or Ewan McGregor playing George Mallory.

Then, in 2019, supported by the *National Geographic* and yet another documentary team, the American climber and writer Mark Synnott arrived at the Rongbuk glacier to begin a new search, equipped with that most modern of expedition essentials: a set of high-altitude drones with remote control cameras. His team included Thom Pollard, the cameraman from the 1999 search, and back home in America, Tom Holzel, the veteran mountain sleuth.

A few years earlier, Synnott had attended a lecture given by Pollard in which he told the tale of the 1999 search expedition. Like so many before him, it wasn't long before Synnott was gripped by the story of Mallory and Irvine, and before long, in December 2018, he and Pollard were setting out to visit Holzel at his home in Connecticut.

Three decades after his own search expedition, Holzel was still keenly interested in the story. He no longer held to his original idea that Mallory and Irvine had separated above the Second Step, but still maintained that the best way to resolve the mystery was to retrieve a camera and hope to find some photographic evidence. Unsurprisingly, Holzel had a theory of where Sandy Irvine's body might be.

In 1984, the American cartographer Brad Washburn had flown around Everest in a Lear Jet, gathering photographic data for a very detailed map. Holzel had obtained one of Washburn's images showing the Yellow Band and blew it up into an eight-foot-by-three-foot print, which he used to attempt to plot the movements of Xu Jing, the Chinese climber who told Hemmleb and Simonson about seeing a body wrapped up in a sleeping bag. After a lot of cross-checking, Holzel narrowed the possibilities down to a notch in the rock where he thought the body might lie.

Synnott's team went out to Everest in the spring of 2019 full of hope, but it was not to be. Their drones did record staggering views of Everest that were used in the subsequent documentary, but after several weeks and a lot of hard work, when Synnott left the fixed ropes and traversed out onto the North Face at 27,700 feet towards the feature where Holzel thought Irvine might lie, he found nothing but rock and ice. Yet another search expedition had failed to find Irvine's body. In the years that followed, Covid put paid to any further search expeditions, with the Tibetan side of the mountain only emerging from quarantine in 2023.

If anyone thought the story was over though, and that there wouldn't be any more twists in the long saga of Mallory and Irvine and their final climb, 2022 would prove them wrong.

Studio portrait, George Mallory, c. 1920.

13

About a Man

Tuesday, 13 June 2023. The main lecture hall at the Royal Geographical Society is full to the rafters for a lecture to celebrate the seventieth anniversary of the first ascent of Everest.

On stage Peter Hillary and Jamling Tenzing are recalling their fathers' dogged climb to the top, the spearhead of John Hunt's British team. There's a message from the new King, Charles III, recalling how the first ascent occurred on the eve of his mother's Coronation, just as the seventieth anniversary has come shortly after his, as well as contributions from Stephen Venables, the first British climber to climb Everest without oxygen, and Kenton Cool, the mountaineer and guide who this year has been up and down for a seventeenth time. He strikes a slightly pessimistic note, worrying about the fate of the world's highest mountain as another wave of commercialism takes over, before morale is restored with the inspiring tale of Hari Budha Magar, a former Gurkha soldier who has just become the first double above-the-knee amputee to reach the summit.

It's a warm-hearted, nostalgic evening, compered by Sue Leyden, John Hunt's daughter. Hillary and Tenzing are the main heroes being celebrated, but you can't talk about Everest's history for long before George Mallory's name comes up. Venables shows Mallory's photo of the Kangshung Face, which he and three Americans climbed in 1988, and Kenton Cool quotes Mallory's famous phrase, 'Because it's there.'

As he and everyone here tonight are quick to acknowledge, Everest today would be almost unrecognizable to Hillary and Tenzing, and even more so to George Mallory and the climbers of the 1920s. Just as the Alps were dubbed 'the playground of Europe' in the Victorian era, so the Himalayas have become 'the playground of the world'. Despite all the complaints and protests about high-altitude rubbish dumps and overcrowding, that process seems unstoppable.

In the twenty-four years since George Mallory's body was found, Everest has seen earthquakes, fist fights, Covid quarantines and huge avalanches, but the numbers of people tackling the world's highest peak just keep on going up. Like Mont Blanc and the Matterhorn, Everest has become essentially a commercial space, where paying clients are led to the summit by increasingly professional Sherpas. In the spring season of 2023, no less than 600 people got to the top – 350 Sherpas and 250 clients.

Many in the climbing world are very critical of this, pointing out that being led up Everest, heavily supported by a bevy of Sherpas, endlessly clipping on to fixed ropes and being offered increasing amounts of supplementary oxygen, isn't really *climbing* Everest at all. That perhaps misses the point: for many clients on commercial expeditions the thrill comes from standing on the summit, not the getting there. If you want to make a really challenging climb of it, then you can avoid the 'yak route' up the South-East Ridge, and go it alone up one of the other ridges or faces, but if your priority is simply to reach the highest point on earth and enjoy the world's most elevated view, does it really matter how you get there?

As I write these words, it's 101 years since the first attempt, and 70 years since the first ascent. In that period around 6,500 people have reached the top, and more than 330 have died trying. In 1921, when Mallory joined Howard-Bury's reconnaissance expedition, there was one glorious moment when he literally found himself walking off the map with Everest just a tiny peak, far away on the horizon. Today it is probably the best mapped mountain in the world, surveyed numerous times from the ground and the air. There's even a good-quality asphalt road on the Tibetan side that goes all the way across the Tibetan plateau, allowing climbers, and tourists, to drive from Lhasa to Base Camp in three to six days.

Since Hillary and Tenzing's triumph in 1953, Everest has gone through several different phases. The 1950s and 1960s were the 'Golden Years' of Himalayan climbing, when all the world's highest peaks were climbed for the first time. On Everest, big national expeditions struggled up the ridges and slopes to plant their national flags on the summit – the first Swiss climbers in 1956, the first Americans in 1963, the first Indian team in 1965. All of these expeditions approached Everest from the southern, Nepali side, though occasionally some Western climbers did stray into Tibet knowing that, at such a high altitude, they would not be intercepted.

In the second phase, the 1970s and 1980s, international mountaineers took on Everest 'the hard way', braving its unclimbed faces and ridges. The first British-born climbers to reach the summit were Doug Scott and Dougal Haston in 1975, after a hard-fought ascent of the South-West Face. In 1980, two Japanese climbers made the first complete ascent of the North Face, and in 1983 an American team climbed the ferociously difficult Kangshung Face on the east side of Everest. When Mallory took his famous photograph of it in 1921, he had declared: 'Other men, less wise, might attempt this way if they would, but emphatically, it was not for us.' Five years after the first ascent of the Kangshung Face, a small Anglo-American team repeated the feat, signalling a new era of 'Alpine-style' Himalayan climbing in which much more compact parties made rapid ascents of the great peaks of the Himalayas and the Karakoram, using minimal Sherpa support and climbing without oxygen.

The third phase, which began in the 1990s and continues to this day, saw the introduction of commercial climbing, led principally by companies from New Zealand and the US. By the end of the decade they were putting dozens of paid clients on the summit every year. The world's top climbers stayed away, setting boot on Everest only to complete bigger challenges such as the Seven Summits, the ascent of the highest mountain on each continent, or more recently the 14 x 8000ers, the much more difficult ascent of the world's fourteen highest peaks, all of which are located in the Himalayas and the Karakoram mountains.

Increasingly the fault line that separates elite mountaineers from most Everest climbers is the use of oxygen. In the 1920s and 1930s, there was an intense debate about the need for supplementary oxygen at high altitude. A lot of eminent scientists said that Everest could not be climbed without it, in spite of what mountaineers like Norton and Somervell had achieved. When Hillary and Tenzing made their historic first ascent using oxygen sets, the scientists felt vindicated, but twenty-five years later the climbers were proved right, when in 1978 Reinhold

Messner and Peter Habeler reached the top under their own steam. As if this weren't enough, Messner repeated the feat two years later, when he made an astonishing solo ascent via the Great Couloir, the route pioneered by Edward Norton in 1924. By contrast, today's commercial clients seem to use more and more oxygen every year, starting very low down on the mountain and consuming up to 6 litres/minute for much of the route, two and a half times the maximum flow-rate of Mallory and Irvine's sets.

The majority of ascents are still made from the Nepali side, using Hillary and Tenzing's route up the South-East Ridge, but some commercial operators prefer the quieter, less crowded approach from the north. Roughly one-third of ascents since 1953 have been made from the Tibetan side, but during the Covid era it was closed to foreigners and only reopened in 2023, too late in the spring season for any commercial companies.

The last couple of years has seen the rise of Nepali-owned trekking and climbing companies, who are increasingly dominating the commercial market. In the past there was a lot of grumbling and resentment over the dominance of foreign companies, with much of the money made on Everest expeditions going out of the country and pay rates for Sherpas generally much lower than for Western mountain guides. 2023 seems to have marked a turning point, with local companies like Seven Summit Treks and Elite Exped rising to the fore. According to their trade body, there are now around fifty Nepali-owned companies, and though the traditional operators from New Zealand, Europe and the US still play a role, gradually their influence is waning.

All this can be traced back to the British expeditions of the 1920s, which helped make the very word 'Sherpa' into a globally recognized brand, but there has been a huge change in their role. In Mallory's day, all the route-finding and rope-fixing was done by the British climbers, who took a paternalistic attitude to their Sherpas and expected them to do little more than carry their equipment and supplies. Today, on commercial expeditions, the situation has been reversed.

Foreign clients are expected to do very little of the technical work and no route-finding at all. Specialist teams of Sherpa 'ice doctors' go in at the beginning of the climbing season, to fix ropes and ladders over the difficult parts of the main routes up the mountain from both north and south. During the expedition itself the support ratio of Sherpas to clients is around 1.5:1, with some clients being supported by two Sherpas in the final stages of the climb. It's worth remembering when you see images of high-altitude queues on the Lhotse Face, the majority of the climbers in the photographs are probably Sherpas escorting their clients.

A high level of support does not of course guarantee success, or safety. According to the American climber and blogger Alan Arnette, spring 2023 was the busiest and 'deadliest season' in Everest's history, with thirteen deaths and four climbers missing presumed dead. Like 1924, it was a ferociously cold year, with high winds and very low temperatures, which led to a high level of frostbite injuries.

The media's latest high-altitude hero is not a public-school Brit like George Mallory, but Nims Purja, a forty-year-old Nepali climber and former Special Boat Service member. He's responsible for the most widely disseminated image of queues on Everest, showing a long line of climbers snaking up to the Hillary Step, a photo that he took in 2019 in the middle of 'Project Possible', an audacious bid to ascend all fourteen 8,000-metre peaks in the minimum time possible. In the end it took him six months and six days. The ensuing Netflix documentary and book were both hugely successful, and if anyone doubted his mountaineering credentials, in January 2021 he and nine other Nepali climbers made the first winter ascent of K2.

Whether, in the future, Nims or other local climbers will push the achievements of the pioneering Himalayan climbers further down the bookshelf into distant memory remains to be seen, but George Mallory at least is remarkably resilient. He still gets the books and the articles and hits the news periodically when one of his ice axes is sold or another collection of letters discovered. None of the other protagonists of the 1924 expedition, however, are remembered outside mountaineering circles, even if they achieved remarkable things.

Edward Norton's ascent to 28,126 feet without oxygen was matched in 1933, but not surpassed until Messner and Habeler's climb forty-five years later. After the 1924 expedition, he continued to climb for pleasure but never went on any big expeditions, focusing instead on his military career before he was forced to retire after a horse riding accident in 1942. When he died in 1954, his climbing partner in 1924, Howard Somervell, wrote his obituary for the *Alpine Journal*, noting that Norton's three lifelong characteristics were 'stability, humility and generosity'.

Somervell survived his former partner by twenty-one years, dying in 1975 in the picturesque town of Ambleside in the Lake District. His climbs in 1922 and 1924 were remarkable achievements, but he always regarded his time as a doctor in India as the most important thing in his life. In fact, he was also an accomplished painter who once exhibited over ninety works at the Alpine Club, and a talented composer who wrote the score for the 1922 Everest film. Like Norton, he never went on any big expeditions after Everest, though he continued to climb for pleasure and went on to become the president of the Alpine Club.

His predecessor was a little more surprising: George Finch. Despite all the problems in 1924, Finch was very loyal to the club, sitting on committees and acting as president between 1959 and 1961. He had continued to climb regularly in the Alps, but in 1931 he was part of an Imperial College Club trip in which three men including one of his close friends fell and died on the Jungfrau. Finch was not directly involved in the accident but he was very disturbed by it. Soon afterwards he had to endure a major operation, after which his doctors warned him off any strenuous climbing. Like Bill Tilman and Charles Evans, two other famous Everest climbers, he took up sailing instead. When he died in 1970 at the age of eighty-two, *The Times* referred to him as 'one of the best two alpinists of his time', the other being George Mallory.

Charles Bruce did not last quite so long. His oversized liver matched his huge appetite for life, but he managed to soldier on for seventy-three years, dying in 1939 just before the Second World War. Though a consummate man of action, he wrote two books about his time in the Himalayas, revealing himself to be a very witty and erudite author. His funeral, according to his obituary in the *Alpine Journal*, was attended by many friends and was 'not a sad one, but was almost merry and bright, and its tone undoubtedly was one that Charlie himself would have been the first to enjoy'.

His nephew Geoffrey Bruce was in some ways an 'accidental mountaineer' who never expected to climb high in 1922 or 1924. Like Edward Norton, he put his military career ahead of his mountaineering, rising to become Deputy Chief of the

General Staff in India. As for the two other members of the climbing team, Bentley Beetham and John de Vars Hazard, neither had an enjoyable or notable expedition in 1924 and both saw their reputations suffer in the aftermath. Beetham was widely blamed for the exclusion of the Quaker climber Richard Graham, and Hazard, Graham's replacement, was criticized for the unauthorized journey he made at the end of the expedition that angered the Tibetan government and for a time jeopardized the chances of further expeditions.

As for Everest's great showman, John Noel, the collapse of Explorer Films did not entirely dent his enthusiasm for Everest or cinematography. He continued to tour Britain and America, showing clips from his Everest films and lecturing about his experiences. He died in 1989 at the splendid age of 99, the last survivor of the 1924 party.

Noel Odell was the only member of the team to return to Everest or take part in any further major Himalayan expeditions. In 1926, he went on a brief American lecture tour and had his portrait taken in Boston by Helen Messinger Murdoch, the same photographer who had immortalized Mallory on Dartmouth Street Bridge in March 1923. After being offered a place on the 1933 expedition and then having to turn it down, in 1936 Odell made the first ascent of Nanda Devi, the highest mountain in India, as part of a small Anglo-American team. In 1938 he returned to Everest with Bill Tilman's British team, but it was another Everest expedition brought down by the early arrival of the monsoon and Odell did not get any further than the North Col. He lived to the tender age of ninety-six, graciously fielding questions on Everest to the end.

Though Odell was a very powerful climber in his own right, he will always be remembered as the last man to see Mallory and Irvine on Everest, though precisely what he witnessed remains a contentious issue. Did he see them climbing the Second Step, as he wrote in his account for *The Fight for Everest*, or at the First Step, as he later suggested? Or even on the Third Step, a lesser feature just below the summit pyramid, as a few more recent commentators have speculated? Odell could be seen as someone who just couldn't make up his mind and whose opinion was constantly swayed by others, but that would do him a disservice.

From very early on Odell was unsure where on the North-East Ridge he had seen them, and as a scientist who was used to being objective, he refused to hide his uncertainty. He was under no pressure in 1924 to revise his opinion. Norton disagreed with him over how and where Mallory and Irvine had died, but he didn't question whether or not they'd climbed the Second Step. Later, in 1933, when the next British expedition attempted Everest and returned with a very negative account of the Second Step and tales of high-altitude hallucinations, Odell's account was put under even greater scrutiny, but he came out fighting, insisting that he hadn't been confused by any rocks or high-flying birds. He had definitely seen Mallory and Irvine on the North-East Ridge, but whether they were on the First or Second Step he still could not be quite sure.

For a few very noisy years, the search for photographic evidence of the 1924 expedition took centre stage. If a camera could be found and a roll of film could be processed with images of Mallory and Irvine at the top of the Second Step – or even better, on the summit itself – then all the arguments over what Odell did or did not see would be irrelevant. But was the camera really ever more than a Hitchcockian MacGuffin? If Mallory and Irvine had reached the summit late in the day, especially if they were in the middle of a snow storm, would there have been enough light to take any photographs?

The most recent, and perhaps final, twist in the camera saga comes from Mark Synnott, the American writer and climber who led the last big search expedition on Everest in 2019. Three years later, at the tail end of the Covid epidemic, he published an article in the online magazine *Salon* about rumours that Irvine's body had been found by 'the Chinese' and taken away, on the pretext of either cleaning up the mountain or in order to hide evidence that Mallory and Irvine had been the first to climb Everest from the Tibetan side. But that wasn't all: according to some reports they had found Irvine's camera and had made a botched attempt at developing the film, destroying any images that it might have held. Subsequently, the Chinese authorities had attempted to erase the evidence and cover the story up. If it was true, the long search for photographic evidence had reached a dead end. Unless some oxygen bottles or some other piece of physical evidence from 1924 were to be found, it would never be possible to say definitively whether Mallory or Irvine reached the summit.

All this has many of the hallmarks of a twenty-first-century conspiracy theory – and as Synnott acknowledges, the evidence chain is complex and unresolved. Nevertheless, several Everest 'sleuths' support this theory, arguing that there have been so many unsuccessful searches over the last two decades that the only credible explanation is that the body has been spirited away. It's equally possible, of course, that after the fatal slip, Irvine never came to rest on the mountain. After all, Mallory's body was found close to some steep cliffs at 27,000 feet – if Irvine had been roped to him, as the evidence suggests, he might easily have gone over the cliffs and fallen far down the North Face, his body never to be recovered.

Today, even if the possibility of finding definitive photographic evidence has now been discounted by many, Mallory is still regarded as one of the most important figures in Everest's history – a climber who inspired so many others by his actions and his words. Some argue that it doesn't really matter whether he reached the summit or not, and that it's his values and his indomitable spirit that make him a heroic figure, but for others who continue to fill web pages and chatrooms with their thoughts on Mallory's final day, analysing and reanalysing all the 'clues', whether he reached the summit or not remains the key question.

In 1999, and for a few years after, the Everest search expeditions brought him back to centre stage. As in 1924, a lot of people *wanted* him to have been the first man to the summit, and no one ever went looking for evidence to categorically *disprove* that he'd reached the top. Now, if the search for a camera is finished, then the debate over whether they reached the summit comes back to two issues: could he and Irvine have climbed the Second Step, and climbed it quickly as in Odell's first report – and secondly, did they have sufficient oxygen to get to the top?

With regard to the first question, the consensus among top climbers has always been that they probably could not have done it. Neither Edward Norton nor George Finch – nor the members of the 1933 expedition – thought the North-East Ridge was a feasible route, because the Second Step was just too difficult. Elite modern-day climbers like Conrad Anker who have climbed it agree that it was too demanding for climbers of that era, in terms of both technique and equipment.

The Second Step was subsequently scaled by Chinese teams in 1960 and 1975, but neither climbed it quickly. The 1960 team took three hours to get up the final ten feet – and only made it using 'combined tactics', with one climber clambering up his teammate's back to overcome the final pitch. The 1975 Chinese team spent two days fixing ropes and a four-section aluminium ladder, which they hammered in at the crux of the Second Step, but it still took them six and a half hours to get from their high camp, at 28,480 feet, to climb the final 540 feet to the summit.

The second question, of whether Mallory and Irvine had sufficient oxygen to reach the summit, is murkier. The problem here is that there is no certainty at all what the final sets looked like, how well they performed, and how much oxygen Mallory and Irvine took. The retrieval of a 1924 oxygen bottle high up on the North-East Ridge in 1999 confirmed that they must have been climbing on oxygen on the morning of 8 June. Mallory's notes found in his pocket implied that he had more oxygen available than had previously been thought, but it is impossible to be precise. In the note that he sent down on 7 June he described his oxygen set as a 'bloody load' for high-altitude climbing, so it seems unlikely that on his summit day he would have carried anything more than the minimum number of bottles.

What you can say is that more and more evidence has emerged that the 1924 oxygen apparatus did not work well and may have contributed to Mallory and Irvine's demise. The new sets for 1924 theoretically had a greater capacity than those taken in 1922, but were put together badly. In a candid, unpublished memorandum sent by Percy Unna to Noel Odell just before they were shipped off to India in February 1924, he admitted that there had been significant production difficulties. Siebe Gorman's 'best man' had only just returned from the US and the Air Ministry's oxygen expert had been away in Mesopotamia. In 1924 the facilities did not exist to simulate the low pressure and intense cold found high on Everest – so, Unna continued, the new sets still had to be considered 'experimental'. Before he left Britain, Hinks explicitly warned Bruce not to criticize the oxygen sets in any of his expedition dispatches because 'a lot of the work is done gratis or at special terms'.

When they were checked in Tibet, everything from the cylinders to the pipework and valves leaked badly, and all of the sets had to be thoroughly reworked by Irvine. Siebe Gorman refused to accept responsibility. When Unna wrote to them in June 1924 to report all the faults that Odell and Irvine had found, their managing director, R. H. Davis, dismissed his complaints bullishly, saying that it was all the fault of the team's oxygen officer, the latterly appointed Noel Odell, who had neither visited their factory nor the British Oxygen Company. 'Had the oxygen officer himself seen the apparatus tested in our works,' Davies wrote, 'he would have been able readily to deal with any of the matters in question in a practical way, and put them right, and the points raised in the report need never have arisen.'

Odell was not to blame. He had left Britain for Iran on 12 December, about a month before he was appointed oxygen officer by the Everest Committee. He simply couldn't have played any role in the testing or approving of the cylinders or apparatus. Andrew Irvine did study a 1922 oxygen set and sent in recommendations for how future equipment could be improved, but his suggestions were ignored.

When they reached Tibet, Irvine did as much as he could to mend and improve the damaged equipment, but everything conspired against him, from the inadequate packaging to the thread size of the small nuts and bolts that held the equipment together. He'd checked before he left England and been told that Siebe Gorman used Whitworth threaded bolts on the new sets, so he'd gone out and bought a set of Whitworth taps and dies, in case he had to remake any screws or bolts. On examination, however, it turned out that Siebe Gorman had actually used British Association threads throughout. It was a small detail, but in the wilds of Tibet, there was no chance that Irvine could have ordered new tools.

Later, in the autumn of 1924, when the expedition returned to London, there were immediate and repeated calls for a commission of enquiry into the appalling state of the oxygen equipment. Odell and Unna were invited to appear before the Everest Committee on 9 January 1925. Odell produced a report in which he reiterated most of his criticisms, but ultimately Unna took responsibility for the problems, saying that he felt that he had not given the team sufficient information about the production difficulties. The Committee, however, exonerated him in the official minutes, recording that any defects were due to 'the haste with which it had been made and assembled' – and in time-honoured fashion, they vowed to set up a subcommittee to 'deal with the whole question'.

It is impossible to read all this without thinking of George Finch, and the peremptory way in which he had been banished from the project. Between the return of the first expedition in September 1922 and the dispatch of the second in February 1924, there was almost eighteen months. There had been no need for haste. If Finch had been allowed to continue developing the equipment and been part of the team, it's hard to believe that things would have turned out the same way.

In September 1925, Bentley Beetham wrote to Hinks to ask for a copy of the original long memo, detailing the operation of the oxygen apparatus. Hinks let him have it, but only with a caution: 'This memorandum must be considered as confidential and no quotations may be made from it nor should any statements be made publicly tending to criticise it in any

way, because that involves many delicate questions.' Whether
those 'delicate questions' referred to the Everest Committee's
relationship with the Air Ministry or the manufacturers Siebe
Gorman – or to Percy Unna's role – remains unclear, but either
way, the problems were hushed up.

It's now much easier to understand why the British climbers
of the 1930s were so reluctant to use oxygen. In the past,
commentators have put this down to continued opposition on
the grounds of 'sporting ethics' or anti-scientific prejudice, but
it's abundantly clear that even though the Everest Committee
spent a huge sum of money in 1924, the equipment sent out to
India was not fit for purpose.

It was of course a huge irony that in June 1924, Mallory,
previously the arch-sceptic, was strapping on a cobbled-together
set for his final climb while George Finch was lecturing about
Everest and licking his wounds back in London. Having seen how
high Norton and Somervell had gone on 4 June, Mallory could
have changed his mind and opted to make a second oxygen-less
attempt with Noel Odell, who seemed so well acclimatized, or
with Sandy Irvine, who had his own profound doubts about
oxygen, but instead he insisted on sticking to the plan that he
had formulated weeks earlier.

Throughout the expedition, and as far back as 1923, Mallory
was concerned about his health and physical fitness. When
lecturing in America he had come down with a mysterious 'liver
chill', and in letters back home to Ruth in 1924 he alternated
between telling her how he felt better than ever and complaining
about his aches and pains. On the approach march he had such
bad stomach issues that Somervell suspected appendicitis; later
in the expedition he suffered from various coughs and throat
issues. Mallory was famously young-looking, but in June 1924

he was almost thirty-eight. Did he feel the onward march of time and believe the only way he could get to the summit was with supplementary oxygen?

A simpler explanation for his conversion is that he had been convinced by Finch's performance in 1922, and was so determined to reach the summit this time that he was prepared to put aside his previous reservations, just to get Everest out of his system.

Perhaps that's the tragedy of George Mallory, the classical hero's 'fatal flaw'. In 1923 his life was at a turning point. He had got the job that he had always wanted, moved to a city that he loved close to many of his friends, and was relishing the opportunity to set up a new house with Ruth and spend more time with his young family. Off the mountain, he was not obsessed with Everest and led a rich and fulfilling life, full of promise.

There were several moments in 1923 when the 'tragedy' might have been averted. If Mallory's Cambridge bosses had refused to give him leave; if Ruth had told him that it was not the right moment to disappear off on a six-month expedition for the third time in four years; if the Everest Committee's money had fallen through or the Dalai Lama had changed his mind… then Mallory might not have left for Everest. None of those things happened, though, and so the die was cast.

When he reached Everest, that sense of obsession really did kick in – some inner force that pressed him to go further than anyone else. In 1921 he had written to Geoffrey Winthrop Young, 'At what point am I going to stop?' There was never a satisfactory answer. At the end of the 1921 reconnaissance, he led the ascent to the North Col with Guy Bullock but later maintained that he could have gone 2,000 feet higher. As Bullock wrote laconically in his diary: 'I was prepared to follow Mallory if he wished to try and make some height, but was glad when he decided not to.' In 1922, Mallory was the prime mover behind the disastrous third attempt, pressuring Charlie Bruce to agree to it against his better judgement, and in 1924 he did the same thing again.

George's great friend Mary O'Malley (also known as Cottie Sanders before she married), the first woman he was romantically involved with, recognized that risk-taking was part of his nature, even though he occasionally tried to pretend it wasn't. She had been part of the climbing parties that Geoffrey Winthrop Young had organized before the First World War in Snowdonia. 'It was comic to hear George talk sagely of prudence,' she wrote to Young in July 1924, 'and do you remember his funny face of protest if one told him so?' O'Malley blamed Edward Norton for being too weak at the climax of the expedition. 'It is bitter to think that as you say,' she continued, 'there was no-one to curb that lovely fearlessness... and say "Not here, not now"... If only [General] Bruce had been there. Oh it is so miserable.'

Young agreed, and was no great fan of Norton, but saw the leadership question in a more nuanced way, arguing that it wasn't just a question of Bruce or Norton giving in too easily, but rather of not giving Mallory enough responsibility. 'In every year,' Winthrop wrote to George Trevelyan, another of the Snowdonia climbers, 'the leadership has lapsed to him, without the responsibility that *might* have steadied his judgement into a cooler detachment.' The italics were his – it was only ever *might*. Young recognized that coolness and detachment were not really part of Mallory's make-up, or for that matter his own: 'I attach no glamour or importance to the circumstance of his death: it was as accidental a consequence of his choice of life, and of his temperament, as my losing my leg.'

O'Malley's criticism of Norton seems harsh. When he returned to the North Col on the evening of 4 June, Norton was physically very weak and on the brink of three days of excruciating snow blindness. In spite of what he and Somervell had just achieved, he still felt like a failure. In the circumstances, could Norton have really pushed back against a third attempt? General Bruce hadn't been able to in 1922.

Perhaps Norton was a little overawed by Mallory, or perhaps he really did think it was worth a final roll of the dice, but Mallory wasn't only putting himself at risk. In 1922 seven porters had died on the ill-conceived third attempt, leaving him feeling distraught and guilty, and in 1924 Andrew Irvine disappeared with him. There's absolutely no doubt that Irvine wanted to go – he wrote in his diary and in letters home how much he wanted to have a 'whack' at the summit – but he was a young, impressionable novice climber with little experience before 1924.

For someone who was such a technically gifted mountaineer, Mallory was remarkably willing to accept beginners. Back in 1914, when he was planning to take Ruth to the Alps on their honeymoon, it was Geoffrey Winthrop Young who had to warn him against it. 'Your weakness, if any,' Young wrote, 'is that you do let yourself get carried away on occasions in the mountains... I think that is your failing, the consequence of your combination of extraordinary physical brilliance in climbing and of power of mental absorption in it, that you do not or at least have not held back from allowing yourself to sweep weaker brethren, carried away by their belief in you, to take risks or exertions that they were not fit for.' It was a comment that equally could have applied to Mallory's relationship with Andrew Irvine. In 1921, Guy Bullock was strong enough to stand up to Mallory, and refused to take his porters over routes preferred by Mallory because he thought them too dangerous, but would Sandy Irvine have been able to say no?

All of these points come with an important caveat: we simply don't know when, where or why Mallory turned back. In 1922, George Finch made his summit bid with Geoffrey Bruce, someone who had even less mountaineering experience than Irvine. Finch had a moment of epiphany at 27,200 feet, when after resolving a problem with Bruce's oxygen set, he realized that this was no place for a partner with so little experience: 'Never for a moment did I think we would fail... And then – suddenly, unexpectedly, the vision was gone... If we were to persist in climbing on, if only for another five hundred feet, we should not both get back alive.' Finch called a retreat and both men got back safely. At a certain point, did Mallory come to the same realization, only for he or Irvine to slip on the way down?

For years the 'mystery of Mallory and Irvine' has revolved around a simple question: did they or did they not reach the summit? But there's another equally valid question: did Mallory call off their attempt before they got near the top, realizing that the conditions and climbing difficulties made it just too risky?

Edward Norton argued forcefully in *The Times* that this was the case, insisting that Mallory 'would have been the last man in the world to chance things when accompanied by a youngster like Irvine'. In his letter of condolence written on 13 June 1924, he expanded on this, telling Ruth that her husband's 'determination was tempered with discretion. He fully realised his responsibility as leader of the climbing party... and he has often told me of his views as to the point at which the leader of a party must turn back for safety's sake, however near the goal.' Sandy Irvine had shown great promise when climbing in

Spitsbergen and Wales, and had performed really well on Everest, but Mallory was fully aware of his limitations.

On 5 June 1924, the day before they left camp, Norton talked through Mallory's plans with him, and undoubtedly would have reiterated the need for safety. Both Norton and Mallory were adamant that there should be no casualties in 1924, and a few weeks earlier had put their lives at risk to rescue the porters trapped on the North Col. In spite of their resolution, two men, Shamsher and Manbhadur, had already died. Would Mallory have risked Irvine's life too?

Arguably, the most important single piece of evidence found in 1999 was not one of the small items recovered from Mallory's pockets, but the simple fact of where his body was located. In 1924 there were plenty of Mallory's admirers who believed that he could have made an all-out dash for the top, even if he realized that he might not get back. As David Pye, his friend and first biographer, wrote, he imagined him at the summit, reaching his goal and then collapsing: 'In that moment of achievement may not the strained cord have snapped, and unconsciousness, the natural refuge of the overwrought body, supervened?'

But Mallory's body wasn't found on the summit pyramid or nearby. It was found at 26,760 feet, to the east of the First Step, just a few hundred feet away from his high camp. The damage to his body did not indicate that he had fallen a long way. If he and Irvine had reached the summit, they would have had to both ascend *and* descend the First and Second steps. If it is hard to imagine them both climbing the Second Step, which none of their contemporaries thought was feasible, then the idea that they could have also managed to down-climb this very challenging rock step at 28,250 feet and then retraced their steps for several hundred feet across the North Face is virtually impossible to believe. Today there's a ladder and a lot of fixed rope at the Second Step, but in 1924 there was no safety equipment in sight apart from the flimsy rope the two men carried.

The alternative possibility – that Mallory and Irvine climbed up to the North-East Ridge, managed to get over or around the First Step and then stopped when Mallory realized how difficult the Second Step was, makes more sense with the position of his body. Perhaps they began their retreat soon after Odell spotted them on the ridge, or perhaps they backtracked and investigated Norton's route before turning around and attempting to climb back down, but either way the fact that Mallory's body was found so far to the east of the summit makes it even harder to believe that he and Irvine reached the top.

Every version of their final day is of course theoretical, and in every instance there are contradictions and problems in fitting all the 'clues' together. It's perhaps why Mallory's story continues to fascinate so many people. Unlike Scott of the Antarctic, who died in a hut after writing a final letter to his wife, or the Swedish balloonist Salomon Andrée, who disappeared but whose diary and photographs were subsequently discovered, apart from a few brief notes, there's no written record of Mallory's final three days.

In some respects, Mallory has always appeared very knowable. He wrote hundreds, maybe even thousands, of letters, many of which survive, as well as books and articles. After he died, much more was written by his friends and biographers, yet there was always an unresolved quality to him – contradictions and loose ends that didn't add up. He had a lot of friends, but from different backgrounds. He was interested in a lot of different things, from poetry to politics, from art to education, from family life to mountaineering, but he was perpetually on the move.

His wife Ruth understood this elusive quality. They were clearly soulmates, but there were things about him that even she just didn't have access to. 'I never owned him. I never even wanted to. We all had our own part of him. My part was tenderer and nearer than anyone else's but it was only my part.'

Mallory's disappearance and death in 1924 was the ultimate loose end – the void he didn't just touch, but fell into. Since then there have been many attempts to fill that void, with mythical projections of Mallory as a medieval knight or, more recently, the incarnation of adventure itself. Like James Dean, Jimi Hendrix, Janis Joplin, John Keats and the Romantic poet Percy Shelley, who Mallory once said had influenced his life more than anyone else, George Mallory died young, full of promise. Before long the myth started to replace the man.

Everyone has their own version of Mallory, but they are all just versions, reflections of what they want to see as well as what he was really like. His famous response to the question 'Why climb Everest?', 'Because it's there', is both the simplest and the most enigmatic explanation of the lure of high mountains, open to many different interpretations.

Everest was the best and worst place for Mallory. The best, because someone like him was needed, with all his energy and drive and sheer guts, if the mountain was to be climbed. The worst, because it was such an unforgiving environment, where instinctive risk-takers needed to tread very carefully.

In 1921 the first expedition was a great adventure and a way to make a name for himself, but by 1924 Everest had become a duty and almost a burden. A lot of his friends sensed his profound ambivalence about going on a third expedition, but it was not in his nature to avoid challenges. Like anyone born with a gift, he was instinctively drawn to exercising it. He was a climber, so he climbed. The problem was the risks were so great.

In 1924 the upper slopes of the North Face of Everest were the ultimate arena to practise his craft, but even a small slip on an Alpine peak or a crag in North Wales could have been fatal. His death might have occurred in an extraordinary place, but as Edward Norton insisted, it was the result of an 'ordinary mountaineering accident'. Whether he was coming down the mountain after a desperate struggle to the summit, or after making a wise decision to turn back when he realized that he and Irvine had reached their limit, the outcome was the same.

The boy who had sat on the rock defying the waves to sweep him away, who had grabbed the back of the milk cart not knowing whether he could hang on or where it would take him, had become the man who dared to singe Everest's 'very nose-tip'. In the end he didn't survive his final challenge, but he never gave up. When the American climbers found his body in 1999, they were struck by his muscular arms, stretching upwards, as if right to the last he was trying to arrest his fall, clinging on to the life he loved, before he was literally frozen into the mountain.

As Ruth Mallory so simply put it at the end of one of her most poignant letters to Geoffrey Winthrop Young in 1924: 'I know George did not mean to be killed. He was not so hard... If only it hadn't happened. It so easily might not have.'

Bibliography and Sources

Published Sources

For a general history of Everest, Walt Unsworth's monumental *Everest: The Mountaineering History* remains unsurpassed. The three major biographies of Mallory are David Pye's *George Leigh Mallory*, David Robertson's *George Mallory* and Peter and Leni Gillman's *The Wildest Dream*. To all these authors I am deeply indebted – particularly the Gillmans for a detailed and exhaustive investigation of every aspect of Mallory's life.

For *Fallen*, I have relied primarily on original documents, as well as some key primary texts.

Archives

The Alpine Club: a key source for Everest and contextualizing documents pertaining to all the Everest expeditions 1921–1953

The British Library, for the T. S. Blakeney Collection

Magdalene College, Cambridge, for George Mallory's Archive

Merton College, Oxford, for Andrew Irvine's Archive

The Mountain Heritage Trust

The Royal Geographical Society, for the MEF collection, the principal source of Everest documentation for the expeditions 1921–1953

Trinity College, Dublin, for access to Richard Hingston's diary

Books

Anker, Conrad, and David Robertson, *The Lost Explorer*, Simon & Schuster, 1999

Bruce, C. G., and others, *The Assault on Mount Everest 1922*, Edward Arnold, 1924

Carr, Herbert, *The Irvine Diaries*, Gastons–West Col, 1979

Finch, George Ingle (edited by George W. Rodway), *The Struggle for Everest*, Cromwell Press, 2008 (originally published as *Der Kampf um den Everest*, F. A. Brockhaus, 1925)

——, *The Making of a Mountaineer*, Arrowsmith, 1924

Firstbrook, Peter, *Lost on Everest*, BBC Worldwide, 1999

Hemmleb, Jochen, Larry Johnson and Eric Simonson, *Ghosts of Everest*, Macmillan, 1999

Hemmleb, Jochen, and Eric Simonson, *Detectives on Everest*, The Mountaineers, 2002

Howard-Bury, Charles, and others, *Mount Everest: The Reconnaissance, 1921*, Edward Arnold, 1922

Hoyland, Graham, *Last Hours on Everest*, Collins, 2013

Holzel, Tom, and Audrey Salkeld, *The Mystery of Mallory and Irvine*, Jonathan Cape, 1986, Pimlico, 1999

Mallory, George, *Climbing Everest*, Gibson Square, 2012

Morris, John, *Hired to Kill*, Rupert Hart-Davis, 1960

Noel, J. B. L., *Through Tibet to Everest*, Edward Arnold, 1927

Norton, Christopher, *Everest Revealed: The Private Diaries and Sketches of Edward Norton 1922–24*, History Press, 2014

Norton, Edward, *The Fight for Everest*, Edward Arnold and Co., 1925

Ruttledge, Hugh, *Everest 1933*, Hodder & Stoughton, 1934

Salkeld, Audrey, *People in High Places*, Jonathan Cape, 1991

Somervell, T. H., *After Everest*, Hodder & Stoughton, 1936

Younghusband, Francis, *The Epic of Mount Everest*, Constable, 1927

Journals and Newspapers

Alpine Journal (various): the key reference source, both during the 1920s and beyond

Daily Telegraph: for coverage of the 1933 expedition

Geographical Journal (various): another key reference, for the 1921 reconnaissance and the 1922 expedition

Himalayan Journal (various): established in 1929, several years after the first Everest expedition, but another key archive source

Newspapers.com: an invaluable source of archival newspapers all over the world

The Times: the Everest Committee's 'newspaper of record'

Films

Climbing Mount Everest, directed by John Noel, 1922

The Epic of Everest, directed by John Noel, 1924

Lost on Everest, produced by Peter Firstbrook, BBC TV, 1999

Selected Secondary Sources

Archer, Jeffrey, *Paths of Glory*, Pan, 2009

Breshears, David, and Audrey Salkeld, *Last Climb*, National Geographic Society, 1999

Conefrey, Mick, *Everest 1953*, Oneworld, 2012

——, *The Last Great Mountain*, Conefrey, 2020

Davis, Wade, *Into the Silence*, Alfred A. Knopf, 2013

Gillman, Peter and Leni, *The Wildest Dream*, Headline, 2000

Green, Dudley, *Because It's There*, Tempus, 2005

Hale, Keith, *Friends and Apostles*, Yale, 1998

Hankinson, Alan, *Geoffrey Winthrop Young*, Hodder & Stoughton, 1995

Hillary, Edmund, *High Adventure*, Hodder & Stoughton, 1955

Holroyd, Michael, *Lytton Strachey*, Heinemann, 1968

Hunt, John, *The Ascent of Everest*, Hodder & Stoughton, 1953

Huxley, Juliette, *Leaves of the Tulip Tree*, John Murray, 1986

Irving, R. L. G., *The Romance of Mountaineering*, J. M. Dent and Sons, 1935

Keynes, Geoffrey, *The Gates of Memory*, Oxford University Press, 1981

Krakauer, Jon, *Into Thin Air*, Macmillan, 1997

Lind, Charles, *An Afterclap of Fate*, Ernest Press, 2006

Lowes, Michael D., *Lure of the Mountains*, Vertebrate, 2014

Macfarlane, Robert, *Mountains of the Mind*, Granta, 2003

Messner, Reinhold, *The Second Death of George Mallory*, St Martin's Press, 2001

Noel, Sandra, *Everest Pioneer: The Photographs of Captain John Noel*, Sutton, 2003

Norton, Hugh, *Norton of Everest*, Vertebrate, 2017

Ortner, Sherry B., *Life and Death on Mount Everest*, Princeton University Press, 1999

Parsons, Mike, and Mary B. Rose, *Invisible on Everest*, Old City Publishing, 2003

Pye, David, *George Leigh Mallory*, Oxford University Press 1927, republished Orchid Press, 2002

Roberts, Alistair, *The Forgotten Man of Everest*, Lulu, 2019

Robertson, David, *George Mallory* Faber and Faber, 1999

Shipton, Eric Earl, *The Mt Everest Reconnaissance 1951*, Hodder & Stoughton, 1952

——, *Upon That Mountain*, Hodder & Stoughton, 1943

Smythe, Tony, *My Father Frank*, Baton Wicks, 2013

Synott, Mark, *The Third Pole*, Headline, 2021

Summers, Julie. *Fearless on Everest*, Iffley Press, 2010

Thompson, Simon, *Unjustifiable Risk*, Cicerone, 2010

Unsworth, Walt, *Everest: A Mountaineering History*, Houghton Mifflin, 1981

Venables, Stephen, *Everest, Summit of Achievement*, Bloomsbury, 2003

Wainwright, Robert, *The Maverick Mountaineer*, Allen and Unwin, 2016

Ward, Michael, *Everest: A Thousand Years of Exploration*, Ernest Press, 2003

Image Sources

Front and back end papers:

The 1924 Everest team. Photo
by Capt. J.B. Noel/Royal
Geographical Society via Getty
Images.

Chapter 1: About a Boy

Page 6: Mallory and Herford at
Pen-Y-Pass in Snowdonia.
Photo by Geoffrey Winthrop
Young, 1913. Photo reproduced
courtesy of The Alpine Club.

Chapter 2: Go West

Page 28: George Leigh Mallory,
1886–1924, English climber,
while on lecture tour in USA
in 1921 or 1922. Photo
reproduced courtesy of The
Alpine Club.

Chapter 3: The Two Georges

Page 48: Arthur Robert Hinks
(1873–1945), Hugh Ruttledge/
Royal Geographical Society via
Getty Images.
Page 49: Colonel Sir Francis
Younghusband. Photo by L.P.P.
Ruddock/Royal Geographical
Society via Getty Images.

Page 56: George Ingle Finch (1888–
1970), 1922 Everest Expedition.
Photo reproduced courtesy of
The Alpine Club.
Page 68: John Noel's 1924
promotional postcard. Images:
author's own.

Chapter 4: To Go or Not to Go

Page 83: Wayfarers' Club Dinner
menu, 28 February 1924. Image
reproduced courtesy of Anthony
Bard.

Chapter 5: The Long March

Page 90: Mallory and Irvine onboard the SS *California*. Photographer unknown.

Page 112: Mount Everest from Base Camp, Mount Everest Expedition 1924. Photo by J. de V. Hazard/Royal Geographical Society via Getty Images.

Chapter 6: Cold Comfort

Page 114: The 1924 Everest Team. Photo by Capt. J.B. Noel/Royal Geographical Society via Getty Images.

Page 118: Map depicting camps on the Ronbuk Glacier. Illustration by Adam T. Burton.

Chapter 7: Trapped

Page 139: Camp on the North Col by a snowy peak, Mount Everest Expedition 1924. Photo by Capt. J. B. Noel/Royal Geographical Society via Getty Images.

Chapter 8: There

Page 157: Map depicting the North-East Ridge. Illustration by Adam T. Burton.

Page 161: The Tigers. Mount Everest Expedition 1924. John B. Noel Collection/Royal Geographical Society via Getty Images.

Page 167: Mount Everest Expedition 1924. Photo by T.H. Somervell/Royal Geographical Society via Getty Images.

Chapter 9: The Boys from Birkenhead

Page 178: Mallory and Irvine leaving North Col for the last climb. China (Tibet), June 1924. Mount Everest Expedition 1924. Photo by Noel E. Odell/Royal Geographical Society via Getty Images.

Page 191: 1924 Everest party. John B. Noel Collection/Royal Geographical Society via Getty Images.

Chapter 10: Your Ever Loving George

Page 194: George and Ruth Mallory. Photographer unknown.

Page 210: Geoffrey Winthrop Young (1876–1958), English climber, poet and photographer, President of the Alpine Club 1941–43, President's Portrait, 1934. Photo reproduced courtesy of The Alpine Club.

Chapter 11: The Searchers

Page 238: The first assault party (Wyn Harris and Wager), China (Tibet), 16 April 1933. Mount Everest Expedition 1933. Photo by Frank S. Smythe/Royal Geographical Society via Getty Images.

Chapter 12: A Tale of Two Photos

Page 250: Vest-pocket Kodak. Photo by Mick Conefrey.

Page 284: Map depicting evidence found on Everest in 1933 and 1999. Illustration by Adam T. Burton.

Chapter 13: About A Man

Page 294: George Mallory portrait. Photographer unknown.

Acknowledgements

This book could not have been written without the help and assistance of many friends and colleagues. I'd like to thank my editor, Ed Faulkner, for commissioning the book, and all his colleagues at Allen and Unwin for helping get it into production; a big word of thanks to my agent Leah Middleton and everyone at Marjaq for all their work and encouragement, and to Gemma Wain, who copy-edited the book so assiduously. For the US publication, big thanks to Claiborne Hancock at Pegasus Press.

There are several excellent biographies of Mallory that I have drawn on, most especially Peter and Leni Gillman's *The Wildest Dream*, David Robertson's *George Mallory*, Tom Holzel and Audrey Salkeld's *The Mystery of Mallory and Irvine* and David Pye's *George Leigh Mallory*. For a general history of the mountain, Walt Unsworth's *Everest* remains the definitive text.

Fallen is primarily based on research in archives of the Royal Geographical Society and the Alpine Club, and I would like to thank them heartily for giving me access to their material in the especially difficult Covid period. I'd particularly like to thank Alasdair MacLeod, formerly of the RGS, for being so positive and helpful with this project, and Eugene Rae, the principal librarian, who was always very accommodating. At the Alpine I'd like to thank Glyn Hughes, the Honorary Archivist, Nigel Buckley, the former librarian, and Beth Hodges, the current librarian. I'm very grateful also to the staff of the British Library, Katy Green at Magdalen College Cambridge, and Julia Walworth and all the staff at Merton College Oxford. I'd also like to thank Francis Russell for giving me access to the archives of his grandfather, George Finch, and for permission to use the photograph of Finch at Base Camp in 1922.

I'm very grateful to the Master and Fellows of Magdalene College Cambridge for permission to transcribe and quote from Mallory's letters; the Warden and Fellows of Merton College Oxford for permission to transcribe and quote from Irvine's letters and diary; and to Nick Mays for access to the *Times* Archive.

A special word of thanks for Tim Jordan, my former writing partner at the BBC, for his close reading of the text and all his advice and good humour, and to Diana Halsall and Jerry Lovatt, who also read and commented on an early version of the text. I'd also like to thank Stephen Venables, Virginia Arnott, Pam Roberts, Alistair Roberts, Adam Rattray, Anne Spencer, Guy Cotter, Brian Hall, Michael Pritchard, George Millikan, Margaret Lewis, Peter Odell, Deanna Parsi, Jonathan Westaway, Mark Horrell, Peter Gillman, Wade Davis, Garrett Madison, David Keitz, Anthony Bard, George Mallory II, Seb Coulthard, Mike Parsons, Mary B. Rose, Jean-Francois Fava-Verde, Jennifer Coulton, Peter Hansen, Jan Faull, John West, Tom Holzel and Tony Astill. For the chapter dealing with the 1999 expedition, I'd like to thank Conrad Anker, Dave Hahn, Graham Hoyland, Jochen Hemmleb, Tom Pollard and Peter Firstbrook for agreeing to be interviewed.

Last, but never least, I'd like to thank my children, Frank and Phyllis, and my darling wife, Stella Bruzzi, for all her love and support.

Mick Conefrey
Oxford

Index